跨文化交际
案例分析

主　编　廖华英
编　者　陈　娟　汤　昱
　　　　罗　晶　向　鹏

北京理工大学出版社
BEIJING INSTITUTE OF TECHNOLOGY PRESS

版权专有　侵权必究

图书在版编目（CIP）数据

跨文化交际案例分析 / 廖华英主编. —北京：北京理工大学出版社，2010.10（2018.2重印）
　ISBN 978-7-5640-3888-5

Ⅰ. ①跨…　Ⅱ. ①廖…　Ⅲ. ①文化交流－案例－分析　Ⅳ. ①G115

中国版本图书馆 CIP 数据核字（2010）第 198039 号

出版发行 / 北京理工大学出版社
社　　址 / 北京市海淀区中关村南大街 5 号
邮　　编 / 100081
电　　话 /（010）68914775（办公室）　68944990（批销中心）　68911084（读者服务部）
网　　址 / http://www.bitpress.com.cn
经　　销 / 全国各地新华书店
印　　刷 / 三河市文通印刷包装有限公司
开　　本 / 710 毫米×1000 毫米　1/16
印　　张 / 15.25
字　　数 / 245 千字
版　　次 / 2010 年 10 月第 1 版　2018 年 2 月第 3 次印刷　　责任编辑 / 梁铜华
印　　数 / 5501～6500　　　　　　　　　　　　　　　　　　责任校对 / 张沁萍
定　　价 / 28.00 元　　　　　　　　　　　　　　　　　　　责任印制 / 边心超

图书出现印装质量问题，本社负责调换

Preface 前言

　　跨文化交际课程是英语学习者了解和掌握不同文化之间差异和交际的一门重要课程,也是一门实践性和应用性较强的课程。许多学生在具体实践中做不到融会贯通,跨文化交际的失误仍然存在。为了使学生能积极融入课堂,培养他们的实际交际能力,授人以渔,举一反三,作者编写了《跨文化交际案例分析》教材。

　　该教材以学生获取知识的认知途径为基本突破口,采取了与普通教材不同的编写方式,从事物的特殊性到普遍性的哲学规律,引导学生根据案例来分析跨文化交际的理论体系和中西方文化的基本差异,从而达到能提高其基本交际能力的目的。通过阅读案例,明确问题;通过分析案例,找出原因;通过制定方案,解决问题。

　　该教材的编写基本涵盖了跨文化交际失误的内容;坚持以案例分析为主,理论介绍为辅;增强其趣味性阅读,案例丰富,具有实用性、现代性、真实性、典型性和价值性特点;课后练习可以对学生进行举一反三能力的培训;全英文编写,适合大学以上各种层次学习者的需求;案例结合日常生活与外贸等相关领域,做到尽量覆盖知识、技能、文化3个方面,达到授人以渔的目的。

　　该教材的使用能在课堂上达到以学生为主,着眼于其能力培养的目的;强调集体合作,而非个体单干的理念;培养学生身临其境地解决问题,并在不圆满的条件下做出自己独立的决策,从而不断提高决策能力,使得抽象的理论形象化、具体化,做到学以致用。

　　该教材适用于高等学校大学英语拓展课程,英语专业选修课程,外贸、外事、旅游、对外汉语等专业的必修课程,也可作为高校英语教师的参考资料。

　　在教材的编写过程中,外教 Peter Kelly 及 Terrence Moeller 提供了一定的案例并对案例进行了必要的分析。东华理工大学教务处对该教材的出版给予了支持。

编　者

Contents 目录

Part I Culture and Communication / 1

    Chapter 1 What is culture? / 3

    Chapter 2 What is communication? / 9

    Chapter 3 Culture and communication / 14

Part II Culture Conflicts and Case Study Introduction / 17

    Chapter 1 Culture conflicts / 19

    Chapter 2 Case study introduction / 23

Part III Case Analyses of Pragmatic Failures in Intercultural Verbal Communication / 27

    Chapter 1 Pragmalinguistic failures / 29

    Chapter 2 Sociopragmatic failures / 44

Part IV Case Analyses in Intercultural Nonverbal Communication / 91

    Chapter 1 Kinesics (body language) / 94

    Chapter 2 Haptics (touch) / 107

    Chapter 3 Appearance and dress / 113

    Chapter 4 Olfactics (smell and taste) / 119

    Chapter 5 Proxemics (body space) / 124

    Chapter 6 Chronemics (time) / 139

    Chapter 7 Paralanguage / 149

Part V Typical Cases in Intercultural Business Communication / 155

    Chapter 1 Value perception conflict / 157

    Chapter 2 Corporate culture matters / 171

    Chapter 3 Corporation system and management / 190

    Chapter 4 Cross-cultural negotiating style / 207

Part VI Tips for Successful Intercultural Communication / 223

    Chapter 1 Tips for ordinary intercultural communication / 224

    Chapter 2 Recommendations for effective intercultural business negotiations / 232

References / 236

Part 1

Culture and Communication

    Culture is to communication what water is to fish. Speakers from different cultural backgrounds may have different interpretations of what it means to be truthful, relevant, brief, or clear with regard to conversation and body language.

    When we discuss culture and communication, we should be aware of the total spectrum of communication, which includes language, non-verbal communication, customs, perceived values, and concepts of time and space. What happens when people from different cultures interact face-to-face?

    People with experience of different cultures, through travel or work, know that they do things in different ways. Common examples are giving gifts, seating guests at dinner, and the way language is used to communicate.

    Learned from childhood, the rules guide our attitude toward communication and our belief in what is correct and what is not. These hidden beliefs determine how a person communicates, and how he or she expects communication to be offered. We all learn to expect messages to be given in certain ways.

Expectations are crucial in cross-cultural communication. Not only do they govern our unthinking reactions and beliefs of what is or is not polite, but also determine what things mean.

For example, Westerners expect disagreement to be clearly stated. It may happen, however, that a Westerner discovers that a Chinese is doing something different to what was agreed upon. He will tell the other, probably patiently and politely, that he is not happy about this. Of course, the Chinese will feel offended because that makes them "lose face." Although both of them are respecting the rules of etiquette, they still think the other is wrong and wonder about whether they can trust each other.

Successful communication is never easy, even when communicating with someone from our own culture. We may try to be clear, but many things can go wrong. Communication is rarely perfect, even with best friends or family members. Different cultural expectations make cross-cultural communication much harder.

Overcoming cultural barriers is difficult, but possible. People must first own an awareness of the foundations of the other people's culture, i.e., not just what the expectations are but why they are so. To communicate with people from another culture we must endeavor to think about communication the way they do and understand why it is important and proper for them to think that way. Then proper tips for the cultural communication should be grasped.

Chapter

1

What is culture?

What is CULTURE? There are hundreds of definitions of culture. Some view culture as the knowledge, beliefs, art, laws, morals, customs, and so on, of a particular group, as distinct from those of other groups; Others think that a culture is a fuzzy set of attitudes, beliefs, behavioral conventions, basic assumptions and values that are  shared by a group of people, and that influence each member's behavior and each member's understanding of others' behavior.

It is mostly agreed that culture can be summarized as the deposit of knowledge, experience, beliefs, values, attitudes, meanings, hierarchies, religion, notions of time, roles, spatial relations, concepts of the universe, and material objects and possessions acquired by a group of people in the course of generations through individual and group striving. Culture can therefore cover everything relating to human life and experience.

Culture is also the coherent, learned, shared view of a group of people about life's concerns that ranks what is important, furnishes attitudes about what things are appropriate, and dictates behavior. For the purpose of cross-cultural studies, culture can be viewed as the shared patterns of behaviors and interactions, cognitive constructs, and effective understanding that are learned through a process of socialization. These shared patterns help identify the members of one culture group while at the same time they distinguish those of another group.

1.1 Characteristics of culture

Cultures around the world share five common characteristics: culture is shared, learned, based on symbols, integrated and selected.

Culture is shared

A culture is shared by a society. The members of the culture share a set of ideals, values, and standards of behavior, and this set of shared ideals is what gives meaning to their lives, and what bonds them together as a culture.

The members in the society mostly agree about the meanings of things and why they should be so. They share symbols of that culture including language, visual symbols, company logos, icons, religious images, and national flags.

As almost everyone belongs to a number of different groups and categories of people at the same time, people unavoidably carry several layers of mental programming within themselves, corresponding to different levels of culture. For example:

- a national level
- a regional and/or ethnic and/or religious and/or linguistic affiliation
- a gender level
- a social class level
- a generation level
- an organizational or corporate level

So in this sense, everyone is simultaneously a member of several different cultural groups and thus could be said to have multicultural membership.

Culture is learned

Culture is not an innate sensibility, but a learned characteristic. Without the advantages of knowledge from those who lived before us, we would not have culture. All of us are born with basic needs — needs that create and shape behavior — but how we go about meeting those needs and developing behaviors to cope with them is learned.

From childhood, people begin learning about their culture at home with their family members and they know how they interact with each other, how they dress, and the rituals they perform. When they grow up, they enter into the community. They are educated and through watching others and participating activities, they form their own relationship and take their place in the culture.

Proverbs are a good way for people to learn their own culture. In colorful and vivid language, they offer an important set of instructions for members to follow. People also learn culture from folk tales, legends, and myths. A trip to any museum in the world quickly reveals how the art of a culture is another method of passing on that culture. In the modern world mass media provides people with abundant and quick access to touching their culture.

That the culture is acquired through the process of learning has several important implications for the conduct of international communication.

First, such an understanding can lead to greater tolerance in respect of cultural differences, and make the intercultural communication more successful in the practical settings.

Second, the learned nature of culture stimulates people in the multicultural environment to learn the other cultures with full of confidence and put it into function as well.

And finally, it leads people to grasp the deeper skills in training programs relevated to the different cultures and lessens the barriers of the global cultures into the slimmest degrees.

Culture is based on symbols

Through the symbols like language, art, religion, money and etc. , the culture can be transmitted successfully from one person to another, and from one generation to the next. The use of symbols is at the core of culture. In this way the ideals and thoughts of one culture can last and its uniqueness can attract people from other cultures.

Symbols tie together people who otherwise might not be part of a unified group. They allow people to package and store their culture as well as to transmit it. The minds, the books, pictures, films, religious writings, videos, computer accessories and the like enable a culture to preserve what is deemed to be worthy of transmission. This makes each individual, regardless of his or her generation, heir to a massive repository of information that has been gathered and maintained in anticipation of his or her entry into the culture.

Cultural symbols can take a host of forms, encompassing gestures, dresses, objects, flags, religious icons, and the like. Yet the most important symbolic aspect of culture is language — using words to represent objects and ideas.

Culture is integrated

In order to keep the culture functioning, all aspects of the culture must be integrated. The language must own its function in describing the ideas and ideals and pass them from one generation to the next. Without the integration of language into the structure of the culture, confusion and dysfunction would reign and the culture would collapse.

Each culture, past or present, is coherent and complete within itself — an entire view of the universe. If we can view cultures as integrated systems, we can begin to see how particular culture traits fit into the integrated whole, and consequently how they tend to make sense in the setting.

Culture is selected

In every culture, only part of behavior patterns from the total of human experience can be presented. The selection of these contents is mostly based on the basic sumptions and values that are meaningful to each culture because each individual has only this limited experience. That is why some cultures attach importance to privacy so much, while other cultures do not. This characteristic is important to all learners of cross-cultural communication.

There are two reasons for that: First, what a culture selects to tell each generation is a reflection of what a culture deems important. Second, the notion of selectivity also suggests that culture tends to separate one group from another.

These characteristics of culture exist in every culture, no matter where the culture is located in the world. The manipulation and sculpting of these characteristics decides how a culture defines itself and sets it apart from other cultures.

There are some other characteristics of culture, e. g. *Culture is a dynamic system* that means culture changes as time goes by. The diet culture, clothes culture, and greeting culture vary greatly in different times. A typical example is the greeting culture in China. In ancient times, people would kneel down before their elders or their masters, and they would bow to each other with their hands folded in front of them if they were friends or of the same social status. After 1911, Chinese people began to adopt the Western way of greeting — shaking hands. From the 1980s, more ways of greeting began to appear, such as waving one's hand and saying "Hi," or hugging each other.

Although cultures do change, most change affects only the surface structure of the culture. The deep structure resists major alterations. Elements such as values,

Part I *Culture and Communication*   7

ethics and morals, definitions of freedom, the pace of life, etc. are so deep in the structure of a culture that they tend to persist generation after generation.

1.2 Three things culture does

Culture ranks what is important

Different cultures have their own value orientation and what is important in one culture may be virtually meaningless to another. Cultures rank what is important. In other words, cultures teach values or priorities. Values underlie attitudes. They also shape beliefs. In business settings or other multicultural environment, it is necessary to understand what motivates the people from other cultures.

Culture furnishes attitudes

An attitude is learned, and it is a tendency to respond in the same way to the same object or situation or idea. Attitudes can change, although change can be difficult. Attitudes are based on beliefs as well as values. Beliefs are convictions or certainties based on subjective and often personal ideas rather than on proof or facts. Belief systems or religions are powerful sources of values and attitudes in cultures. Culture furnishes attitudes in its function.

Culture dictates how to behave

Behavior comes directly from the attitudes about how significant something is — how it is valued. Values drive actions.

1.3 The components of culture

The components of culture mainly include the attitudes, beliefs, customs, traditions, art and achievements of society that are passed on to each generation. But the most interesting fact about culture is that everyone has a culture of its own, which decides the different understanding to the components of a culture.

To make it easier to understand, normally culture includes the following components that can be put together to form **Emeralds(祖母绿)**:

> *Environment* — *geography, climate and places in the country*;
> *Math, science, tools and technology* — *inventions, buildings, roads,*

bridges and aqueducts;
Economics — money, trade, jobs;
Religion, spiritual beliefs — religious practice, mythology;
Arts, language, writing, architecture;
Laws and government;
Daily life — home, school, entertainment, dress, food;
Social structure — social levels, roles and classes.

Chapter 2

What is communication?

Everyone communicates and has a preconceived notion of what communication is and how it takes place. The origin of the word "communicate" can be traced back to the Latin word "communis," which means "common." And it has a close relationship with "commonality." Etymologically, it's obvious that the precondition of communication is what people is having and sharing in common. For people sharing the same culture have a lot in common, so the  communication between them is much smoother than that between people of different cultural backgrounds.

Communication can be defined as that which happens whenever meaning is attributed to behavior, or to the residue of behavior. When someone observes our behavior or its residue, and gives meaning to it, communication has taken place regardless of whether our behavior is conscious or unconscious, intentional or unintentional.

Judging from this definition, we can say that communication is a form of human behavior, and the aim of which is to satisfy people's need to interact with others. And all people have such kind of need, and this need is met through the act of communication. Communication is a kind of symbolic activity and a dynamic process of encoding and decoding. When people give the verbal or non-verbal signs meanings, communication takes place.

Because communication is a process of encoding and decoding, it is complete only when the initiator's behavior is perceived by the addresee. These transactions must include all conscious and unconscious, intentional or unintentional, verbal or non-verbal, contextual stimuli that act as cues about the quality and credibility of the message. When cultural dimension is taken into consideration, the issue will be more complex. Symbols are used by all cultures to represent realities; however, the symbols used to represent the realities are quite different in various cultures. We can take the action of greeting for example. In some culture, smile in a casual manner is regarded as a proper way of greeting, whereas in another greeting involves of bowing formally in silence, and in yet another a hug will do.

2.1 Characteristics of communication

Communication is the basis of all human interaction. Whether we live in a city in Canada, a village in India, a commune in Israel, or the jungles of Brazil, we all participate in the same activity when we communicate. The results and the methods might be different but the process is the same.

Normally, the main characteristics of communication can be summarized as follows.

Communication is dynamic

Culture is an ongoing, ever changing activity. When people communicate, they are constantly affected by each other's messages and as a consequence, people undergo continual change. Each time one is influenced, one changes in some way and people never stay frozen when in communication.

Communication is symbolic

Communication involves the use of symbols. Symbols are things used to stand for, or represent, something else. Symbols are not limited to words; they also include nonverbal display and other objects (e.g, the flag). Within a culture, there is sufficient agreement that people can communicate with relative clarity on most topics of communication.

Communication is interactive

Obviously, communication must take place between people. When two or more people communicate, their unique backgrounds and experiences serve as a backdrop for the communication interaction. Also, interaction implies a reciprocal situation in which each party attempts to influence the other.

Communication is irreversible

The moment we have said something and the other has received and decoded the message, we cannot retrieve it. We are all familiar with the phenomenon that we unconsciously or unintentionally send a message to someone and this sometimes results in what is called "put your foot in your mouth."

Communication takes place in a physical and a social context; both establish the rules that govern the interaction. Communication never occurs in isolation or vacuum. We always interact with others within specific physical surroundings and under a set of specific social dynamics.

2.2 Types of communication

Communication is a process of exchanging information, thoughts, ideas and emotions. The process involves four key factors, namely message sender, message, communication channel and message receiver. The whole communication process is like that the message sender encodes the message and sends it through the communication channel, while having received the message, the receiver decodes the message, processes the information and sends an appropriate reply via the same communication channel. It can occur via various processes and methods and, there can be various types of communication according to the channel used and the style of communication.

Types of communication based on communication channels

Based on the channels used for communicating, communication can be broadly divided into *verbal communication* and *non-verbal communication*.

Verbal communication can be further divided into oral and written communication. Oral communication refers to the spoken words in the communication process. Oral communication can be of different forms, it can be a face-to-face communication or a conversation over the phone, and it can also be a chat over the Internet. As for verbal communication, factors such as voice modulation, pitch, volume, and even the speed and clarity of speaking have a great influence on it. Written communication involves any type of interaction that makes use of the written words. The effectiveness of it depends on the style of writing, vocabulary used, grammar, clarity and precision of language.

Non-verbal communication generally refers to body language, facial expressions and visuals, diagrams or pictures used for communication. It includes the overall body language of the person who is speaking, which will include the body posture, the hand gestures, and overall body movements. The facial expressions also play a major role while communicating since the expressions on a person's face say a lot about his/her mood. On the other hand, gestures, like a handshake, a smile or a hug, can independently convey emotions. *Non-verbal communication* can also be in the form of pictorial representations, signboards, or even photographs, sketches and paintings.

Types of communication based on style and purpose

According to its style and purpose, communication can also be classified into formal communication and informal communication. Each of them has its own set of characteristics.

Formal communication refers to communication that has to occur in a set format. Business communication or corporate communication is a typical example of this sort of communication. As its name shows, the style of formal communication is very formal and official. Official conferences, meetings and written memos and corporate letters are the usual forms of this type. Formal communication can also occur between two strangers when they meet for the first time. The characteristics of formal communication are straightforward, official and precise.

Informal communication refers to free unrestrained communication between people who are acquainted with each other. Informal communication requires two people to be on a similar wavelength and hence occurs between friends and families. Unlike formal communication, it does not have any rigid rules and guidelines; it even does not necessarily have boundaries of time, place, and fixed subject for that matter since we all know that friendly chats with our loved ones can simply go on and on.

2.3 Barriers to communication

There are a number of factors that act as hurdles when it comes to effective communication. Some of the main communication barriers are listed below.

Physical barriers

Physical barriers are often due to the nature of the environment. One physical barrier is often created by marked out boundaries for individuals. In the workplace, such barriers can be caused by the different seating arrangements for staff members of different status. This distance factor can be a hindrance in normal workplace communication. Whilst distractions like background noise, poor lighting or an environment that is too hot or too cold can all affect people's morale and concentration, which in turn interferes with effective communication.

Lack of communication skills

If the message given out by the sender is not clear, then it becomes a barrier. When the sentences of the sender are not completed or there is a long pause in between two words or there is no consistency in what is being said, barriers will be created to successful communication. In such a situation, the listener doubts the credibility and authenticity of what has been said. Low confidence or lack of self-esteem is a typical instance of lack of communication skills, which will cause failure of communication.

Language barriers

If a person uses a lot of jargon or buzzwords during conversations, there will be language barriers to communication. This is because that not all people are familiar with those specialized terms. Hence, they may not even understand certain parts of the message and would feel left out.

Barriers of attitude

Barriers of attitude are mainly caused by personal conflict between individuals. If it happens, it will badly damage any interpersonal relationship as both the individuals involved delay the communication. Such an inflexible attitude is usually seen among employees of an organization when they are not motivated, or are dissatisfied with poor management.

Emotional barriers

This barrier is associated with the mental state of an individual during communication. If an individual is in a bad mood and this is reflected in his or her words of communication, the listener may lose interest and fail to listen to the message.

Barriers to communication make our life complicated and their effects are usually destructive. So identifying these barriers and being aware of these factors will make it easier for us to overcome them. When we are communicating, do not overlook the fact that such a barrier may exist. Act patiently, and make persistent efforts until you see an improvement in the situation.

Chapter 3

Culture and communication

Culture and communication are directly linked. On the one hand, culture is learned, acted out, transmitted, and preserved through communications. Communication — our ability to share our ideas and feelings — is the basis of all human contact on the other hand. The reciprocity between culture and  communication is crucial to the understanding of intercultural communication, because nearly all communications are cultural-specific.

Communication behavior, to a large extent, is dependent on culture, and culture is the foundation of communication. If we fail to pay attention to the cultural factors while communicating, pragmatic failure will follow. We can frequently find instances of pragmatic failure in communication, which are simply due to the lack of cultural knowledge.

Intercultural communication happens when people from different cultures have reached a certain degree of understanding regarding their differences. To understand each other, both sides must have some knowledge or awareness of the norms or customs that exist in the two cultures concerned. Verbal and nonverbal communications can contain implied meanings, as well as certain degrees of symbolism. For the success of communication, background knowledge concerning values, norms and perceptions is necessary in order for clear, effective communication to take place.

All communication is cultural-specific, it's confined by the ways we have learned to speak and give nonverbal messages. The way we communicate is not the same from day to day, because factors like context, personality, and mood interacting with the variety of cultural influences influence our choices. Communication is reciprocal, so an important influence on its effectiveness is our relationship with others. Do they hear and understand what we are trying to say? Are they listening well? Are we listening well in response? Do their responses show that they understand the words and the meanings behind the words we have chosen? Is the mood positive and receptive? Is there trust between them and us? Are there differences that relate to ineffective communication, divergent goals or interests, or fundamentally different ways of seeing the world? The answers to these questions will give us some clues about the effectiveness of our communication and the ease with which we may be able to move away from conflicts.

Part II

Culture Conflicts and Case Study Introduction

    Like underground rivers, cultures run through our lives and relationships, giving us messages that shape our judgments, attributions, perceptions, and ideas of self and others. Though cultures are of great power, their influence upon conflicts and attempts to resolve conflicts are often unconscious, in imperceptible ways.

    Culture is an essential part of conflicts and conflict resolution. When two cultures collide, the true suffering occurs. What is definitely "right" in one culture may appear to be "wrong" in another.

    Case analysis is one of the most general and applicable methods of analytical thinking, depending only on the division of a problem, decision or situation into a sufficient number of separate cases. Analysing each such case individually may be enough to resolve the initial question. For most instances of studies of teaching applying this method, they describe the experience for both teacher and learner as exhilarating. Through the analyses of the cases, students learn how to think, how to plan, and how to act in specific contexts.

Chapter 1

Culture conflicts

In every conflict we can find the shadow of culture because conflicts arise in human relationships, which are cultural-specific. Cultures affect the ways we name, frame, blame, and attempt to tame conflicts. Whether a conflict exists at all is a cultural question. Culture is inescapable from conflicts, though culture does not cause conflicts. When differences surface in families, organizations, or communities, culture is always present, shaping perceptions, attitudes, behaviors, and outcomes.

"This concludes my lecture on non-verbal communication. Any comments or questions?"

1.1 Cultural differences

Differences of cultures can become most explicit when people from different cultural backgrounds interact with each other or in circumstances involving business. Personal space, manner, forms of address, time and gestures are possible areas where cross-cultural differences can take place. This can be exemplified by norms surrounding personal space, which vary from culture to culture. Personal space refers to the acceptable distance that exists between people during conversations. While an American may have a one-to-two-foot comfort zone, someone of a different culture may consider six inches to be an acceptable personal area.

No two individuals or groups hold identical beliefs and manifest uniform behaviors, and whatever characterizations we make about one culture or cultural group must be thought of as variable rather than rigidly structured. Nevertheless, there are several key elements that distinguish each perspective clearly from the other. To specify these factors is also to identify the points of connection that tie different nations together to constitute either the Eastern or the Western cultural world.

In order to make it clearer, some main cultural differences between America and China will be described as follows.

Social structure

The social structure of China emphasizes formality and hierarchy, which extends to business, institutions, and family life. For example, children are expected to respect their elders and the older a family member is the more respect he commands. However, there is greater fluidity in America between groups with workers, managers, children and adults often making joint decisions and enjoying social occasions together.

Collectivism vs. individualism

In China, people value collectivism, often considering how their actions will affect their friends, neighbors and colleagues before making a decision. Decisions are more commonly made for the greater good as opposed to personal gain. On the contrary, Americans prioritize individual goals and motives over collective ones. Individualism is often actively encouraged to stimulate ambition and a drive to achieve business and personal success.

Morals and values

Humility and respect are of great importance in Chinese culture. People are expected to respect each other and to be modest when discussing achievements, or to not discuss them at all. While Americans openly discuss, play up and praise success, and humility even being seen by some as a weakness.

Additionally, Chinese have a strong sense of right and wrong. In America, questions of morality are regarded as gray areas, being a matter for discussion as opposed to being set in stone.

Freedom of expression

For Chinese, it is better to save face by respecting and honoring the opinion of others, even if you believe what they are saying is incorrect, than to demand that others agree with your way of thinking. This is because they are strictly bound by protocol. Americans are much more direct, and they are encouraged to debate contentious issues even if it leads to confrontation.

1.2 Cross-cultural conflicts

Cross-cultural conflicts can be defined as conflicts generated, and perhaps exacerbated or perpetuated, by cultural differences among the groups involved in the conflicts. A person's cultural background, to a large extent, tells his or her worldview, moral code, judgments, and ideas or perceptions about others. Of course, these aspects of a culture can be incorrect or misinformed, leading to conflicts with people from other cultures or groups. The power of culture is strong, however, and it can be difficult to overcome cross-cultural conflicts, as evidenced by the numerous conflicts between different cultures that continue to rage around the world today.

History

The history of cross-cultural conflicts is very long, which can be traced back to the very beginning of civilization and the emergence of distinctive cultures around Mesopotamia in ancient times. From the Roman and Persian conquests and subsequent persecutions of groups who did not conform to their laws and societies, to the Crusades of the Middle Ages, to the cross-cultural conflicts that cropped up around the Age of Exploration and Colonialism in the 1500s through the 1800s, this type of conflicts has a very long and violent history.

Considerations

The issue of religion is an important consideration when studying cross-cultural conflicts. The force of religion is extraordinarily powerful in the lives of many people throughout the world, and if one feels that their religious beliefs are called into question or its authority is threatened by another faith or group who do not practice (or perhaps respect) the same faith, one may feel compelled to protect that faith, even by violence.

Geography

Through the overview of the cross-cultural conflicts historically occurred or currently taking place throughout the world, we can find that geography plays an important role. Perhaps the most famous areas of current conflicts are the Middle East and countries in Africa. Both examples involve different tribal allegiances and religious affiliations that have led to distrust and prejudice. The disturbing events have been an outpouring of violence and acts of revenge, which have caused these conflicts to spiral beyond control. It can be particularly difficult to overcome cross-cultural conflicts in countries where governments and societies are unstable, as they are in many Middle Eastern nations.

Effects

The consequences of cross-cultural conflicts are very serious, though those fightings may not even know or understand the roots of the conflicts. Cross-cultural conflicts can lead to a divided world in which conflicts are promoted. Heightened tensions, discrimination and even violence in places where cross-cultural conflicts lead to distrust and fear are accumulated. This kind of violent conflicts occurs all over the world, from the Middle East to South America.

Prevention/solution

Cultural fluency is the key to understanding those who are different from us and preventing or overcoming cross-cultural conflicts. Through cultural fluency, one knows more about other cultures and becomes more understanding of the complexities involved in other cultures. People must become familiar, and therefore more comfortable, with other cultures. This heightened awareness should humanize other cultures and lead to greater communication, peaceful interaction and cross-cultural understanding.

Though the relationship between culture and conflict is intertwined with each other, some approaches to conflict resolution minimize cultural issues and influences. Since culture is like an iceberg — largely submerged — it is important for our analyses and interventions. Unacknowledged icebergs can be more dangerous. If we don't know their size or position, it is difficult for us to make choices about them. Acknowledging culture and bringing cultural fluency to conflicts can help people of all cultures make more intentional and flexible choices.

Chapter

2

Case study introduction

2.1 What is a case?

A case is a story. Cases recount real (or realistic) events or problems as objectively and meticulously as possible so that students experience the complexities, ambiguities, and uncertainties confronted by the original participants in the case (be they foreign policy decision makers, medical doctors, or government officials). As they "inhabit" a case, students must figure out key  components from the real messiness of contradictory and complicated information. Cases force students to

- tell essential from peripheral information,
- identify the problem(s) in question and define its context and parameters,
- find out a set of possible solutions,
- formulate strategies and recommendations for action,
- make decisions, and
- confront obstacles to implementation.

The formats of case vary from one to another. They can be a movie clip, a radio/TV news story, formal written cases, a lead newspaper article, a picture, a mathematical word problem, a piece of art. No matter what format they have, cases

- illustrate issues and factors typical of the kind of problems in question,
- reflect theoretical frameworks,
- emphasize prevailing disciplinary assumptions and principles, and

- reveal realistic complexities and tensions.

2.2 Why use cases?

Case teaching can promote learning by engaging students in very powerful ways. The reason why teachers use cases is that they believe that if students are at the center of the process, they can learn more. Students and course content are actively connected together by case teaching, which shifts responsibility for learning to students so that they can discover (or construct) a body of knowledge and master life learning skills simultaneously.

Though process is emphasized, it does *not* mean that facts, theories, and concepts are sacrificed. Good cases are chocks full of information and require students to apply text-based theory to analyze complicated, real world events. What make it different is that active learning promotes deeper understanding and improved retention.

The cases used in the class should

- *be interesting and real;*
- *relate course content to students in an extraordinarily powerful way;*
- *demonstrate the application of and the limitations of concepts and theories;*
- *make students take responsibility for their learning; and*
- *contribute to students' subsequent successes, graduate programs and careers.*

The goal of case teaching

Cases work in classes where teachers want students to
- *improve their methodology in analyzing material — both quantitative and qualitative;*
- *enhance their ability to use new materials to support their arguments (learn to use empirical evidence to support their claims and why it is important to do so);*
- *improve their ability to listen to and to communicate with others;*
- *contest or refute the points of others, using reasoned argument;*
- *build on points made by others to develop a response that draws on the best thinking of a group;*
- *develop hypothetical solutions to problems; and*
- *examine the consequences of decisions they make.*

2.3　Case analysis

Methodologically, case analysis is qualitative. It organizes data according to its utility in explaining and predicting the behavior of a group and the possibility that a given member will also display that behavior. It is used to identify current practices and to shape future responses.

Analysing each such case individually may be enough to resolve the initial question. The principle of case analysis is invoked in the celebrated remark of Sherlock Holmes, to the effect that when one has eliminated the impossible, what remains must be true, however unlikely that seems.

2.4　Case-based teaching

Case-based teaching is one of the best ways to help cultivate communicative ability. It is a flexible model. If a teacher uses leading questions to direct students toward a moral or process he or she deems "correct," the model is not far removed from direct instruction. However, if students are allowed to formulate their own opinions of a case by improving group-coordinated research activities, debate, or simulated decision-making, the model is more closely aligned with social constructivism.

Just as a child learns to ride a bike by getting on it, students in a case-based course actively engage in course material. They simultaneously learn curricular content — knowledge — and *how* to learn — skills and competencies such as writing, speaking, listening, and critical thinking. Case learning depends on inductive reasoning, and in case learning, content is the very foundation. As students apply knowledge and evaluate options to solve the problem at hand, case learning sharpens their skills of communication and critical thinking. During case discussions, students should listen carefully to each other, respect opinions of others, and work collectively to solve a problem. Thus, case teaching can make students learn to value the contributions of others while strengthening their own ability of creative thinking and effective communicating.

Part III

Case Analyses of Pragmatic Failures in Intercultural Verbal Communication

As far as the communicative channel is concerned, communication can be classified mainly into verbal communication and nonverbal communication. Verbal communication refers to how people communicate by verbal means, i.e. through the oral use of words or in a written way. A five-minute talk with a friend, a bargaining on the market, and a speech for hours are all cases of verbal communication. The most frequent pragmalinguistic failure is the transplant of words, phrases and structures of the mother tongue.

In intercultural communication, people often meet such problems as when a native speaker cannot understand the meaning of the sentences that have been said by a language learner, even though the sentences have no grammatical mistakes. For example, an American remarked to a Chinese interpreter, a young lady who had graduated from a Chinese university: "Your English is excellent, really quite fluent." The Chinese lady demurred, "No, no. My English is quite poor." Then the American appeared a little puzzled, for he had not expected such an answer.

Why should such a phenomenon appear? It is mainly because both parties ignore the differences between their cultures. Linguists call this kind of phenomenon "pragmatic failure."

Pragmatic failure is the inability to understand what is meant by what is said. In intercultural communication people from different cultures speak the same language, but their communication may break down due to cultural differences in ways of thinking, rules of speaking, social values, lexical connotations, and other factors. Pragmatic failure does not refer to the errors of language use in making sentences, but refers to the errors of inappropriateness when speaking; or the errors of not getting the expected communicative effects caused by the inappropriateness of speaking manner, the expression inconsistent with custom.

From the various definitions of pragmatic failure, we can sum up the common characteristics of pragmatic failure as follows.

1. Pragmatic failure is not caused by the misuse of words, phrases, tenses, or violating the grammar rules.

2. The communicative participants cannot talk effectively, that is, they find it hard to understand each other so there is no point in continuing the conversation. The sender and receiver seem like two persons with a hearing disability. What is even worse, they may take offence and become angry.

3. Pragmatic failure often happens between people from different cultures, so we talk of "intercultural pragmatic failure." Pragmatic failure occurs because different cultures have different customs, norms, social conventions, values, ways of thinking, and taboos. Neglecting the cultural differences leads people to use correctly formulated sentences in an inappropriate context or to an inappropriate addressee.

Pragmatic failure falls into two categories: ***pragmalinguistic failure*** and ***sociopragmatic failure.***

Chapter 1

Pragmalinguistic failures

Pragmalinguistic failures occur when the pragmatic force mapped on to a linguistic token or structure is systematically different from the normally assigned to it by native speakers. It is related to the inappropriate expression of language, or misunderstanding of the other's utterance. In a word, it is related to the language itself.

It includes two levels:

1. The speaker misuses English expressions by violating the conventions of native English speakers, or transfers the Chinese meanings and patterns into English through not knowing the correct English expressions.

2. The hearer misunderstands the illocutionary force that the speaker wants to express, or the speaker has not expressed the illocutionary force clearly.

Both the two levels of pragmalinguistic failure are related to the language itself.

In the actual language communication process, verbal communication failure is unavoidable and it can happen between unacquainted communicators as well as between two familiar communicators. It even happens between people that live together.

There are seven kinds of classifications of phenomena of verbal communication failures:

incorrect understanding about the communication purposes of the speaker and the hearer;

ignorance of the pragmatic elements in word meaning;

violating the fixed relation of meaning categorizations;

the existence of speech acts and fixed mindsets;

responses to description;

differences between the speakers;

differences in contextual cognition.

Here is a conversation between an American friend and a Chinese guide:

An American friend: Thank you.

A Chinese guide: It's my duty to do so.

It is known that both Chinese and English have the same expression "Thank you!" for gratitude, which presents no problem. But the foreigner felt a little surprised at the reply. In English, a proper reply might be "It's my pleasure" or "I am glad to be of help," while "It's my duty to do so" implies that the Chinese guide did not want to do it, that he did it only because it was his duty and he had no choice. In point of fact, in China, the above reply is very polite, expressing the force of humility. The communication breakdown like this is mainly due to the different illocutionary force of the same utterance in English and Chinese.

Pragmalinguistic failures will be categorized into three aspects: *lexical*, *syntactic*, and *textual*.

Section 1   Lexical failure

Compared with phonetics, phonology and syntax, meaning is a much less well-known area of language because people from different cultures attach different associations to the same words. As a key component of language, words have self-evident importance and indispensability. To language learners, having a good command of words is one of the preconditions to  master a language. Then there is the problem that all the language learners have to solve: Does the meaning of a word in one language remain the same when the word is translated into another language?

The question might be surprising to some people; after all, "a book" is "一本书" and "tiger" is "虎." But are the answers to these questions always "yes"? Are the meanings of equivalent words exactly the same in both languages?

The reason behind this is that a language user wrongly believes that two words from two languages are totally equal in their cultural connotations and associational or extensional meanings. In fact, the vocabulary of a language is not merely an inventory of arbitrary labels referring to objects, entities, or events. Words also convey many kinds of cultural meanings that add to, transform or manipulate basic senses of words.

If the speaker pays no attention to differences embedded in words, it will be difficult for the hearer to understand him or her. Communication breakdown will take place. For learners of a foreign language, it is essential that they know not only the denotations of words, but also the connotations, especially cultural connotations — covert symbolic meanings expressing cultural values and shared assumption transmitted through words.

The denotation of a word is important in communication and should be given the same attentive consideration. Serious mistakes have been committed because of ignorance of a denotation: sometimes misinterpreting an innocent or well-meaning remark, causing harm or ill feeling; sometimes taking sneers for compliments, leading people to laugh up their sleeves. Thus words should be used with care.

In order to avoid pragmatic failure at the lexical level, people should pay great attention to those culture-bound words and try to learn the historical background and the cultural knowledge behind them instead of automatically memorizing them.

Case 1 Is 龙 a dragon?

Huang Guangqin studies in America. One day she had a chat with her hostess Susan about family relationships and child-raising.

She said, "In China, the parent is more likely to make the decision for the child, and the children are not supposed to make their own decisions when they're young."

Susan said, "Really? But in America, every person is encouraged to act independently and be responsible for his actions, so children are encouraged at an early age to start making decisions. This allows them to learn to express their individual desires and make choices."

Guangqin said, "But whatever the parents do, they do it for the sake of their children since all the parents in China hope their children will be dragons."

After hearing that, Susan felt very surprised, "Dragons? Why do your Chinese parents hope their children will be *Monsters*?"

Discussion:

1. What is the conflict of the case?
2. Why does Susan think that Chinese parents hope their children will be *Monsters*?

 Case analysis:

Here pragmatic failure results from the negative lexical transfer. Susan and Huang Guangqin do not know that there exist differences between the words with surface similarity. They do not know of culture conflicts and they take it for granted that two words (龙/dragon) from two cultures are identical in every connection. They therefore use their own cultural concept to understand the target language, which causes a breakdown in communication.

In China, "龙" is the symbol of royalty, good fortune, power and even used as the symbol of China, so we often hear the following sayings, "龙凤呈祥,望子成龙,""中国是一条东方巨龙," while "dragon" in English refers to a very fierce, terrible, mythological beast and is seen as the embodiment of a monster in Western countries. When the Chinese refer to the four developed areas in Asia they speak of the "four dragons." However, in English newspapers and magazines these are referred to as the "four tigers of Asia." In Chinese culture, the dragon is a holy animal, symbolizing power and royalty. Hence, Chinese are proud of calling themselves the descendents of the dragon. However, according to Christianity, the dragon is a creature of ill omen, just like the serpent in the Garden of Eden that induces Eden and Eve to break the rule and eat the forbidden fruit. *Collins Cobuilt English Language Dictionary* explains it in this way, "If you call a woman a dragon, you mean that she is fierce and unpleasant." So the Chinese idiom "望子成龙" is translated as "wish one's child to be somebody." The literal translation is unacceptable as it will give rise to different cultural associations.

Some other examples can be found. "Family" in English usually only refers to husband, wife and children, while "家庭" in Chinese includes not only husband, wife, child but also grandparents. The English word "owl" does not have any impolite meaning and can even be used to praise people, as in "You are as wise as an owl." But its Chinese counterpart "猫头鹰" is always used to express the feeling of

Part III *Case Analyses of Pragmatic Failures in Intercultural Verbal Communication*   33

being unlucky. Chinese usually use "虎" to convey the meaning of power, courage and masculine beauty — "虎将，虎虎生威，生龙活虎," because we treat "虎" as the king of beasts. By contrast, in English "tiger" gives place to "lion" to refer to a person or a country that is considered to be strong or powerful, and which other people respect or fear. So, in English history, King Richard is known as "Richard the Lion Heart" on account of his boldness and chivalry.

From the above examples, we can see that the associative meanings of English words are not equivalent to those of Chinese words. Neglecting the differences will lead people to bring their original values and attitudes into the process of intercultural communication. It is one of the most common failures resulting from inappropriate understanding of the associative meanings of words.

Case 2   No, she is from Africa!

Mr. Golles works in an international company in China. Once he commented on his secretary Dobbie with his colleague, Wang Fei.

"I think Dobbie devoted herself to the post. She is a really white person."

"A white person?" Wang Fei was surprised, "No, she is from Africa."

 Discussion:

1. Can you find any conflict in the case?
2. How do you understand "the white person" here?

 Case analysis:

The apparent failure of the case is the misunderstanding of the "white" since Wang Fei only knows the surface meaning of "white."

In fact, "white" in the western culture is usually an esteem color. It is considered pure. The word "white" stands for honest and upright, such as "a white soul," "a white spirit," and "white hand" (廉洁). Emerson, a famous American writer mentions "the gray past, the white future." "White" also stands for good luck, such as "one of the white days in somebody's life"(某人生活中的吉日), "white-haired boy"(宠儿) and etc.

Since there exists great difference in geographical location, history background, religious belief, climate and etc., the same color words will make people connect different cultural meanings. Consequently, pragmatical errors might occur and communications between languages might fail to function.

China is a country where red is admired, black is despised and white is rejected. For instance, during Chinese Lunar New Year period, red couplets are attached to doors. Brides wear red clothes, covered with red piece of cloth when in marriage ceremony. But in most cases, red is derogative in English and it is associated with cruelty, disaster, anger, potential danger, war and death, etc. "Red light district" is a well-known euphemism indicating some locations where sexual business is going on.

Green is a sort of color full of vigor and energy underlying "life, youth, hope, peace and energy" both in Chinese and English. But comparatively speaking, green has more associative indications in English such as "green hands"(新手), "be in the green"(血气方刚), which associate with "inexperienced, premature or naive," etc. More than that, green is connected with jealousy such as "green with envy." So more color words, more cultural meanings. Learners could find very interesting phenomena about color words in the following paragragh:

"Mr. Brown is a very white man. He was looking rather green the other day. He has been feeling blue recently. When I saw him, he was in a brown mood. I hope he'll soon be in a pink again."

People might get puzzled with the sentences when reading them, though the words and the structures are both simple, and eager to know what they are talking about.

 Case for students' practice:

Liang Hong, a visiting Chinese lives in London. After seeing signs with T. G. I. F. and hearing people talking about T. G. I. F. parties, he asked, "What does T. G. I. F. mean?" He was told that the letters stood for "Thank God it's Friday" and they would have Weekend Parties. He was surprised. Why Friday? Why not Saturday or Sunday?

Part III   *Case Analyses of Pragmatic Failures in Intercultural Verbal Communication*   35

Section 2   Syntactic failure

Syntax is the study of the rules governing how words and phrases are put together to form sentences in a language, or the study of the relationships between elements in sentence structure. The choice of words, which belongs to the syntactic field, reflects a particular culture. Correct use of each word does not guarantee the  correct intended meaning of a sentence; perhaps you choose the right words in communication but you are still not understood and the hearer cannot grasp your intended meaning. Then communication breakdown occurs.

Here is an example:

An American visitor: Is this a good restaurant?

A Chinese friend: Of course.

Generally, "of course" in English has the meaning of "Yes, indeed," or "Yes, certainly." But this does not mean that it can be used to express the force of certainty in any case. Sometimes it implies that the speaker has asked about something that is self-evident, and sounds at best peremptory and at worst insulting. The same is true of the above example, with "of course" implying "a stupid question." As a result, the foreigner felt offended though the Chinese only meant to convey the force of certainty.

The real meaning of a sentence does not equal the accumulation of the meanings of each word in the sentence, and furthermore it is not the result of the direct translation from the mother tongue. As foreign language learners, we should neither understand sentences in a target language according to our mother language habits nor take everything for granted without considering the possible differences between the two languages concerned. Otherwise, we may well not express our intended meanings and communication will be doomed to failure.

Case 1   Is the curtain beautiful or not?

A Chinese paid a visit to an American friend. After he learned that the beautiful curtains were made by the friend's wife, he said to the friend, "Well, I didn't expect she could make such beautiful curtains." The hostess was upset by this remark and this spoilt the visit.

Discussion:

1. What caused the hostess to be unhappy?
2. What would you say if you wanted to praise the curtains?

Case analysis:

The main conflict of the case is the improper phrasing of the compliment. The visitor used Chinese grammar to praise the hostess.

We know that the equivalent Chinese utterance "哎呀，没想到她还能做这么漂亮的窗帘" is an expression of admiration. However, the illocutionary force of the original English utterance is quite the opposite; it implies that the speaker previously thought that the friend's wife was not skilled in sewing and thus incapable of producing such delicate curtains. So the utterance was interpreted as ironical and rather insulting by the hostess and certainly not perceived as compliment it was intended to be. Such a mismatch of illocutionary forces may often result in pragmatic failure in intercultural communication.

Complimenting as a kind of speech act is frequently used in interpersonal communications, and compliment with compliment response constructs as one aspect of people's communicative competence. Both Chinese compliments and American compliments can be interpreted as formulaic in basic semantic and syntactic patterns, topics on compliment. Both Chinese compliments and American compliments, however, contain their own peculiar emphasis within these aspects. American compliments are formulaic in nature and lack of originality in terms of syntactic structure and semantic items and remain in the range of limited adjectives and verbs while those in Chinese are much more specific and original. Chinese show more implicit compliments, whereas American compliments are much more highly formulaic to be as explicit compliment. Chinese compliments favor the topics on achievements and abilities, while American compliments concentrate more on the topics on appearance and possession.

Part III *Case Analyses of Pragmatic Failures in Intercultural Verbal Communication*   37

Case 2 Be polite, please!

A man was trying to make his way through the gangway of a crowded train. With great effort, he managed to get to his seat-row, but the way to his seat was blocked by a stout lady carrying several packages. He wanted to ask her to make a way for him, saying, "Excuse me, make a way please." Her response was simply to ignore him and not move.

 Discussion:

1. What is the reason for the conflict?
2. Can you find anything wrong with "Excuse me, make a way please"?

 Case analysis:

Linguistically, this is a request made directly in the form of an imperative. It sounds more like an order than a request, which makes it understandable why the person addressed should not comply with the request.

The above sentence is acceptable to Chinese because Chinese learners of English are taught that imperative sentences can perform the speech act of request but, in fact, English-speaking people seldom use imperatives to express requests. This sentence threatens the hearer's face. In this case, a native speaker would say "Excuse me, do you think you could let me pass?", which unquestionably sounds tactful and polite. Here, in order to save the hearer's face, a negative politeness strategy is employed, which emphasizes the hearer's right to freedom.

In language-based communication, some communicative strategies are often used. More often than not, non-native speakers cannot employ them skillfully enough. As a result, the utterances they make sound impolite or even offensive to native speakers, which results in communication breakdown. For example, when a foreigner seems to have lost his way, a Chinese student wants to help him and goes over to him, "What can I do for you?" The foreigner would look at the Chinese student in hospitality. He did not know whether the student would really want to help him or not. If you want to help somebody in western countries you must try to know if he needs help or not. "What can I do for you" is too direct. If he were unwilling to accept the help, the speaker would feel embarrassed and would not get out of the predicament. In this situation, the speaker can say, "Can I help you at all?" Because he expresses it unsurely even if he were refused he would not be abashed.

Case 3   A rather bumpy start!

Yang Yang has invited a Canadian friend, Julia, to her home for a meal. Unfortunately, the occasion gets off to a rather bumpy start.

Yang Yang: Hi, Julia, welcome! Come in, come in!

Julia: Thank you for inviting me. This is a lovely room.

Yang Yang: My room is very small and untidy. Please sit down and have a cup of tea. You must be tired on such a hot day.

Julia: Oh, your room is perfectly clean and tidy! And as for the walk, I'm very strong, you know. I usually walk for at least an hour every day. Don't you think walking is a good way to keep fit?

Yang Yang: Yes, I do. Dinner is ready. Please sit at the table.

Julia: Wow! So many dishes — four! They all look delicious.

Yang Yang: I'm sorry I'm not a very good cook. These are all cold dishes.

Later on in the meal, just before they finish the cold dishes, four hot dishes are placed on the table.

Julia: Another four! There's only two of us eating.

Yang Yang: Never mind, please try more. I am sorry I have prepared so little. If there were more people, there would be eight cold dishes and eight hot dishes, because you are my distinguished guest.

Julia: No, it's not too little. It's more than enough, "Gou le, Gou le."

 Discussion:

1. Why is Julia surprised? What's wrong with their conversation?
2. How can Yang Yang be a better host to her Canadian guest so she can help

Part III *Case Analyses of Pragmatic Failures in Intercultural Verbal Communication*

her learn about Chinese culture?

 Case analysis:

Julia was surprised by Yang Yang's remarks denigrating her flat. However, Yang Yang was probably just being politely modest and the flat was not really untidy. Julia certainly seemed to think it odd that she should say so.

Julia also seemed surprised by her remark about being tired from the walk. Yang Yang was undoubtedly just trying to be polite by showing concern for her guest. We often show our concern by saying something like "You must be tired. Have a good rest." Westerners are sometimes sensitive about such comments; they feel it implies a lack of stamina. Julia was not offended. She just wanted Yang Yang to know the walk over to the flat was not a problem for her.

This pragmatic failure is mainly due to the insensitivity of non-native speakers to the target language. They take it for granted that the utterances they used have transmitted the same meaning both in their mother tongue and in the target language.

Communication would have been perfect if it had gone along the following lines:

Yang Yang: Hi, Julia, welcome! Come in, please.

Julia: Thanks for inviting me. This is a lovely room.

Yang Yang: Thank you. Please have a seat. Would you like a cup of tea?

Julia: Yes, I would.

Yang Yang: Was it difficult to find my place?

Julia: No, your directions were very helpful.

Yang Yang: It's only May, but it's quite hot outside today. How long did it take you to come here?

Julia: It only took 30 minutes to get here. You're right, it is hot, but I don't mind the hot sun.

Yang Yang: Julia, dinner is ready.

Julia: Wow! So many dishes — four of them! They all look wonderful.

Yang Yang: Thank you. I prepared them by myself. I hope you like them. Please help yourself.

Julia: They're delicious. I do enjoy Chinese foods.

Yang Yang: I'm glad you like them. But leave some room for another four hot dishes.

Julia: Really? Another four! This is a real feast!

Yang Yang: You're right. You know in China, numbers have significance, even the number of food dishes we serve a guest. We prefer even numbers but not the singular ones. The figure "eight" is a lucky number in Chinese, and two sets of eight dishes would be prepared for distinguished guests. I am sorry I didn't prepare that many for you — my distinguished guest.

Julia: But I thought it would really be too much food. When there are only two people eating, four hot dishes plus four cold dishes is considered a feast. I feel honored indeed. How sweet you are!

 Case for students' practice:

Li Hua was a freshman in a university and had an American teacher named Alan. One day Alan, while talking on the subject of poetry, wrote something by Chaucer on the blackboard, and asked the students what it meant. Li Hua knew little about this great British poet, let alone his poems, just like her classmates. To tell the truth it would have been difficult for Li Hua to answer the question, even if the writing had been translated into Chinese. There was a long silence during which everyone was afraid to answer and they lowered their heads. Unfortunately the teacher chose Li Hua to answer the question. She mustered up all her courage and said, "Sorry, I don't know." That was always the reply to difficult questions in Chinese classes. She expected him to go on and ask one of the other classmates, as a Chinese teacher would do.

To her surprise he spent the rest of the class explaining how childish her answer was. "As an adult, you should at least have some idea about a question, no matter how difficult it is. Even though your answer is totally wrong, it's much better than 'I don't know.'"

She didn't know why she couldn't say "I don't know." It was always safe for her to say that in her Chinese classes.

Section 3 Textual failure

In discourse analysis, text is defined as a continuous stretch of sentences or utterances. It can be as short as a sign (e.g., No Smoking) or as long as a novel. But here "text" refers to a sequence of sentences deliberately composed by the author with

Part III *Case Analyses of Pragmatic Failures in Intercultural Verbal Communication*   41

determinate beginning and end, which are internally cohesive and coherent and can be analyzed into smaller, sequentially ordered units.

In the research on intercultural communication, the structure of discourse in different cultures has been given more attention. The research found that students with different backgrounds tend to adopt different ways to organize their discourses.

Most native speakers of English would try to go directly to the key points, which can be attributed to the emphasis on the values of egalitarianism and individualism in many Western societies. In contrast, most Asians prefer to use the strategy of indirectness in order to show their politeness and respect for the other person. Usually, the structure of Chinese discourse is developed in this way: the minor points are presented first and then from the step by step analysis the conclusion is derived at the end, which is also called the pattern of climaxing.

It is known that writing styles reflect cultural knowledge, historical background and also modes of thinking of the authors. If foreign language learners do not know the differences behind the two languages, it goes without saying that they will put their own culture or modes of thinking into the target language writing, with the result that when native speakers read these articles they feel confused.

Case study   Why is English important to scientists?

The following example is a Chinese student's composition.
Why Is English Important to Scientists

Today English is the most widely used language. When a scientist draws a conclusion after a long period of study, he wants to let other people know his discovery. How should he do so? If he writes the paper in his native language, only some people will understand it. If he writes it in English, then more people will know it and other scientists may discuss it and form different opinions. It is good for the development of science. Other scientists can learn about their work. English, as a useful tool, is helpful for the scientists to communicate information. If every scientist knows English, he can see others' opinions without difficulty. So English is important to scientists.

Case analysis:

Chinese students' spiraling pattern is a longstanding product of Chinese social and historical culture. Whenever English writing based on the spiraling pattern is used to communicate interculturally, communication will break down. The reasons are as follows.

(1) In the eyes of native speakers, an English thesis by Chinese students is clumsy, though there may be no defect in it with respect to grammar and rhetoric.

(2) When reading a non-literary English text, Chinese learners of English do not excel in distinguishing generality from particularity so they usually fail to catch the main idea of the text even though they may know all the component words.

In contrast, English narration and description are simple, direct and plain. English-speaking people try to use as few modifiers as possible and, when necessary, the simplest and the most precise will be chosen. The function of adjectives cannot be questioned. They are like paints that brighten and bring scenes and events to life. But if they are not used with care, they can have the opposite effect — quickly kill interest and produce boredom. A poor command of modifiers is the weak-point for Chinese learners of English. They do not realize that it is meaning that gives power to an essay, so they always overuse or misuse modifiers that make their writing sometimes appear bombastic and perhaps a little ridiculous. All too often, they try to dress up their works by resorting to a host of adjectives and adverbs that have become overused and long lost their flavor, like "great," "marvelous," "wonderful."

A study of English writing will show that good writers often choose their words with precision. This can be best illustrated through the words of Ophelia in Shakespeare's play *Hamlet*, "Now see that noble and most sovereign reason, like sweet bells jangled, out of tune and harsh." Could there be a better choice of words — the unusual choice of "jangled" following the delightful use of "sweet" — to suggest the incongruity of reason and madness? Or to reflect the torment in Ophelia's mind?

Differences in thinking patterns between Chinese learners of English and native speakers are found to have contributed a great deal to the differences in writing styles. The most important and typical thinking pattern of an English text is the "General-Particular Pattern," or "Linearity," which is characterized by the combination of simplicity and directness. In English writing by native speakers, topic sentences or broad outlines of the text will generally be found at the outset.

If a foreign language learner intends to write a good essay in the target language, he must take into account the differences between the target language and his native tongue and word his essay according to the features and patterns in the writings of the target language.

Orientals prefer indirectness, i. e. , they do not like coming straight to the point, instead, they prefer deducing the viewpoint by means of an "Approach by Indirection." Chinese students are not familiar with the "General-Particular Pattern." They often unconsciously use the Spiraling Pattern, which is rooted in the style and textual structure of Chinese writings. Whenever expounding a theme, most Chinese students do not start with the issue under discussion, but resort to devious methods by analyzing the other aspects concerned so as to provide a hint of their own viewpoint.

Cases for students' practice:

Can you avoid the next textual failures?

1. It is interesting to note that iconic models only represent certain features of that portion of the real world that they stimulate. For example, a map will only contain those features that are of interest to the person using the map. Similarly, regarding architecture, models will be limited to including only those features that are of interest to the person considering employing the architect.

2. For decades, alligator weed had been surely, and not so slowly, taking over the lakes and rivers of much of the South. It fouled the boat propellers and knocked water skiers off their balance; it grew so thick in some lakes that a person could walk on the water. For twenty years, the Army Corps of Engineers had spent 4 million dollars annually on herbicides to control the weed and failed!

Chapter 2

Sociopragmatic failures

Having knowledge of word meanings and grammar rules is far from enough to maintain communication. The inappropriate utterance will be treated as impolite behavior, which is worse than those mistakes caused by lack of linguistic competence. It is said that to be bilingual, one must be bicultural, thus indicating that sociopragmatic  failure occurs when communicators deliver inappropriate messages due to lack of knowledge in respect of the other culture.

Sociopragmatic failure occurs when the interactants fail to observe the other's social and cultural customs. Sociopragmatic failure mainly derives from the influence of one's native culture in intercultural communication; and always occurs when non-native speakers produce socially inappropriate behavior or fail to choose the appropriate language because of lacking the knowledge of cultural differences.

Sociopragmatic failure finds its way in many aspects of daily communication, such as ways of greeting and addressing people; ways of expressing modesty and apology, inquiring or offering, bidding farewell or making an introduction, and view of value system as privacy. These failures may directly lead to serious misunderstanding or even breakdown in intercultural communication.

It stems from cross-culturally different perceptions of what constitutes appropriate linguistic behavior, i.e, what to say and what not to say.

What to say

Free and non-free goods offer us a useful framework within which to discuss sociopragmatic failure. Free goods are those which, in a given situation, anyone can use without seeking permission. Generally speaking, what an individual regards as free goods varies according to relationships and situations.

Perceptions of what are freely available topics differ greatly in different cultures. It is quite acceptable for Chinese to ask a person about their income, the cost of their house, politics, religion, marital status, etc. Americans consider these topics as matters of privacy. It is considered impolite, rude, even unfriendly, to ask such questions. In English there are such expressions as "to poke (or push) one's nose into other people's business" or "meddle in other people's affairs. "People who do so are told "Mind your own business," "It is none of your business."

Accordingly, the following examples taken from a textbook in China are pragmatically inappropriate and seldom used in everyday conversation by native speakers:

What is your name?
My name is Li.
How old are you?
I am forty.
Are you writing to your wife?
Yes, I am.
How often do you write to her?
Once a week.

What one should say

Chinese and Americans have different perceptions of what are proper and inappropriate manners of linguistic behavior. As is known to all, it is proper for Chinese to press their guests many times to take more food by saying "Take your time and eat more." "Come on, taste this." "Eat slowly." and the like, whereas in America it would be unusual to do so.

Indeed, American recipients always feel embarrassed since it seems that their Chinese hosts are behaving impolitely by forcing them into a situation in which they could not find polite refusal strategies. Generally American hosts do not offer food more than once or twice and "Help yourself." is usually what is said.

Many English-speaking people tend to address others by using the first name such as Tom, Michael, Linda, Jane, etc. rather than calling the person Mr. Summers, Mrs. Howard or Miss Jones. This is especially common among Americans, even when people meet for the first time. This applies not only to people of roughly the same age, but also of different ages. People of different social status do the same. For example, it is not at all uncommon to hear students addressing their professors by their first names. "Morning, Joe!" is not a sign of disrespect or familiarity but rather an indication that the professor is considered affable and has a sense of equality. This, of course, is quite counter to Chinese custom. We would imagine the reactions of adults if children were to call a grandparent by his or her first name, or a student were to do the same when addressing a teacher.

Sociopragmatic failure can be categorized as: *forms of address*, *invitations*, *greetings and saying goodbye*, *presenting and receiving gifts*, *compliments*, *family relationships and child-raising*, *friendship*, *taboos*, *euphemisms*, and *different ways of thinking*.

Section 1   Forms of address

Address forms are common phenomena in human verbal communication in daily life across cultures. They make up one of the most important parts of language word systems and reflect the speaker's and addressee's role and identity, family and social status, intimacy or remoteness of their relationship as well as their likes and dislikes.

The norms of addressing are good examples indicating that people's daily communication is tied up with cultural awareness. People would usually choose the most appropriate way to address other persons according to their cultural background and tradition. Addressing expressions are considered as an important part of the social intercourse etiquette with the functions of maintaining, strengthening and even establishing all kinds of interpersonal relationships.

Address terms include pronouns, proper names, titles, kinship terms, etc. In using address terms, there are variations across cultures. Some cultures emphasize one type of address forms such as pronouns, while others emphasize proper names, titles or kinship terms.

The English address system includes personal names, titles, pronouns, kinship terms, nominal phrases, etc. The Chinese address system includes pronouns, proper names, titles, and kinship terms.

The choice of addressing expressions fully reflects the social relationships of power and equality among people. For the addresser and addressee, the change of

Part III *Case Analyses of Pragmatic Failures in Intercultural Verbal Communication*   47

addressing expressions embodies the change of their feelings and the change of close or distant relationships. Each language usually has its own addressing systems and rules. The forms of address in every language also reflect the social status of the speaker, addressee, or the relationship between them. Without knowing the correct form of address, one could not even start a conversation. Even worse, one might often put oneself at the risk of causing misunderstanding. The address forms can be divided into two kinds: *kinship terms* and *social terms*.

Case 1   Hello, Granny!

Linda Walker is an American teacher in her fifties who has just arrived in China and has asked her new colleagues to call her Linda. She has been invited for dinner to the home of her young Chinese colleague, Xu, who is also an English teacher. When Linda arrives, she is introduced to Xu's five-year-old daughter.

"Hello, granny," says the little girl in English.

"No, not granny," the mother hurriedly corrects. "This is Linda."

"But why? She's so much older than you! How can you be so impolite!"

The little girl is puzzled and protests in Chinese. Fortunately, Linda does not understand Chinese, though she can sense something is wrong from the little girl's reaction.

 Discussion:

1. Why did the little girl think it was impolite to call Linda by her first name?

2. Suppose you were the mother, what would you explain to both the little girl and Linda?

 Case analysis:

Such awkwardness is due to different attitudes towards age in different cultures. Chinese people would like to use family terms to address non-family members in order to show their politeness and respect. As the little girl sees that Linda is much older than her mother, she thinks she should call her "granny" out of politeness and respect.

English-speaking people are accustomed to address others by their first names. In America, people also use a title plus first name, but in most informal situations, even the people who have a higher status like being addressed by their first names. For example, many college students call their professors by their first names. Part of the reason for this is that informality is the characteristic of Americans. Chinese people are used to addressing the family members or relatives, even friends or strangers, by using kinship terms. At a party a Chinese student introduced one of his friends to a foreigner. "This is my brother." "Your brother?" The foreigner was doubtful. The student used "brother" to show that his friend was as close as a brother. This the foreigner did not know and explained his scepticism.

This is called the extensive use of kinship terms. It means to address those who are not the relatives of the addresser. Since China is a country with a long history, it has had many large families since a long time ago. And among family members, there were very close relations because people in the past did not move too much and they lived together. As a result, they must have a detailed and clear system to address their family members, for they met each other very often or nearly every day. So it is no wonder that we call someone by kinship terms even if he/she is still a stranger to us, for example, when asking the way, we had better call an older man "*Daye*," otherwise we are considered to be impolite.

When we use these kinship terms to address those who are not our relatives, we never think that we are using a kinship term. It has become so natural that people use them unconsciously.

Case 2   Just call me Robert

A visiting American scholar, Professor Robert Johnson, is teaching in Zhejiang University. His wife Rebecca and six-year-old son David have been living with him in Hangzhou for one year. David attends the kindergarten attached to Zhejiang University and is rapidly picking up Chinese. Chen Yilian, one of Professor Johnson's students, came to visit one weekend. When she arrived, Rebecca was momentarily away from the home. Below is the conversation.

Part III *Case Analyses of Pragmatic Failures in Intercultural Verbal Communication*   49

Prof. Johnson: Hello, Chen, please come in! How are you today?

Chen Yilian: I'm fine, thank you. And you, Professor Johnson?

Prof. Johnson: Fine too, thanks. Just call me Robert.

Prof. Johnson: Dave, this is Chen Yilian from Zhejiang University. Say hello to her.

David: Hi, Yilian Ayi.

Chen Yilian to David: You speak very good Chinese. But you can call me Chen Ayi.

 Discussion:

1. Why does Prof. Johnson address Chen Yilian as Chen but asks her to address him as Robert?

2. And why does David address her as Yilian Ayi?

 Case analysis:

Prof. Johnson has taken the Chinese student's surname for the given name, since the order of the surnames of Chinese and English names is just the opposite. That is the reason he addresses Chen Yilian as Chen, and asks her to address him as Robert. According to American custom it is quite normal in less formal settings for people to address each other by their given names alone, regardless of differences in age or status.

The combination of Yilian Ayi (given name + Auntie) reflects the mixture of two cultures. On one hand, we have the extended use of kinship terms preceded by a person's surname in Chinese culture; on the other hand, we have the conventional use of kinship terms followed by the given name in the American culture. This example shows the combination of the Chinese sequence, i.e. name plus kinship term with the American use of the given name.

Since David has lived in China for a year, he has been influenced by Chinese culture in addition to the American culture of his parents. So, from his point of view, it is appropriate and polite to call the Chinese student Yilian Ayi. However, Chen Yilian follows the Chinese tradition and thinks it is appropriate for a child to address an adult using the surname. In American culture, unless a child is told otherwise, it's only proper to address an adult by his or her surname. David hasn't yet learned this.

Another ordinary rule of address is demonstrated with people's names. Both English and Chinese people have a surname (family name) and a given name (first name), but they are different in the order and usage. In Chinese, the surname comes first and it is followed by the given name, but in English the order is reversed, as can be seen from the following examples: 李(surname)达(given name); Brad (given name) Pitt (surname). This frequently gives rise to misunderstanding.

In China, it is very common to address others by their titles. In Britain, titles are mainly reserved for royalty, government officials, military, religious and law circles, such as Queen, Prince, President, Senator, Judge, Father, General, Colonel, etc. In contrast, Chinese title terms like "主任,部长,科长," are classified in more detail and used on more occasions than in English, with the result that corresponding words for many Chinese titles cannot be found in English. For example,"这位是海信集团的李经理" cannot be translated as "This is Manager Li from Hisense," because "manager" is not a title in English. The proper equivalent would be "This is Mr. Li, a manager from Hisense." In most cases, "陈主任" or "陈部长" should be "Mr. Chen," instead of "Director Chen" or "Minister Chen." Meanwhile, occupation can also be adopted as an address form in both English and Chinese cultures. Some title terms can be occupation terms at the same time, such as "司机,""老师,""医生," "律师,"etc., in Chinese, and waiter, boy, usher, conductor, Father, Sister, etc. in English. "Surname + occupation" is often used in Chinese to show the respect of the speaker for the addressee, while people may adopt this practice in English, e. g. "Doctor Smith," without such an intention or effect.

 Cases for students' practice:

1. A group of Chinese children were playing football, and the football was kicked out of the playground. At that moment an Englishwoman was passing by, so the children said to her, "Aunt, could you please pass the ball to us?" Undoubtedly, the Englishwoman felt strange when she was addressed by a group of children as "Aunt."

2. Two men met on a plane from Tokyo to Hong Kong. Chu Hon-fei is a Hong Kong exporter who is returning from a business trip to Japan. Andrew Richardson is an American buyer on his first business trip to Hong Kong. It is a convenient meeting for them because Mr. Chu's company sells some of the products Mr. Richardson has

come to Hong Kong to buy. After a short exchange of conversation they introduced themselves to each other.

Mr. Richardson: By the way, I'm Andrew Richardson. My friends call me Andy. This is my business card.

Mr. Chu: I'm David Chu. Pleased to meet you, Mr. Richardson. This is my card.

Mr. Richardson: No, no. Call me Andy. I think we'll be doing a lot of business together.

Mr. Chu: Yes, I hope so.

Mr. Richardson (reading Mr. Chu's card): Chu, Hon-fei. Hon-fei, I'll give you a call tomorrow as soon as I get settled at my hotel.

Mr. Chu (smiling): Yes, I'll expect your call.

When these two men separated, they left each other with very different impressions of the situation. Mr. Richardson was very pleased to have made the acquaintance of Mr. Chu and felt they had gotten off to a very good start. They had established their relationship on a first-name basis and Mr. Chu's smile seemed to indicate that he would be friendly and easy to do business with. Mr. Richardson was particularly pleased that he had treated Mr. Chu with respect for his Chinese background by calling him Hon-fei rather than using the Western name, David, which seemed to him an unnecessary imposition of Western culture.

In contrast, Mr. Chu felt quite uncomfortable with Mr. Richardson. He felt it would be difficult to work with him, and that Mr. Richardson might be rather insensitive to cultural differences. He was particularly bothered that Mr. Richardson used his given name, Hon-fei, instead of either David or Mr. Chu.

Section 2 Invitation

A native English speaker decides to hold a party. He gives his invitation a month ahead of time to his Chinese friend Wang and then does not mention it any more. When the date for the party approaches, Wang is not sure whether the invitation is still valid or not after such a long time. Due to a different attitude to time, the communication is affected. In the same context, a Chinese will give the invitation one or two days before the party is held.

Therefore, in intercultural communication, misunderstandings often occur on such occasions.

In China, when we extend our invitation, we may give a very exact time at the beginning. However, interestingly, the invitees usually will not say exactly when they will come. They may say "I may be there about ten o'clock on Sunday," "I'll arrive at the restaurant as soon as possible after the meeting. Don't wait for me. You eat first!" These answers all sound indefinite to the invitors, but they tell them that the guests will come and so they will wait for them. We are used to such answers and do not take offence.

For example:

A：明天来我家吃饭吧！

B：不去了，添麻烦了。

A：麻烦什么呀，来吧。菜都是现成的，好做。

B：还是算了吧，不想麻烦你。

A：一点都不麻烦，你不来我也要烧饭吃呀。来吧，你再拒绝我可要生气了！

B：那好，你千万别费工夫，我们就随便吃点好啦！

This is an example of the Chinese way of extending an invitation. Although the first refusal of an invitation sounds hypocritical, it is a sign of politeness.

In Chinese culture, when receiving an invitation, people like to decline several times even if they have mentally decided to accept. They usually reply with some ambiguous words like "太破费了(It will squander money)," "以后再说吧(We'll talk about it later)," or "不好意思(I feel embarrassed)," etc., to show their politeness. But it will confuse English-speaking people by not knowing whether the invitation has been accepted or not. In fact, it is regarded as impolite or a loss of face to accept an invitation directly without a polite refusal first. Consequently, Chinese people tend to accept an invitation only after the other party firmly insists.

By contrast, in English culture, an invitation without exact time or arrangement and not given a week or two ahead of time, is not a real invitation. For example:

S (a Chinese student): It's really horrible we haven't seen each other for so long.

A (an American student): I know. We have to arrange something.

S: How about dinner? Why don't we go out to dinner together?

A: That's a good idea.

S: What days are good for you and Joe?

A: Weekdays are the best.

S: Weekdays are bad for us. Don't you ever go out to dinner during the week?

A: Well, we do, but we usually don't make plans till the last minute. Joe gets home late a lot, and I never know what his schedule is going to be.

S: Okay, well, look, why don't you tell me when you want to go out, any week night is good.

A: Okay. I will.

S: Really! Don't forget.

A: Okay, I won't. I'll call you.

In English culture, people will express their real intention clearly without any ambiguity to avoid causing trouble for others.

In cross-cultural communication, special attention should be paid to making a request, or it will become a demand. If a Chinese invites his or her western friends to dinner, he or she would say, "Could you come to dinner on Saturday evening please?" The pragmatic force of the sentence is not an invitation, but a demand. Thus it becomes rather impolite. The right expression should be, "Would you like to come for dinner on Saturday evening?"

Case 1   The host-guest relationship

Sarah and Daniel are a young American couple who are teaching English at Zhejiang University. They are learning Chinese, enjoying their new life, and eager to know more about the Chinese people. So they were pleased when Chen Li, their Chinese Colleague, invited them to her home for dinner on one weekend. When Sarah and Daniel arrived, Chen Li introduced them to her husband Wang Bing. She asked them to sit down at a table with eight plates of various cold dishes, served them tea, and then disappeared with her husband into the kitchen. Sara offered to help in the kitchen but Chen Li said she didn't need help.

A half-hour later Chen Li came back, sat down and the three began to eat. Wang Bing came in from time to time to put hot dish after hot dish on the table. The food was wonderful and much more than Sara and Daniel could eat. They kept wishing Wang Bing would sit down so they could talk to him. Finally, he did sit down to eat, but quickly turned on the TV to show them all its high tech features. Then it was time to go home.

Sarah and Daniel were disappointed by this experience, but returned the invitation a month later. They wanted to prepare a nice American meal, and felt lucky to find the appetizers of tomato juice, olives, and even some cheese in the hotel shop. For the main course they prepared spaghetti and a salad with dressing made from oil, vinegar, and some spices found in the market.

When Chen Li and Wang Bing arrived they were impressed by the apartment and asked the price of the TV, video camera, vacuum cleaner and other items. Sarah politely refused to answer their questions, and then asked them to sit at the dining table. Chen Li and Wang Bing were surprised when Sarah and Daniel also sat down at the table and started to eat with them. Chen Li and Wang Bing took small bites of the appetizers, ate only a little spaghetti, and didn't finish the salad on their plates. Sarah urged them to eat more but they didn't, and they started to look around expectantly.

Sarah and Daniel talked about their families and asked the Chinese couple about theirs. After a while, Daniel cleared the table, then served coffee and pastries which the Chinese couple barely ate.

After the couple left, Sara and Daniel felt upset and puzzled because their Chinese guests hadn't eaten much. Yet when they left Chen Li's home, they were extremely full.

Discussion:

1. How did the Chinese couple's understanding of the host-guest relationship influence the way Chen Li and Wang Bing entertained Sara and Daniel?

2. How did Sarah and Daniel's understanding of the host-guest relationship influence the way they entertained Chen Li and Wang Bing?

3. How are the differences in both Chinese culture and American culture, with regards to food and dining, contributing to the communication difficulties?

Case analysis:

Sarah and her husband entertained their Chinese guests as American hosts do, by offering their own favorite food and carrying on a conversation with their guests. They didn't realize Chen Li and Wang Bing weren't eating very much because the food and flavors were unfamiliar, and they were expecting more food to follow as would have been the case at a Chinese dinner. The meal wasn't enough in the eyes of the Chinese guests.

In the West, the guests don't walk around someone's house without permission, and it's impolite to ask personal questions. Asking the price of an item is considered a personal question, and usually wouldn't be answered even if someone were to ask. So when Chen Li asked about the price of the furniture, Sarah refused to answer to protect her own privacy.

Chen Li and Wang Bing should try to learn about American culture. Then they could discuss with Sarah about the different ways of entertaining guests in both cultures. And by learning more about American culture, they will respect her privacy and understand why she didn't answer the questions about prices. Sarah and Daniel should also learn about Chinese culture. They would then also know what to talk about and how to adjust.

In China, when entertaining friends at home, the host shows his or her hospitality by the quantity and the expense of the food offered to a guest. Number 8 is very lucky and important in China. The eight cold dishes and eight hot dishes are offered for the most distinguished guests; and the more a guest eats, the happier the host will be. Normally, a host would not let a guest, especially a distinguished guest, help in the kitchen, unless the guest insists. It's usual for one host to accompany the guests and the other to do the cooking. Chen Li and Wang Bing regarded Sarah and Daniel as their honorable guests by offering eight cold dishes and eight hot dishes, and didn't let Sarah help in the kitchen.

It is common for Chinese guests to walk around the host's home commenting on the furniture and asking the price. A Chinese host would be proud to answer the questions. So at Sarah's apartment, Chen Li and Wang Bing, being good Chinese guests, kept asking the price of their furniture and other items.

In the West, hospitality is not shown by the quantity of the food served. Quality is always important, and hospitality is shown by preparing special dishes the hosts hope their guests will enjoy.

A good host and hostess spend time conversing with the guests. At a home dinner party, either the host or hostess may temporarily leave the guests to finish preparing the meal. When the guests are invited to sit at the dinner table for the meal, both the host and the hostess will also sit down to eat and enjoy a warm conversation with their guests.

When entertaining guests from a different culture, look for an opportunity early in the conversation to ask if the guest is familiar with your cultural traditions for a dinner meal. If the guest says, "yes," you can say, "We're delighted to have you join us tonight." If the guest says, "no," you can explain the highlights of what to expect for the evening. This gives the guest new information about your culture and enlightens the guest on what to expect during the evening. By learning about the other's culture, each will be able to ask questions in areas that may be different and confusing. This new knowledge will give each person greater understanding about another's culture, and the differences will be respected.

Case 2 Thank you! I will try!

A Chinese researcher, visiting America, was invited by his supervisor to dinner at home. He kept saying "Thank you," adding all the time "I will try to come." This irritated the American supervisor who wanted a simple "Yes" or "no." He had no idea whether the Chinese had accepted his invitation or not.

 Discussion:

1. What does the researcher mean by saying "I will try!" in Chinese way?
2. Why was the supervisor irritated?

 Case analysis:

The Chinese, when he receives the invitation, acts in a way that is tactful and appropriate in Chinese culture. The American professor, with his very different cultural background, cannot infer the implication from the Chinese researcher's speech act; he does not know whether the researcher will come or not, whether he is accepting or not. From his point of view, the Chinese violates the quality maxim of Grice's Cooperative Principle. Miscommunication thus occurs. To be brief, that is to avoid obscurity of expression, to avoid ambiguity, to be brief (avoid unnecessary prolixity), and to be orderly.

 Case for students' practice:

A Chinese student saw a non-Chinese at a busy traffic intersection who was having trouble finding his way to his destination. Since she was learning English, she offered to help him, which he much appreciated. They had a friendly conversation, and at the end exchanged telephone numbers. He called her the next day and invited her to go to his apartment at 9 p.m. that evening. She was unsure about what to do. A Chinese man would never do such a thing. Perhaps this was simply a cultural difference and the invitation was proper.

Section 3 Greetings and saying good-bye

Greetings and saying good-bye are effective ways of establishing and maintaining social contact. There exist differences in greetings and saying good-bye in English and Chinese, especially regarding content and meaning. Neglecting these differences and expressing oneself according to his or her own cultural practice will result in inappropriate language. This will lead to misunderstanding, and possibly a negative reaction on the part of the listener and, eventually, lead to pragmatic failure.

Greetings

Greetings, being an indispensable link for emotional contact and enhancing understanding between people, play an extremely important part in daily life and communication. When greeting, people of different cultural backgrounds often cause misunderstanding and hence commit pragmatic failure. Therefore, we must make our greetings in accordance with customs. If we do not, it may appear meaningless and even convey a meaning very different from that we wish to convey. Whatever the way one chooses, it is necessary to make the words as polite and as appropriate as possible.

Saying good-bye

Greetings occur at the beginning of a personal interaction, while saying good-bye takes place at the end of a personal interaction. The latter serves to strengthen the relationship between the two parties. Westerners tend to deliver the information showing their enjoyment and pleasure for a meeting by saying "It is a wonderful party. I really enjoy it. But I have to go now" or "It is nice to meet you. I hope we will meet again soon." In contrast, Chinese would take a very different way to express the similar meaning with the word of "sorry," "I am sorry to have brought you trouble. You had spent a lot of time to prepare all of these" or "I am sorry to have wasted a lot of your precious time."

Case 1 Have you eaten lunch?

Robert, a British teacher of English in China, went to the bank. He was asked by the bank clerk, "Have you eaten lunch?" He was extremely surprised and said, "I haven't had lunch? So what?"

1. Why was Robert extremely surprised?
2. What are the different interpretations of the greeting by the two people involved in this situation?

In British culture, this question would be regarded as an indirect invitation to lunch and it also indicates a young man's interest in dating the girl if this happens between unmarried young people. However, the clerk simply intended it as a greeting.

In China, the ways of greeting are rather flexible in a sense; they depend on the situations and environment when they meet. We prefer to say "Where are you going?" or "What are you going to do?" to show our consideration. People may just give a smile in answer or simply reply "go out for business," "to have a walk." We are aware that the questions are just a way of greeting one another, so we usually won't take them seriously. However, the ways of greeting are diverse in Chinese and English. Chinese greetings sound strange and ridiculous for westerners, such as "Have you had your meal?" "Where are you going?" "Where have you been?" "Are you going to work?" etc.; native speakers of English will treat them as real questions and may find them offensive. Here greetings in one culture become pragmatic failures that lead to miscommunication in another culture as most English-speaking people will not interpret them as greetings but as inquiries and invasions of their privacy.

At present, more and more Chinese learners of English have realized the differences shown above, and avoid using the Chinese way of greeting to greet native speakers of English. However, there are still some breakdowns in this area. A better understanding of cultural differences in greeting will definitely overcome the cultural clashes and improve human relations in intercultural communications.

Case 2 Nice meeting you

The conversation was between Gao Tiantian, a Chinese high school female teacher of English, and Sunny, a female visitor from America. They met at Tian'anmen Square for the first time.

Sunny: Nice to meet you.

Gao Tiantian: Nice to meet you, too.

(After chatting for a while)

Sunny: Nice meeting you.

(The Chinese teacher, Gao Tiantian, continued talking.)

Sunny: Sorry, I have to go.

 Discussion:

1. What does Sunny mean by saying "Nice meeting you."?
2. What's wrong? Why?

 Case analysis:

In this case, the English native speaker wanted to end the conversation by saying "Nice meeting you," but the Chinese teacher of English did not understand the discoursal force of the sentence and continued talking.

Generally speaking, in different cultures, the guest has to decide when it is appropriate to leave. In Chinese culture, when the guests decide to leave, they may put a sudden end to the conversation and immediately get up to leave. However, if the host or hostess is from an English-speaking culture, they may be taken aback by such a sudden move since in their culture the guests will signal several times before eventually leaving.

Usually when Chinese guests are ready to leave, they would say "You are so busy, and I will not disturb you any more," or "You must be tired, so I am leaving now," which may make the Western host experience a sense of abandonment. In fact, in their culture guests usually find some reasons for leaving related to themselves rather than to the host, such as "Well, I am really enjoying talking with you, but I must go soon, for I have to get up early tomorrow," or "Thank you for such a wonderful dinner, but I have to go." Chinese guests prefer to say "I'm leaving now," when bidding farewell to the host. In addition, when there are a lot of guests, a guest may say "I will go first." Such utterances would not be acceptable in English culture as "I'm leaving now" can only be said to other guests, but not to the host, while "I'll go first" can only be said to the host. If a man is leaving earlier and declares "I will go first" loudly to all the guests, this would be unpleasant and have a disturbing effect.

Because of the different procedures and rhythm, the Western hosts sometimes feel the Chinese guests leave too eagerly; they are not even prepared when the guests have already stood up to leave. Chinese guests are used to chatting more after leaving the sitting room: They often feel the Western hosts are not hospitable when the latter accompanies them directly to the door and says good-bye.

According to Chinese culture, when the host sees his guests off he often says "Walk slowly," "Be careful on the way," etc. Native English speakers might feel unhappy hearing those words because they are wondering why they should go slowly and why they are considered as children since they are adults and know how to care for themselves. By contrast, hosts in English-speaking country usually just stand at the door, smile at the guests and say "see you" or "take care."

Case 3 Any movie you like will be fine!

One American friend invited a visiting scholar to watch a movie. The following was the conversation between them.

American: What kind of movie do you like?
Chinese: I don't care. It's up to you.
American: Since I live here, I can go any movie I like

Part III Case Analyses of Pragmatic Failures in Intercultural Verbal Communication   61

at any time. But if you have any movie particular in your mind, I will take you to that.

Chinese: I don't mind. Any movie you like will be fine.

 Discussion:

1. Can you find any conflict in the case?
2. What do you think of the American's reaction to the answer of the Chinese?

 Case analysis:

This is a typical sociopragmatic failure. The Chinese visiting scholar dealt with the situation in America according to the experience in China. In Chinese practical social customs, when being invited, the guest always follows the arrangement of the host and is unwilling to put too much trouble for the host. So when asked about any advice to the arrangement, the guest normaly tries not to show his or her different opinions. That's why the visiting scholar in the case answered like that.

However, the scholar should follow the customs in America and express his own ideas and requirements. In order to satisfy the guest, the host would like to accept the choice of the guest and then decide what should do next although he has his own plans. In this situation, the host hopes the guest answer in this way: "I think I would like to see an action movie or cartoon movie or movie starred by Stephen Seagal..." "I have no idea, can you give me some suggestions?" or "What would you suggest?" or "Any good suggestions?"

 Case for students' practice:

An American invited a group of Chinese students to his house. He and his wife had spent a great deal of time preparing food and hoped that the Chinese would enjoy themselves. They came at about 8:00 at night and right away seemed to be enjoying themselves. There was a lot of dancing and singing and good conversations. Then, almost suddenly, one of them said "Thank you" to the hosts and said it was time to go. After that, all of the Chinese began to get ready to leave. The American and his wife couldn't understand why this happened. They felt insulted because everyone left *so early and at the same time.*

Section 4 Presenting and receiving gifts

In China, when being invited to a meal, people usually bring fruits and flowers, or two bottles of spirits, but never bring just one bottle because even numbers are favored by Chinese people and considered good luck, while odd numbers, especially the number one, might give the impression that the person is stingy.

In America, when an adult is invited to a dinner party, it is regarded as polite to bring a small, relatively inexpensive gift for the hostess, such as a box of candy, chocolate or a bottle of wine. Two bottles of wine are not necessary, since it might suggest the hostess does not prepare enough wine for her guests.

Unless asked, it is not customary to bring food. If you are invited to do so, however, a dish of food large enough to feed the whole group is appropriate. The hostess will usually tell the guests what type of dish to bring. Never bring a friend, a relative, or children to a party, especially a dinner party, unless they have been invited to attend with you.

In the West, opening a beautifully wrapped gift in front of the giver and expressing appreciation is considered polite. Furthermore, giving a surprise is appreciated, so guessing what's inside can frequently become part of the process of receiving and opening a gift. The situation is very different in China. Normally the gift is put aside and opened later, after the visitors have left. The main reason for doing so is to show that the host is welcoming the guests for themselves, not for the gifts. Therefore, opening a gift in front of a visitor would be regarded as impolite and greedy, and the visitor would think the host is only interested in the gift. In addition, many gifts used to be presented without being wrapped. But now, influenced by Western culture, more and more gifts are beautifully wrapped. Also, the people usually tell the receiver what is inside when offering the gift, which is also part of the reason why the gift isn't immediately unwrapped, but set aside.

Case 1 Who's the gift for?

Lin Bao recently moved to Los Angeles as a sales representative for an international conglomerate. He has already been able to bring new business to the company by developing professional relationships with several new clients. He knows it's important to do a good job and provide good service to these clients so they will continue doing business with him rather than the competitors.

It's early December and Lin Bao knows this is the season many businesses give gifts to their clients. The gifts are usually not extravagant, but a gesture to show appreciation for a client's business.

Lin Bao has one client named Ann in Beverly Hills who has been very nice to work with, and he wants to buy her a nice gift. So he buys a bottle of perfume, has it wrapped in red paper which has pictures of Santa Claus, then takes it back to his office and places it on his desk so he can deliver it to Ann the next day.

Lin Bao's manager enters his office:

Manager: Lin Bao, who's the gift for?

Lin Bao: It's for my client Ann.

Manager: That's nice of you to buy her a holiday gift, but we haven't known Ann very long so I recommend you re-wrap it in different paper. It's best to select either a plain color without any Christmas artwork, or one with a winter scene, perhaps gold or silver metallic. By the way what did you buy as the gift? Remember we have a price limit on gifts we can purchase for clients.

Lin Bao: Yes, I read the company regulations and the price of gift doesn't exceed the dollar limit. I bought a small bottle of perfume.

Manager: I'm afraid you'll have to return it to the store and select another gift.

 Discussion:

1. Why is the manager telling Lin Bao to select another gift, and also giving specific directions for the wrapping paper?

2. Do you know any differences between Chinese and Western cultures in respect of the giving of gifts?

Case analysis:

There are two problems with the gift Lin Bao selected for Ann. In fact, December is a gift-giving season because of Christmas and Hanukkah. Since Lin Bao doesn't know whether Ann is Christian or Jewish, the red paper with the pictures of Santa Claus is only appropriate for Christians who celebrate Christmas. Red and green are traditional Christmas colors. The Jews do not celebrate Christmas. December is the timeframe for their eight-day religious celebration of Hanukkah. Blue and silver used together are traditional Hanukkah colors.

Unless you know for certain the religious affiliation of a client, or a friend, select wrapping paper and cards that don't reflect either religion. That's the reason the manager suggested plain colored paper, in addition to gold or silver.

The gift of perfume is not appropriate as a business gift for an American client. Just as articles of clothing are not appropriate. These are considered too personal. Traditional holiday gifts may include calendars, appointment books, candy, wine and gourmet food items in a nice gift basket (but not pork products, unless you know the recipient isn't Jewish).

Case 2　A gift from a Chinese student

Dongxie did his graduate study in an American university. He came back to China for a summer vacation. When he went back to his program, he paid his supervisor a visit and presented him a gift.

The professor opened the gift. It was a ginseng with its many tiny roots spreading out in a very artistic pattern. It clearly was an expensive gift.

The professor's eyes shone at the ginseng, but he then began to feel uneasy. "Dongxie, I appreciated your kindness, but I can't take this as a gift."

"Why? Don't you like it?" It was Dondxie's turn to be uneasy now.

"Oh, sure, I love it. But I can't accept it."

"Why?"

"Because I didn't do anything to deserve it."

Part III *Case Analyses of Pragmatic Failures in Intercultural Verbal Communication* 65

 Discussion:

1. Do you think ginseng is a good gift to be presented?
2. Why didn't the professor accept the student's gift?

 Case analysis:

Chinese people love giving gifts. It is important to know that gifts are a major part of the Chinese culture. For example, the Chinese would much rather reciprocate a gift with another gift than to send a "thank you" card. When visiting someone in China, especially if you are a guest in their house, it is imperative that you bring a gift (whatever the monetary value) to show respect to the host. Usually, the value of the gift is an indication of how important the receiver is in the sender's eyes. Most people giving gifts are concerned about whether the gift will be seen as valuable enough. Sometimes an inexpensive gift means a loss of face.

Dongxie may have a practical reason in giving the ginseng to his supervisor, but most Chinese people will take it as something usual for a student to do this to a professor out of a sign of respect. He chose ginseng because it is a typical Chinese product and because it is expensive. But being rejected by the professor made Dongxie fell embarrassed because of the suspicion of bride.

The gift, as a social gesture, may be expected in some cultures and could be considered a bride in others. To give a proper gift one must understand the culture of the receiver.

In America, people do occasionally receive the gifts out of the appreciation for the friendship and assistance. For them, value of the gift could be small like a book, a CD, or a pen. In this case, Dongxie's supervisor understood not only how special the gift was, but how expensive, and knew it was more than Dongxie could easily afford.

 Case for students' practice:

Wu Mei is going to the United States for a vacation and will be visiting friends Carol and John whom she met there during her last vacation. She's looking forward to seeing them again, and wants to bring them a gift from China. She selects a set of *eight beautiful silk place mats that are frequently used on American dining tables, and has them gift-wrapped in red paper.*

When Wu Mei arrives at Carol and John's home she presents her red gift-wrapped box. Carol immediately accepts it, then starts removing the paper and opening the box, as John stands next to her, watching. Carol and John are both very pleased with the place mats and tell Wu Mei they will always think of her when they use them on their table.

John then tells Wu Mei they will spend the evening on the patio since the weather is so nice, and leads her to the patio table where they will eat dinner. After they all sit down, Carol starts asking Wu Mei about her trip and the other friends she's visited so far on her vacation. The evening is filled with good conversations and an American dinner of charcoal grilled steaks, salad, corn on the cob, garlic bread, and ice cream for dessert.

Wu Mei has a nice evening, but is puzzled by two things.

First, Carol immediately takes the gift Wu Mei has presented.

Second, Carol and John hasn't given her a gift in return.

Section 5 Compliments

Giving a compliment is a common social phenomenon existing in every language and every culture; it reflects people's communication activity at different levels. We can use compliments to greet people, express thanks or congratulations, encourage people, soften the bitterness of criticism, start a conversation or even overcome embarrassment. Concerning compli-

ments and compliment responses, the pragmatic rules are various in different cultures.

Compliment is defined as a speech act which explicitly or implicitly attributes credit to someone other than the speaker, usually the person addressed, which is positively valued by the speaker and the hearer. As a kind of social language, compliments cannot only shorten the distance between the communicators, but also make friendly contacts in order to maintain a normal interpersonal relationship. The speaker, when praising other people, desires a response from the listener. Appropriate compliments and responses to compliments that occur in intercultural communication can facilitate successful communication. The compliment must show sincere expression of positive feelings to the complimentee and it is a kind of face-to-face interacton.

People compliment another individual by passing a favorable judgment or opinion. In doing so, the speaker expresses a commonality of taste or interest with the addressee, thus reinforcing or, in the case of strangers, creating at least a minimal amount of solidarity. In addition, compliments often serve to strengthen or even replace other speech act formulas, and it is common to find compliment expressions in situations of thanking, apologizing and greeting. On such occasions, compliments act as the "social lubricant serving to create or maintain rapport."

In Western culture, the topic of compliments ranges from a person's talent, competence, achievement, appearance, house, car, or even wife or husband and child. And their response to compliments is always positive. Furthermore, comments on someone's appearance or possessions are the most common type of compliment. No matter what her age, social status, or occupation is, the appearance of the female is always to be complimented. The people who express compliments can be either female or male. For example, a male compliments his female superior, "You look so pretty when you smile. You should do it more often." or a male can say to his female colleague, "Join us for dessert. With your figure, you don't have to worry about the calories!"

However, in Chinese culture, complimenting someone on their appearance is only done between females. Generally, Chinese men would be shy to compliment a woman on her beauty directly. This case may happen between lovers, and the response from the girl would be a smile and a blush. If a man compliments a Chinese woman on her appearance, it may cause embarrassment to both persons.

Quite a lot of cases in intercultural communication show that not all the compliments would serve a good function and the responses would be made to make both sides of the communication satisfied. Misunderstandings of compliments and inappropriate responses to compliments would twist the communication and cause negative feelings.

Case 1 Am I really so old?

Li Hong is a new teacher in a middle school. One day, one of her Chinese colleagues, Yang Zhen, introduces her to their middle-aged expatriate teacher Maggy.

Yang: Li Hong, this is Maggy, our English teacher from America. And Maggy, this is Li Hong, our new colleague.

Li and Maggy: How do you do!

Maggy: Your sweater is so smart.

Li: Oh, it is only an old one. I bought it last year.

Maggy: You are so young and smart. I am sure you are a good teacher.

Li: No, no. I am just a newcomer. I should learn from you old teachers.

Maggy looks surprised and thinks, "I am really so old?"

 Discussion:

1. What does Li mean by saying "Oh, it is only an old one, I bought it last year."?

2. Why does Maggy question herself she is really so old?

 Case analysis:

Li Hong comes from a collectivistic culture that emphasizes deference to people older than oneself and the modesty displayed on the part of the young. Maggy comes from an individualistic culture which values assertiveness and free expression of feelings.

As a young and new teacher, Li Hong showed her respect to Maggy with a formal greeting. When Maggy complimented Li on her sweater and herself, Li reacted in a typical Chinese way by overusing modesty in front of a teacher older than herself. She did this by saying that her sweater was an old one and that she should learn from Maggy, an old teacher. Li's responses are perfect between Chinese people but go down badly in cross-cultural situations like this. She did not realize that her expression of respect could be interpreted negatively since individualistic cultures do not associate as much deference with age as collectivistic cultures do. Therefore, Maggy, coming from an individualistic culture, was surprised when Li called her an "old teacher." Maggy did not understand that the word "old" here was meant as a compliment, meaning that she had richer teaching experience. Both Li Hong and Maggy communicated only from their cultural perspectives and thus caused miscommunication.

To avoid miscommunication, Li Hong and Maggy should learn more about each other's culture and adjust their behavior accordingly. When Maggy complimented Li on her sweater and herself, Li could simply reply "thank you." Moreover, she could use her non-verbal language to show her respect to Maggy, for instance, with a smile, a handshake, etc. As to Maggy, she could use fewer complimentary words or more objective questions to reduce Li's nervousness. She should also understand that one of the key values in collectivism is the deference paid to experience and old age.

Case 2 Where, where!

In the late 19th century, a Chinese government official went to visit an English diplomat with his wife and an interpreter. After the routine greetings, the English diplomat said to the official, "Your wife is very pretty." The official responded, "哪里,哪里" (A Chinese modest way) to deny the fact. Then the interpreter translated it as,

"Not at all!" The diplomat was astonished and said, "Of course she is." Hearing this reply, the official was very annoyed, as he considered it an insult according to his own cultural background.

Discussion:

1. What do you think of the Chinese official's response to the compliment?
2. What would your answer be to it?

Case analysis:

It is quite common for people to exchange compliments or praises in English speaking countries and China. However, ways of expressing praises or compliments are quite different and the responses to them are varied.

In this case, the misunderstanding seriously undermines communication. We can see differences in replying to compliments in different cultures. Chinese people usually regard modesty as a virtue. There is a saying, "Modest is the traditional virtue of the Chinese nation." Therefore, when being complimented, most of them tend to reject the compliment, replying politely with something like "Not at all," "You flatter me" or "I feel ashamed" to show their modesty and not to be suspected of being arrogant and conceited.

But to Westerners, a person will not reply to a compliment like this as this might give an impression of dishonesty. In their opinion, honesty is the best policy. They think it impolite to refuse sincere praise. So they will see the compliment as affirming a truth and should be accepted with pleasure. Usually the native speakers of English will respond with "Thank you," "Thank you for your encouragement," "I am glad to hear that, "and the like.

 Case for students' practice:

A famous Chinese actress married a German. One day when she was acting, her husband was there watching, saying again and again that she was the best actress. The actress's colleagues present asked her afterwards to tell her husband not to praise his own wife like that in public. On learning this, the German wondered what he did wrong.

Once the actress and her husband were talking with their Chinese friends at a party. Her husband politely praised a Chinese lady on her beauty. The lady's husband said that his wife was moderately good-looking when young, but now she was old and no longer so. The lady nodded in agreement with a smile. The actress's husband was surprised.

Discuss why the German was confused in the first situation and surprised in the second.

Section 6 Family relationships and education

The differences in roles and relationships between people occur within different cultures. The most important relationships are between parents and children, husband and wife, and those between friends. Moreover, there exists a gender difference between males and females, not only in cross-cultural but also in

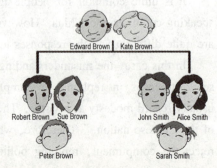

mono-cultural communication.

The most important relationship in the family is that between parents and children. Arranged marriages are therefore to be expected in China. It is the children's duty to support his parents. Respect and obedience to parental wishes are expected of the children. Parents are responsible for their children's education and marriage; household shrines exist for them and graves must be tended regularly.

The most important relationship in the family is that between husband and wife in Western countries. Parents do not arrange marriages for their children, nor do children usually ask their parents' permission to get married. Parents feel that adult children should make major life decisions by themselves. Societal and familial treatment of the elderly reflects the values of independence and individualism. The elderly's financial support is often provided by government-sponsored social security or welfare systems that decrease their dependence on the family. Older people often seek the company of their own friends and avoid becoming too emotionally dependent on their children. It is a common practice for families to place their older relatives in nursing homes because of physical disabilities or illness, rather than care for them in their homes. Many older people do not want to have to rely on their grown-up children. The same spirit of independence that guides child-rearing and young adults also affects older people.

Nevertheless, more and more Chinese families are being influenced by Western cultures, which have caused great changes to occur within those families and the relationships between family members.

In the West, especially in the United States, it is common for parents to put a newborn baby in a separate bedroom when the child is a few weeks old. Part of the reason is economic; that is, many houses are large enough to offer each child a separate room. However, Americans have other reasons for physically separating their children soon after birth. Parents like to preserve their privacy. By having their own rooms, the children will also be able to have privacy when they are older. In addition, the children will eventually learn to be responsible for their own living space. This is seen as a first step toward personal independence.

Americans have traditionally held independence, and the closely related value of individualism, in high esteem. Parents try to instill these values in their children. American English expresses these value preferences: at a certain age, children should "cut the (umbilical) cord" and are encouraged not to be "tied to their mother's apron strings." In the process of their socialization, children learn to "look out for number one" and to "stand on their own two feet." However, children are not autonomous.

Parents are emotionally and financially responsible for their children until they become adults.

The main characteristics of American parent-child relationships are the following:

Children are encouraged to make decisions and to be responsible for their actions;

Children are encouraged, but usually not forced, to "leave the nest" and begin independent lives;

Adult children make major life decisions by themselves;

Parents do not arrange marriages for their children, nor do children usually ask their parents' permission to get married.

Case 1　The right to choose

Iris is an American and has married a Chinese researcher, Ren Hua. They have a three-year-old son, Dave. One morning before breakfast, Iris kept asking Dave to choose between two different breakfast cereals and two different kinds of fruit juice. Dave was busy playing with a toy and wasn't listening to her. Then Ren  Hua told Iris that it wasn't necessary or proper to ask a child to choose his/her breakfast, and it was better just to give him what she thinks is best for him. Iris was puzzled, and argued that a child should be given the right to choose.

1. What's the problem?
2. Why were they disagreeing?

Iris and Ren Hua have different ways of educating their son based on their own cultures. Iris gave her son a choice for breakfast, which would allow him to eat what he preferred. She was offering cereal and juice, both healthy for breakfast. The choices offered to the son were the flavors.

Part III *Case Analyses of Pragmatic Failures in Intercultural Verbal Communication*   73

In individualist cultures like America, as we saw earlier, every person is encouraged to act independently and be responsible for their actions, so children are encouraged at an early age to start making decisions. This allows them to learn to express their individual desires and make choices. Critical in this process is the parent's responsibility to only offer a child choices that are safe and in the child's best interest.

The parent is responsible for offering choices in a situation that the child can reasonably handle. Offering a child choices allows for the child's needs and desires to be met, but it must be paired with teaching that child about responsibility and accountability for the choice. This will teach independence and consideration.

In a culture or hierarchical society like China, parents are more likely to make decisions for their children, and the children are not supposed to make their own decisions when they're young. This breakfast incident points out the differences in the cultural values for nurturing children. No doubt neither Iris nor Ren Hua could have imagined the differences they would encounter while rearing a child!

Case 2   Red rabbit or white rabbit?

Johnson, an ambassador to China, sent his son David to a kindergarten in Beijing during his stay in China. David had one favorite hobby, drawing. Once Johnson went to the kindergarten to meet his son, David looked upset and showed his drawing with 60 marks on that. The red rabbit David drew was vivid and lovely, and he thought it was the best one he had drawn. Johnson patted on his head and said, "Never mind. Next time you will do better."

"But the teacher said it was the color that spoiled the drawing. I am not allowed to paint it in red anyway because all the rabbits are in white or gray in the world."

Johnson felt annoyed and after talking over with his wife he sent his son back to his own country.

 Discussion:

1. Do you think it is the scores that make Johnson decide to send his son back?
2. Could you give any suggestions to the teacher if you were Johnson?

Case analysis:

In this case, the conflict lies in the different ideas about children's education. The teacher in the kindergarden took the drawing the best one only when it shows the reality and vividness, but Johnson regarded the imagination and creativity in children as the most important part in education. So he sent his son back in order not to be affected by Chinese education concept.

The object of American family education is raising the children into a social man who has the capacity of conforming to the series surroundings and independence. By contrast, Chinese parents are always keen for their children to get on, have a good job and live in a bed of roses.

American family education is rich in content that attatches importance to the children's harmony development of physical power, cognition, sociality, language and emotion, which is called competence-oriented education. Chinese family education gives emphasis to ensure that the children could develop in all-round way, morally, intellectually, physically and aesthetically.

What is much ignored in the Chinese family education is the potential, which includes the learning ability and creativity. Apparently, Chinese parents attach more importance to children's learning. However, the real mainspring of society is the creative ability. After school, the Chinese parents always ask their children "What do you learn at school?" or "What scores have you got today?" While the American students would be asked "Have you raised any questions today?" or "How do you like the classes today?"

Different education aims, contents and methods may lead to different results. Generally speaking, the characteristics of American children and teenagers are active, cool-headed, easy-going, independent, bold, creative and sociable. Meanwhile Chinese children even college students are superior in grade points. However they show negative tendency on their characters: passive, timid, dependent, etc. In a word, they are lack of the ability of adapting themselves to the new surroundings.

 Case for students' practice:

Bob and Helen are vacationing in China for a month. They have brought their 5-year-old son Tommy with them. Because he's a noisy and energetic child they've found the trip exhausting.

They marvel at the Chinese children they see who are his age.

Helen: You know, Bob, I never gave much thought to how Tommy behaved. I just thought he was being a typical boy. But I see all these children at his age who sit quietly and pay attention to what their parents or grandparents tell them to do.

Bob: I know what you're saying. Maybe we need to look at how we are training him. He'll be starting school this fall, and he can't even stay seated for a one-hour train trip.

Helen: You're absolutely right. It's important that he's able to sit in the classroom and pay attention. I've always wanted him to play and enjoy himself while he's a very young child. But I can see that I need to help him learn how to sit quietly in order to read or listen.

Section 7   Friendship

Friends are an important part of our daily lives. They are both a basic functional network and an emotional support system for individuals in society. What we do to make friends and to sustain friendship is part of our daily activities.

In China most people expect their friends to help them when they are in need. We have a lot of Chinese sayings concerning friendship: "为朋友两肋插刀" (People can take any risks, even risk their lives, especially among male friends, to do everything for their friends regardless of whether it is right or wrong); "有难同当，有福共享" (People can not only share bitterness and hardship but also happiness with their friends). Other proverbs and sayings such as "一个篱笆三个桩，一个好汉三个帮" (As one fence needs three stakes, a good guy needs three fellows), "在家靠父母，出门靠朋友" (It is your parents that you can rely on at home, but it is your friends that you can count on when out in the society), show that friendship really counts and is of great importance.

Having friends is the reflection of a good personality. The more friends you have the more sociable and likeable you are. Your life will be better if you have more friends, and will be worse without friends. One needs a friend to help out when difficulties occur, and one needs a friend to give emotional support in times of trouble. What is more, one needs a friend to offer financial support when there's a lack of money. So, in other words, one cannot be without friends in life.

In general, Americans have casual, friendly relationships with many people, but deeper, closer friendships with only a few. Friendship requires time and commitment; and depending on the Americans' commitments to family, which is a priority, and time required for work or school, various types of friendships will be developed. Men and women socialize relatively freely and develop a variety of relationships. Single and married people of the opposite sex may be close friends and share personal problems without being romantically involved. Some married men and women consider themselves to be best friends as well as spouses. College students and others may even live with someone of the opposite sex for practical reasons only.

Many people around the world characterize Americans as friendly. They tend to smile and talk easily with others even if they are strangers (in big cities, this is less common). They may even disclose personal information in encounters with strangers whom they will never see again.

Case 1 Who pays the bill?

Zhang Qiang has just met a new American friend, Manfred, who came to Hangzhou Normal College two months ago to learn Chinese. One day Zhang Qiang invited Manfred to go to dinner with him and two of his Chinese friends.

It was a very nice meal with lots of dishes that Manfred hadn't eaten before. He kept finishing everything Zhang Qiang and his friends put on his plate, until he was ready to burst. Even when dinner was over, Manfred saw that there was still a lot of food left on the table, which surprised him since he had eaten so much.

What was more of a surprise to Manfred was when it was time to pay the bill. Zhang Qiang and his friends fought over who would pay. At last, Zhang Qiang won. However, from the point of view of Manfred, it might be better for them all to "go Dutch," for the meal was very expensive and it was too much for one person to pay for.

Part III *Case Analyses of Pragmatic Failures in Intercultural Verbal Communication*   77

 Discussion:

1. Why was Manfred surprised and puzzled?
2. How would you explain to Manfred about the Chinese way of entertaining friends in the way that Zhang Qiang did?

 Case analysis:

As a newcomer to China, Manfred didn't understand the Chinese way of eating out with friends. What he found at the Chinese restaurant was quite different from the usual way it occurs in America, especially for students.

In America when people have dinner together, their individual plates are usually given to them with portions of food already placed onto each one. It's therefore not standard behavior to take food from someone else's plate. Also, it's a common practice to eat everything on your plate, so as not to waste food. If the portions are too large or it is something you can't eat, you can certainly leave food on your plate.

Many times students or young adults have limited incomes because they are just starting out in life. In order to have enjoyable meals at restaurants, they will frequently "go Dutch," which means everyone pays his or her share of the bill. This sense of equality allows them to feel comfortable about "splitting the bill." In China, when having dinner with friends, normally a new friend is given special treatment by having more and more food placed on his or her plate. The guest does not need to finish the food if he or she really doesn't want to.

The Chinese favor generosity. The more generous a person is, the more respectable he or she will be among friends. Therefore, in front of their friends, people try to be generous in order to save face, even though they may not have the money to be that generous. It is quite common for friends to fight over who will pay the bill to show their generosity. In some Western cultures, like the Irish and the Polish, this may also happen.

Case 2 Could you lend me money?

Zhong Min had a very good American friend Sue. The two usually ate lunch together and Zhong Min often asked Sue for advice on problems she faced adjusting to

American society. Sue gave Zhong Min a lot of advice and helped her improve her English. Once Zhong Min urgently needed a large sum of money ($2,000) to pay her tuition fee. Since she had no other friends in the States, she asked Sue for help and promised that she would return the money soon.

Zhong Min was disappointed when Sue didn't seem happy to lend the money. Though Zhong Min returned the money two months later, the two didn't get along well from then on.

Discussion:

1. What's the problem? What are the differences between what American and Chinese people expect from their friends?

2. What would you say to both so they could get to know each other better?

Case analysis:

Zhong Min asked to borrow money from her American friend Sue, which is rarely part of Western friendship. Sue may not have had a lot of money of her own and might not have been in a position to lend $2,000, even to a friend. For example, for a young person, $2,000 would probably be the equivalent of two months' wages.

As an American, Sue would like to help her Chinese friend Zhong Min. But she didn't expect Zhong Min to ask to borrow such a large sum of money. This goes beyond the normal and expected boundaries for an American friendship. Zhong Min, being Chinese, regarded Sue as her good friend, and considered it natural to ask her to lend the money she urgently needed, regardless of the sum.

Zhong Min should try to learn about American culture so she will not do something to create an unpleasant experience for herself or her American friends. Then she can have a discussion with Sue about the differences regarding expectations in friendships within the two cultures. She can also ask Sue to explain the details for applying for a loan at a bank so that in future if she needs money, she will know the procedure.

Sue should learn about Chinese culture. She can talk with Zhong Min about the different expectations of a friendship in both cultures. This discussion would allow Sue to tell Zhong Min whether or not she would be able to lend her money in future and, if so, how much. Zhong Min would therefore know whether or not to ask. This could repair the difficulties in the relationship.

In the West, people prefer to be independent and equal rather than dependent, so they don't feel comfortable in a relationship in which one person is giving more and the other person is dependent on what is being given. Friends spend time together in activities, helping each other with projects, and providing emotional support. They rarely borrow or lend money to each other; instead they get a loan from a bank if money is needed.

Often in the West, it is usual for people to save money for future expenses. Expenses that are routine or expected are planned for in this way. Then, when the expense occurs, the money is available without the person having to borrow. Friends may occasionally borrow very small sums of money from each other, but it is quickly paid back. Since credit cards can be used for most purchases, this habit of borrowing is now diminishing.

In China, people expect their friends to be loyal, and even take risks for them. They not only give emotional support to each other, but will help find a job, solve a problem, in addition to helping out financially by giving money to each other over a long period of time. So when a friend is in need, naturally the first one he or she thinks to ask for help is his or her best friend.

Case for students' practice:

Peter and Guangcheng were talking when a friend of Guangcheng passed by. "Hi, Hua Ma, when are we going to meet? You've been back from the States for two weeks now!" Guangcheng greeted him loudly.

"How about Saturday? I am sorry but I've been really busy. There are so many friends I have to see." When Hua Ma left, Peter could not help asking, "Is he a good friend of yours?"

"Oh, yes! We are the best of friends. He went to the States for half a year and came back a while ago."

"If you're best friends, how come he said he needed to see others first?" Peter could not understand.

Section 8　Taboos and euphemisms

Different cultures have a great number of taboo topics. Those words, phrases and topics that imply something bad or unrefined cannot be used in intercultural communication. Concepts of value are the main causes of miscommunication. Thus, people should choose appropriately what to talk about and how to do so.

Taboo is one way in which a society expresses its disapproval of certain kinds of behavior believed to be harmful to its members, either for supernatural reasons or because such behavior is held to violate a moral code. In fact, taboo is culture specific. Cultural patterns, customs, and ways of life are expressed in language; culture-specific world views are reflected in language.

Euphemism is the avoidance of words that may be seen as offensive or disturbing to the addressee. Taboo and euphemism are actually two sides of the same coin. Cultural taboo is a unique phenomenon, representing the characteristics of a certain culture and protecting a culture from being offended. Different people from different cultures have their own taboo terms. If the participants do not have knowledge of taboos in other cultures, conflicts in intercultural communication can easily arise.

The English and the Chinese both have certain areas of agreement on taboos, though there still exist some differences. Talking about sexual intercourse and certain parts of the body is a taboo in both cultures, as well as excreta and acts of human excretion. What is taboo or not taboo depends on the context. Some expressions denoting some body functions are avoided on formal occasions but quite normal in doctor-patient conversations when the patient complains about their physical problems to the doctor.

In respect of women, for example, it is impolite to ask about their age. Age is considered a taboo for Westerners, especially for ladies. Their cultural background makes them treat "old" as "useless" and "outdated." That is why it is no longer acceptable to speak of "old people" and "old women"; we must now employ the terms "senior citizens" and "elderly ladies."

Also it is commonly known that privacy, individualism, income, and religion are sensitive topics in intercultural communication. The number "thirteen" and the day "Friday" are considered unlucky. According to the Bible, Jesus was betrayed at the Last Supper by his disciple, Judas Iscariot, when there were 13 of them gathered together to eat, and Christ was put to death on a Friday. However, they have no special significance in the Chinese tradition. Thus it is evident that religion and belief are very important fields in which taboo terms are to be found. In England, for example, no one will live in a house or apartment that has the number 13 and it is known for some people not to leave the house or even get out of bed on a Friday that is also the 13th of the month for fear of something bad happening to them.

Death is an inevitable stage at the end of one's life's journey. People use euphemisms to respect the dead, or to remember them, sometimes to praise them, sometimes only to avoid direct mention of death. There are hundreds of euphemisms relating to "death" in both Chinese and English. Here are just a few examples meaning "to die" in English: "to pass away," "to go west," "to go to heaven," "to fall asleep in the Lord," "to be in Abraham's bosom," "to leave this world," "to join the silent (great) majority," "to go to one's eternal reward, ""to cross to the other side, "and so on.

To get along with people from other cultures, we need to understand that people from different cultural backgrounds will have a unique way of doing things, analyzing situations and reacting to circumstances. What is considered an act of politeness in Chinese culture might be regarded as an intrusion upon a person's privacy by a native English speaker. To show warmth and concern is regarded as a polite act in Chinese culture. That is why when two Chinese meet each other even for the first time, they might ask about each other's age, marital status, children, income and the price of an item. In contrast, in Western culture it may be regarded as impolite to ask a person such questions that are considered very personal.

Case 1 Conversations at work

Wu Chang arrived in San Francisco to begin working as a manager for a manufacturing company. After being at his new assignment for a few months, he hired Linda, a new female employee, to work as his assistant.

Linda was very good at her job and she was a very friendly person who treated everyone she met with the same smile and pleasant conversation.

Wu Chang was invited to a cocktail party that would take place the following Saturday at his apartment complex. Since he was new to San Francisco and hadn't met many single women, he decided he would invite Linda to be his date for the party.

The following conversation took place the next morning at work.

Wu Chang: Good morning, Linda, how was your drive to work?

Linda: Hello, traffic was very heavy this morning, but fortunately I had left early enough so I made it to work with time to spare.

Wu Chang: Well, that was good planning. Linda, I've been invited to a party Saturday evening and I would like you to accompany me.

Linda: That's very nice of you to ask me, but I already have plans for Saturday evening and won't be able to go with you.

 Discussion:

1. What subject is discussed in this case that is not appropriate in the United States?

2. Is this subject appropriate to discuss in your culture?

 Case analysis:

Wu Chang's asking Linda to attend the party, even though he considered the invitation a social occasion and not work related, is not appropriate. Even if this invitation had no influence on future decisions within the company, if Linda were not given a promotion she felt she deserved, she might consider her refusing the invitation as the reason she didn't get promoted.

In a work environment, there are civil laws that protect an employee from undue pressure from a superior to fulfill a social or personal request. Then when that request is not complied with, and in consequence the superior limits the employee's opportunities for advancement or pay increases, the employee can sue the company and that superior in a civil court. This is especially important in a male-boss-female-subordinate or female-boss-male-subordinate situation. It's called sexual harassment, and the civil law is based on situations when a boss may pressure a subordinate for personal favors, including sexual favors, in order to keep his or her job.

Any conversation requesting personal favors from a subordinate, no matter how innocent that request may appear, can be construed as sexual harassment; especially if the subordinate feels opportunities for advancement were withheld following his/her refusal to comply with the request. Therefore, it is imperative that supervisors in any capacity should not ask a subordinate to engage in any activity that does not come within the realm of the person's job description.

Case 2 Conversations during meals

Wang Ming lives in Salt Lake City next door to Bob and Helen. He has been invited to a dinner party at their home. Wang Ming knows that Bob was recently in hospital and is concerned about his health. When everyone is seated at the dinner table, Wang Ming turns to Bob and says, "Bob, how are you feeling?"

Discussion:

1. What subject is discussed at the dinner table in this case that is not appropriate, especially in the United States?

2. Is this also a subject that is not discussed at the dinner table in your culture?

Case analysis:

Wang Ming is very concerned about his friend Bob's health. However, a conversation about health, or illness, is never appropriate during meals. In fact, discussion of illness is never an appropriate subject of conversation. Should someone start talking about his illness, you can respond by saying, "I'm sorry to hear that. I hope you're doing better." Or "I hope you're feeling fine now." Don't ask for details about the illness.

In the United States, when a person asks, "How are you feeling?" the question is not taken literally, and you would not expect the response to be a list of the other person's aches and pains. It is meant as a generic greeting, and the standard reply is, "Oh, fine. Thank you," even if that person isn't in good health.

Case 3 Sensitive conversational topics

Bill and Cathy are getting married and moving to a new town in Orange County when they graduate from college. Since they'll both be working downtown, they have stopped to visit Sue, the Human Resource Director at the company where Cathy will be working.

Sue: Have you found an apartment yet?

Cathy: There are actually several that we like. I've marked them on this map for you to see since each one is in a different neighborhood. We're trying to decide so we are hoping you can answer a few questions for us.

Sue: Sure, I'll be happy to help if I can.

Bill: It's important for us to live near our church because we both want to sing in their choir. After all, we both studied music during college. And during the holidays there can be rehearsals in the evenings as the choir is preparing special musical programs.

Sue: Well, I can't talk to you about religion. In fact many of our employees are very active in their own churches, but they don't discuss their various religions while they are at work. It isn't appropriate, even while on breaks or at lunch.

Cathy: Oh Sue, we don't want to talk about religion with you. We know that's not a topic for conversation at work. But we want to know, in your opinion, which apartment will be the best location for traffic coming to work, as well as being conveniently situated for attending The Crystal Cathedral.

Sue: Oh, I can help you with that. It would be this apartment you have marked in blue on your map. The Crystal Cathedral has a wonderful choir. Let me know when they have their Christmas pageant and I'll buy tickets to go and see it.

 Discussion:

1. What topic of the conversation is acceptable, and what topic area is not acceptable?

2. What conversational limitations do you find?

Part III *Case Analyses of Pragmatic Failures in Intercultural Verbal Communication*   85

 Case analysis:

Sue was careful not to discuss religion, but she was able to answer Bill and Cathy's question about an apartment location's proximity to the church Bill and Cathy planned to attend.

Religion is not a topic that is banned, but is one that a person must be very cautious about when discussing. As a general rule, it is not one that should be discussed. As America was a country founded on the basis of religious freedom, the population practices religions of all faiths. This religious diversity can cause verbal conflicts if discussed at inappropriate times, or with many people. Each person is allowed to believe in his or her own religious beliefs, and must be able to practice those beliefs. Many people's religious faith is deep seated; some consider it their personal business and are not ready to discuss it with others. These religious rights should be honored so caution must be used regarding discussing any religion, or one's own religious beliefs.

 Case for students' practice:

Li Xiaopeng and John are both engineers who work together in the same office, and have become friends.

They are attending an engineering conference. At a lunch break, they're invited to join another group of engineers. In this group are several female engineers.

As the conversation takes place during lunch, one of the men sitting next to John starts to talk about a hot new movie he's heard about. He starts to describe the action, and then starts to talk about the body of the female who's the star in the movie.

John (interrupts): Sam, let's change the subject. Tell me about your golf game last weekend.

(When Li Xiaopeng and John return to the conference)

Li Xiaopeng: John, why did you interrupt Sam when he was talking about the movie?

John: I was concerned, especially with women at our table. I wasn't sure exactly how much detail Sam would go into and didn't want the women to feel they were being insulted. Plus, I didn't want Sam to be embarrassed. He just wasn't thinking. You know how guys can sometimes talk.

Section 9   Different ways of thinking

People of a certain culture have a culture-peculiar way of conceiving the world, observing things and thinking about questions. Every culture has its individual thought patterns, and its own way of perceiving the world. The world can be divided into the Orient and the Occident in terms of geography and culture, China is a representative of the Orient while English-speaking nations are representatives of the Occident. Owing to the different geographical surroundings, philosophies, modes  of production, historical traditions, ways of life, economic systems and so on, Chinese and Western thought patterns have different characteristics.

Chinese and Westerners think in a lot of different ways. Chinese prefer synthetic, imagery, subjective, objective, cyclical and group-oriented thinking modes, etc., while Westerners prefer analytic, abstract, objective, linear, and ego-centric thinking modes.

This means that Eastern people are conservative, introvert and inactive, put more emphasis on harmony, and like a common and stable life; while the Western people are more open-minded, extrovert, and active, like a changeable life and emphasize competition.

In this way, their different ways of thinking lead to their different understanding of each other's behavior. If Chinese see somebody is talkative, they might think that person wants to be the focus of attention.

Case 1   What are the responsibilities in a family?

Steve and Mary are living in Dallas, Texas. Mary's parents live in Denver, Colorado and she's talking to them on the phone. When she gets off the telephone, she asks Steve to sit down and have a cup of coffee with her.

Mary: Steve, I've just talked with Mother and Daddy. I think it's time that we had them come live

with us.

Steve: Is your Dad's health getting worse?

Mary: Yes, I think so. He's not able to take care of the yard anymore and you know how he always loves working in his garden. So for him to say he's not able to get out and work with his flowers, you know he's not feeling well at all.

Steve: I'm sorry that he's gotten that sick. You know we bought this house with the extra bedrooms so we'd have a place for them to live, if they ever needed it. And since your brother lives in New York City, in a very small apartment, our house will be the best place for your parents. We have a yard and your father can enjoy being outdoors, even if he's only able to sit and rest in a chair.

Mary: Let's call them and talk about their moving in with us. I know it'll be difficult for them leaving all their friends, but I also think they realize it will be best for them. Plus, we don't have the winter snowfall, which will be better for them when they need to go places during the winter months.

Discussion:

1. What topic does the case mainly talk about?
2. Does the situation and how the family is resolving it surprise you when you read this case?

Case analysis:

In this case, Mary is the daughter and has a larger home with a yard that will provide a more comfortable environment for her parents. Her brother, the son, lives in a very small apartment without the space to accommodate the parents.

The traditions for taking care of one's family are very diverse within the American culture. Each family has its own cultural heritage, since immigrants founded the country just over 200 years ago, and ongoing immigration has been part of the growth in the United States.

In addition, families make decisions based upon what is best for the parents. Even though Americans are brought up with the spirit of individualism, families are still important. And most children do care for the elder members in their family. This responsibility does not fall exclusively on a son. In fact, it's more common to have a parent, or parents, move in with a daughter and her family, than with a son and his family.

Case 2   Lovers become strangers!

Xiaoxin and Peter are newly-weds. Though they spent a lot of time with each other before getting married, they never really lived together. There are some minor problems that occur. One day Peter came home looking unhappy.

"What happened?" Xiaoxin asked.

"Nothing much, I'm just very tired," Peter said.

"I can tell that it's more than that."

Peter gave her a quiet look, went into the bedroom, and threw himself on the bed.

Xiaoxin followed him in and said, "Don't you want to talk about it?"

"No, I don't."

"Perhaps I can help," Xiaoxin suggested.

"Xiaoxin, sometimes you just have to give me some space. All I need now is some privacy," Peter yelled.

Xiaoxin was in tears. Her husband seemed to have become a stranger to her.

 Discussion:

1. Why does Peter refuse to tell Xiaoxin the fact?
2. What would happen if Xiaoxin married to a Chinese husband?

 Case analysis:

The idea of collectivism in China seems to have penetrated into people's emotional life in the sense that most people believe in the fact that couples, or even good friends, are supposed to share every secret thought in their lives. As a result, when a marriage is experiencing problems, relatives, friends, and even employers of the couple will attempt to concern themselves with the problems and try to find a solution. Xiaoxin was well-intentioned, hoping she could help to give Peter some relief. Peter's reaction made her feel rejected and unworthy. But Peter's reaction is very common for Western people. They are trained from childhood to be expected to solve problems by themselves. The idea of talking about problems, thus revealing a sense of inadequacy or weakness, is frightening to most of them, especially when talking to a wife or lover. They don't want to be seen as being soft or weak.

 Case for students' practice:

One Chinese visiting scholar once studied in the United States. He presented his first paper to his tutor. In this paper, he used "we" instead of "I" to state his viewpoint. When the paper was returned, to his puzzlement, on it there was an eight-big-word comment, "Who gives you the right to represent me?"

Part IV

Case Analyses in Intercultural Nonverbal Communication

Nonverbal communication as well as verbal communication is the carrier of culture. It is also a very important form, which supplements and improves the verbal communication. In some specific circumstances, it plays an important role that verbal language can't take.

We communicate with much more than words. In fact, research shows that the majority of our communication is nonverbal. Nonverbal communication includes our facial expressions, gestures, eye contact, posture, and even the tone of our voice. If we see someone with a clenched fist and grim expression, we do not need words to tell us this person is not happy. It is significant in human interaction because it is usually responsible for first impression; it has value in human interaction because many of our nonverbal actions are not easily controlled consciously.

When we interact with others, we continuously give and receive countless wordless signals. All of our nonverbal behaviors — the gestures we make, the way we sit, how fast or how loud we talk, how close we stand, how much eye contact we make — send strong messages. The way you listen, look, move, and react tells the other person whether or not you care and how well you're listening. The nonverbal signals you send either produce a sense of interest, trust, and desire for connection or they generate disinterest, distrust, and confusion.

4.1 The characteristics of nonverbal communication

Compared with verbal communication, nonverbal communication has its own characteristics.

Nonverbal communication is culture-specific

One culture has a different set of nonverbal communication signals from another. These forms are deeply influenced by cultural background. We learn a set of gestures, movement habits, styles of dress, and so on within one cultural setting and that may not even be close to what someone has learned in another culture.

Nonverbal communication is often ambiguous or contextual

By themselves, gestures, movements, objects, and so on may tell us only part of the story. We need to see the context, the relationship, the accompanying verbal behavior, if any and the responses. Although we can make a tentative conclusion about the nonverbal meaning, we must keep it tentative unless we get more information from the situation or other cues about the message. All the factors together can help to dissipate the ambiguous nonverbal behaviors.

Nonverbal communication is non-structural

In contrast to the spoken language, nonverbal communication may or may not be systematized, has no rules or regularities or a dictionary. It is difficult to ask for clarification and is generally impossible to control. Most of them are unintentional and have no rules to follow.

Nonverbal communication is continual

We are continuously communicating. Even if we close the door and turn off the light to avoid our friends, we are giving our friends a message that they are capable of understanding. So we are always communicating through nonverbal communication.

Part IV *Case Analyses in Intercultural Nonverbal Communication*

4.2 The functions of nonverbal communication

Nonverbal behaviors can be used to communicate in a variety of situations. There are several functions of nonverbal communication.

To complement

Nonverbal communication behaviors are used to reinforce our verbal communication. We can tell someone that we are pleased with his or her performance, but this message takes on extra meaning if we pat the person on the shoulder at the same time. We are reinforcing our message and complementing our words.

To substitute

There are quite a few hand signals and gestures that are commonly used which take the place of verbal messages. Americans can say "I don't know" or shrug their shoulders to express the same meaning.

To highlight

Nonverbal signals may be used to emphasize a portion of verbal messages. This type of behavior usually strengthens, or adds to the significance of the communication. Saying "I love you" is nice, but is even nicer when followed by a hug or a kiss from someone you care about.

To report

Nonverbal cues are often used to verify whether the listener understands the verbal message.

To regulate

We often regulate and manage communication by using some forms of nonverbal behaviors. We nod our heads to indicate to our communication partner that we agree and that he or she should continue talking. Our nonverbal behaviors help us to control the situation.

There are many ways to classify all possible nonverbal behaviors. Mostly **kinesics, haptics, appearance and dress, olfactics, proxemics, chronemics and paralanguage** are included.

Chapter

1

Kinesics (body language)

Kinesics, commonly known as body language, body movements, body behavior and so on, refers to all expressions and movements that send communicative nonverbal messages. In general, kinetic cues are those visible body shifts and movements that send messages about one's attitude toward the other person, one's emotional state, and one's desire to control one's environment.

Body language has three major functions: assisting, substituting and expressing or concealing emotions.

Usually, the body movements and expressions are common in many cultures and can play communicative functions: Nonverbal communication is an intrinsic part of every society, and the subtle differences between them are the key to understanding and appreciating the unique qualities of each culture.

There are also universally recognized patterns of nonverbal communication within the mainstream of society that are as much learned as they are an innate part of the human condition. A smile and an outstretched hand show welcome; a frown is a sign of displeasure; pouting has the same meaning — displeasure, bad humor, resentment; the wrinkling of one's nose is a sign of dislike, disgust or disapproval; nodding one's head means agreement — "yes"; shaking one's head from one side to the other means "no"; a handshake is the most common gesture that goes with a greeting; waving an outstretched hand with open palm is the gesture for "goodbye"; leaning back in one's seat and yawning at a talk or lecture shows lack of interest, boredom; a pat on the back of a man or boy indicates approval, praise, encouragement; gritting one's teeth may express anger, fury or determination; men do not commonly hug or embrace when meeting; when you follow what the speaker says, you might show an interested look, wear a smile, make some notes or keep your eyes on the speaker; if you don't understand, you might consciously or unconsciously twist your body, bury your head, avoid the speaker's eyes, wear a blank expression, knit your eyebrows or bite your pen.

In general these gestures have become the accepted norm in most cultures. The following are examples of where these cultural norms diverge.

British, Australian, New Zealander, German and American colleagues will usually shake hands on meeting, and again on departure. Most European cultures will shake hands with each other several times a day, and some French have been noted to shake hands for up to 30 minutes a day. Indian, Asian and Arabic cultures may continue to hold your hand when the handshake has ended. Germans and French give one or two firm pumps followed by a short hold, whereas Brits give three to five pumps compared with an American's five to seven pumps. This is hilarious to observe at international conferences where a range of different handshake pumping takes place between surprised delegates. To the Americans, the Germans, with their single pumps, seem distant. To the Germans, however, the Americans pump hands as if they are blowing up an airbed.

When it comes to greeting with a kiss on the cheek, the Scandinavians are happy with a single kiss, the French mostly prefer a double, while the Dutch, Belgians and Arabs go for a triple kiss. The Australians, New Zealanders and Americans are continually often confused about greeting kisses and inadvertently bump noses as they fumble their way through a single peck. The Brits either avoid kissing by standing back or will surprise you with a European double kiss.

When Italians talk they keep their hands held high as a way of holding the floor in a conversation. What seems like an affectionate touch of the arm during an Italian conversation is more like a "preemptive strike," preventing the listener from raising his hands and taking the floor. To interrupt an Italian you must grab his hands in mid air and hold them down. As a comparison, the Germans and British look as if they are physically paralyzed when they talk. They are daunted when trying to converse with Italians and French and rarely get an opportunity to speak. French use their forearms and hands when they talk, Italians use their entire arms and body, while the Brits and Germans stand at attention.

If a Saudi man holds another man's hand in public it's a sign of mutual respect. It is not advisable that you do it in Australia, Texas or Liverpool, England.

Body language is the universal language and nothing short of paralysis can prevent it. The most common cultural differences exist mainly in relation to territorial space, eye contact, touch, frequency, and insult gestures. Most foreign cultures do not expect you to learn their language, but are extremely impressed by the traveler who has taken the time to learn and use local body language customs. This tells them that you respect their culture.

Usually four elements of body language are included: *facial expressions*, *eye contact*, *gesture*, *and posture*.

Section 1 Facial expression

Communication is as natural as mother's milk and reflected in the wide variety of ways that people exchange information, not only with words, but also using their face and body.

The human face is extremely expressive, and able to express countless emotions without saying a word. Unlike some forms of nonverbal communication, facial expressions are universal. The facial expressions for happiness, sadness, anger, surprise, fear, and disgust are the same across cultures. We constantly read expressions from people's faces. In fact, facial cues are the single most important source of nonverbal communication.

Facial expressions have their own features: They are innate and universal. Therefore, the expressions for happiness, sadness, disgust, fear, anger, and surprise (the six basic emotions) are recognized by most cultural groups as having the same meaning. However, variations exist. Some facial expressions and their interpretations vary from one culture to another. Recent research has shown that Easterners and Westerners place a different emphasis on facial expressions. Westerners predominantly look at the eyes and the mouth in equal measure, whereas Easterners favor the eye and focus less on the mouth.

Case Study Is smiling always the right thing?

Peter is the general manager of an American company in China. Recently, Jun Chen, one of the Chinese managers made a mistake at work that caused difficulties that required a considerable effort to fix. Jun Chen was very upset about what had happened and came to Peter's office to make an apology. With a smile on his face, he said, "Peter, I've been very upset about the trouble I've caused to the company. I'm here to apologize for my mistake. I'm terribly sorry about it and I want you to know that it will never happen again." He looked at Peter with the smile he had been wearing since he walked into the office. Peter found it hard to accept the apology.

He looked at Jun Chen and asked, "Are you sure?"

"Yes, I'm very sorry and I promise this won't happen again," smiling even more broadly than before.

"I am sorry but I simply cannot accept your apology. You don't look sorry at all!" Peter said angrily.

Jun Chen's face turned red. He had not in the least expected Peter to react negatively. He was desperate to make himself understood. "Peter," he managed to smile again, "trust me, no one could feel sorrier than I do about it."

Peter was furious by now, "If you are that sorry, how can you still smile?"

Discussion:

1. Why did Jun Chen wear a smile when he made the apology?

2. Do you think it reasonable that Peter became so angry with Jun Chen? Why or why not?

3. What are the different interpretations of a smile by the two people involved in this situation?

 ## Case analysis:

The conflict was caused by the misunderstanding of the cultural difference in the application of body language. For Jun Chen, smiling is a way to show his sincerity and politeness while, for Peter, smiling when apologizing is a way of showing disrespect to the other person.

The act of smiling is a universal form of body language, but sometimes misunderstanding or conflict occurs in intercultural communication simply because people from different cultural backgrounds treat a smile in different ways. It is taken for granted that smiling means the same thing because "the whole world smiles." This failure to recognize the cultural differences of smiling often leads to unexpected cultural conflicts.

For Chinese, smiling not only expresses feelings of happiness, but also of sorrow when one has offended another person. It is desirable for a Chinese to apologize with a smile, as this is a sign of humility and is a cover for their embarrassment. Jun Chen probably was not even aware that he was smiling when he first went into the office to apologize, yet he did make an effort to smile when he saw Peter getting angry. For Jun Chen, the smile was an important part of the apology. As a result, he could not understand why Peter got angry when he made a sincere apology. For Americans, the way Jun Chen acted indicated that he was only going through the motions of apologizing. His smiling is interpreted as smirking, as showing that he was not really sorry for the mistake; it is seen as a sign of disrespect. In such a situation, Jun Chen is expected to keep his eyes lowered while apologizing and adopt a serious, contrite air.

In Chinese society, Chinese people seldom smile to strangers. A person, no matter if he is walking down a crowded street or sharing a table with another person in the dining hall, will normally show no facial expression at all and pretend that the other person is not present. If someone smiles to you in China, you might assume that he is going to ask you to do him a favor, such as showing him the way to some place, or that he wants to sell you something. You might also think that there is something wrong with your appearance or dress. Therefore, smiling to strangers is usually avoided in China. In contrast, in America and many other Western countries, smiling to a stranger is a sign of friendliness, a sign that you wish that person well. Many visitors to China initially have the impression that the Chinese are not friendly as they seldom respond to their smile.

In American society, American people often smile to strangers to be polite. This is especially true when the space is narrow and the number of people around is small. For example, when one person gets in an elevator with one other person already in the elevator or when two strangers walk past each other in an empty hall, they are likely to exchange a brief smile. A smile to a stranger merely acknowledges the presence of the other.

Smiling to a stranger of the opposite sex is even more complicated. Assume an occasion in which a man shows interest in a woman he sees for the first time by staring at her for a long time. A smile from the woman in such a situation has opposite meanings and leads to totally different results in America and China. For an American woman, the smile is a soft warning that may effectively stop the man from staring at her. But for a Chinese woman, the smile conveys her good impression of the man and may encourage him to take further action. If this situation takes place in an intercultural environment, the different meanings of smile can bring rather awkward consequences.

Case for students' practice:

Huihua, a Chinese student, and *Mary*, an American student studying Chinese in China, were on their way to a bookstore. As they arrived at the bookstore, they saw a young man walking down a flight of stairs. In his hurry, he missed the last two steps, and fell to the ground. He struggled to get back on his feet while people around him laughed. Fortunately, he seemed to be okay.

Mary was worried. She found Huihua smiling a little and was not comfortable at all. "Tell me, Huihua, how could people laugh when someone fell like that? Don't they care at all? Shouldn't they go up and ask the young man whether he was hurt?"

Huihua said, "They could see he wasn't really hurt."

"But I still don't understand. A fall is a fall. In my culture, the last thing people would do is laugh."

Section 2   Eye contact

It has been said that "The eyes are the window of the soul." Why? Perhaps it is because through eye contact with another individual can we read their thoughts and intentions. In some case it is unavoidable, and for that reason an insincere person will divert their gaze to hide their intentions, and a sincere person will look straight at another individual, as if to say, "I have nothing to hide."

The customs and significance of eye contact vary widely between cultures, with religious and social differences often altering its meaning greatly. Eye contact and facial expressions provide important social and emotional information; people, perhaps without consciously doing so, probe each other's eyes and faces for positive or negative mood signs. In some contexts, the meeting of eyes arouses strong emotions. In some parts of the world, particularly in Asia, eye contact can provoke misunderstandings between people of different nationalities. Keeping direct eye contact with a work supervisor or elderly person leads them to assume one is being aggressive and rude — the opposite reaction in most Western societies.

Showing that you are physically attracted to a member of the opposite sex is strictly prohibited in Muslim cultures. This means that eye contact between men and women is only allowed for a second or two.

In many Western cultures, failure to look someone in the eye can be interpreted as being "shifty-eyed," and the person judged negatively because "he wouldn't look me in the eye." Nevertheless, the seeking of constant unbroken eye contact by the other participant in a conversation can often be considered overbearing or distracting by many, even in Western cultures.

Case study Unacceptable staring

Sophie and Robert is a couple from England. When they first came to China, they felt uneasy because people liked staring at them (especially at Sophie). Some children or men even quickly walked past her and turned back to look at her several times. When a man stared at Sophie, she had no other choice but to stare back at him. Such things often happen to foreigners in China. In 2003 in Nanjing, when a foreigner wearing a T-shirt printed "ten warnings to Chinese" including number one "don't stare at a foreigner" entered a restaurant, people felt upset and criticized him. Given this very hostile reaction, he was obliged to get rid of his T-shirt.

Discussion:

1. Why do you think Sophie stared back at the man who stared at her?
2. Why did people from Nanjing criticize the Westerner when they saw him?
3. How would, say, an Englishman, react if a Chinese wore a T-shirt in Britain listing ten warnings to English people? How could these offenses be communicated in a more subtle way?

 Case analysis:

In China, less well educated people like staring at strangers whom they see as very different from themselves. This is the only way they can satisfy their curiosity and it would be a very hard habit to overcome.

Regarding the second situation, as more and more Westerners are to be seen in the big cities of China, they no longer give rise to the same curiosity. The reason the people in the restaurant feel insulted and show their feelings is because they see the Westerner is demonstrating a lack of respect for their country and its people.

Staring at a stranger is a Western cultural taboo, unlike in China. Many people here feel quite free to stare at anything they like and are particularly inclined to do so if it is something they are not used to seeing. The fact that they cannot communicate with outsiders makes them even more curious.

Most Western visitors, at some point during their stay in China will have the disconcerting experience of being stared at. Interpreting this as rudeness is unproductive. However, this idea does not alter the fact that this staring often embarrasses them and makes them feel self-conscious, this in turn leading to antipathy and misunderstanding on their part. So, on their side, Chinese parents and teachers could instruct children from an early age not to stand and stare when they see someone so physically different from themselves. The wise response on the part of the person who is the object of such staring is simply to ignore it. Very often curiosity brings the Westerner to China or is certainly present during their stay. So it makes better sense to accept this equally innocuous form of curiosity and not misinterpret it.

 Case for students' practice:

Mr. Brown is a teacher from England and has recently arrived in China. He has been recruited by a university on the mainland. A few days after his arrival he met with one of his female students on campus and praised her for a piece of writing she had done for his course. In response, the student avoided eye contact, looked down at the ground and said nothing. Mr. Brown was puzzled and unhappy at this reaction. He went away wondering what he had done wrong.

Section 3 Gestures

A gesture is a form of nonverbal communication in which visible bodily actions communicate particular messages, either in place of speech or together and in parallel with spoken words. Gestures include movement of the hands, face, or other parts of the body. They differ from physical non-verbal communication that does not communicate specific messages, such as purely expressive displays or displays of joint attention. Gestures allow individuals to communicate a variety of 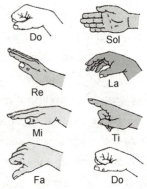 feelings and thoughts, from contempt and hostility to approval and affection, often together with body language in addition to spoken words.

Gestures are woven into the fabric of our daily lives. We wave, point, beckon, and use our hands when we're arguing or speaking animatedly — expressing ourselves with gestures often without thinking. However, the meaning of gestures can be very different across cultures and regions, so it's important to be careful to avoid misinterpretation.

It is estimated that the human body can produce over 270,000 discrete gestures. Care should be taken in using gestures because different cultures interpret gestures in different ways. Understanding human behavior is a difficult task. No two people behave in precisely the same way, nor do all people from the same culture gesticulates in uniform manner.

Although we are normally not aware of it, most of us use gestures when we are talking. We have found that gestures used within one culture are quite different from those used in another culture. Suppose we take the sign for beckoning as an example. In America, when a person wants to signal to a friend to come, he or she makes the gesture with one hand, palm up, fingers more or less together and moving towards his or her body. In Japan, when beckoning to someone to approach, one extends the arm slightly upwards and cups the hand, with the fingers pointed down, making a clockwise motion. In Germany, a beckoning motion is made by tossing the head back. This is common in America as well.

Part IV *Case Analyses in Intercultural Nonverbal Communication*

Case study This "Ok" is not that "Ok"!

Jun Jie was an overseas student at the University of Lyon in France. He lived with an elderly couple, Monsieur and Madame Deville, in a large, spacious and comfortable house. Their four children had long since grown up, now had their own families and lived elsewhere. The Deville's rented their rooms out to students in order to retain that lively and family atmosphere that had existed when their children were at home.

Mme Deville and her husband had graduated from Lyon University many years previously and both had sympathy for the difficulties that an overseas student might experience. The first problem was the language so Mme Deville offered to give Jun Jie French lessons without requiring any payment in return. Jun Jie was very moved and soon came to regard her as a mother.

After Jun Jie had been staying in their home for five months, M. Deville asked him, "How do you feel about your life here?" Jun Jie was very pleased with his living conditions and used the gesture "okay" to show his satisfaction. To his surprise, M. Deville became very angry and said, "If you are not satisfied with the life here, you can leave."

Seeing that he had been misunderstood and had created an embarrassing situation, Jun Jie repeatedly apologized and kept on saying how satisfied he was. Eventually, he succeeded in appeasing Monsieur Deville.

Discussion:

1. What made Monsieur Deville angry with Jun Jie?
2. What would you do if you found yourself in such a situation?

Case analysis:

The conflict in the case is the different understanding of the gesture "OK." "Making a circle with one's thumb and index finger while extending the others" means "okay," "praise" in China. But to French people, the gesture indicates zero, i. e. "worth nothing," "very unsatisfactory." That is why Jun Jie found himself in such an awkward situation.

The most widely recognized American sign for "OK" was popularized in the USA during the early nineteenth century, apparently by the newspapers that, at the time, were starting a craze of using initials to shorten common phrases. There are many different views about what the initials "OK" stand for, some believing it stood for "all correct" which may have been misspelled as "oll correct," while others say that it means the opposite of "knock-out," that is, K. O. Another popular theory is that it is an abbreviation of "Old Kinderhook," from the birthplace of a nineteenth century American president who used the initials as a campaign slogan. There are also those that argue that it is of Greek, American Indian and even African origin. We may never know which theory is the correct one, but it seems that the circle represents the letter "O" in the "okay" signal.

The "okay" meaning is common to all English-speaking countries and, although its meaning is fast spreading across Europe and Asia, the gesture for okay has other origins and meanings in certain places. For example, in France, as we saw, it means "zero" or "nothing"; in Japan it can mean "money"; in some Mediterranean countries it may be used to infer that a man is homosexual. For overseas travelers, the safest rule to obey is, "When in Rome, do as the Romans do." This can help avoid any possible embarrassing circumstances.

 Case for students' practice:

Wenjun attended the annual boat-rowing competition between Oxford University and Cambridge University. The former just managed to defeat the latter. As Wenjun was studying at Oxford, he went with his classmates to a bar to celebrate. Maybe because he had drunk a little too much, he made the "V" sign with the palm turned inward to other classmates. As a result, the atmosphere became a little tense. Fortunately someone understood his mistake and showed him how to produce the correct gesture.

Section 4 Posture

Posture, as a form of body language, is largely determined by the culture. The way one stands and sits offers insights into a culture's deep structure and often reflects a person's attitude toward people one is with.

In many Asian cultures, the bow is much more than a greeting, and it signifies that culture's concern with status and rank. For example, in Japan low posture is an indicator of respect. The manner of sitting, standing and moving can also communicate a message and reflect a certain culture's life style. The Thai people use a similar movement called the wai. The wai movement — which is made by pressing both hands close together in front of one's body, with the fingertips reaching to about neck level — is used to show respect. The lower the head comes to the hands, the more respect is shown. Also, the higher the hands, the higher the respect. In Thai tradition it was a sign that the person was unarmed. He offered his unprotected head as a sign of vulnerability and mutual trust. Noteworthy is the use and misuse of the wai in foreigner circles.

As we saw, in the United States, people can be very casual and will often spread themselves out in chairs in a very relaxed way. When standing, they may slouch or lean against something. In many countries, such as Germany and Sweden, such a posture is considered a sign of bad manners. This is also true in the US, although it may be more casual.

It is not uncommon to see an American woman sit with her legs crossed even during public meetings, whereas in many other countries, this is avoided. It may be because the life style is more formal or because the hot climate makes such a posture uncomfortable.

Case study Posture in the classroom

Mr. Cohen is an expatriate teacher from the United States teaching in a university in China. He likes to conduct his class in a very casual way. This is particularly noticeable in the way he dresses and sits in class. He invariably wears jeans and a T-shirt and sits on the teacher's desk with his legs stretched out and his two feet resting on the edge of the student's desk in front of him. Once the senior teacher responsible for teaching affairs spoke to him about his very informal posture in class and told him that it was not acceptable, Mr. Cohen was annoyed at this criticism as he felt that by acting in this way in class he would help students to relax more and be ready to talk more.

Discussion:

1. As an English major student, what do you think of the posture adopted by Mr. Cohen in class?
2. What do you think of his view that this would encourage students to talk more and profit more from the oral interaction with a native speaker of English?

Case analysis:

To Mr. Cohen, a casual posture will make students feel relaxed and create a more harmonious atmosphere in the classroom, whereas the senior teacher considers that such behavior will undermine discipline and respect for the teacher.

For Chinese, the teacher should be an example. He is the authority and students should be able to look up to him in every way. They are required to sit upright in class and to answer the teacher's questions seriously and with respect when spoken to. In the United States, free expression and a relaxed atmosphere in class are encouraged, which explains why Mr. Cohen adopts the attitude he does. However, it would be wrong to generalize to all Western countries, as the story shows.

Case for students' practice:

Once Andy, who taught English in one Chinese university, went to the airport for a traval to Shanghai. When he arrived there he found so many people there. He couldn't find any chair to sit. After settling the concerned procedures and feeling very tired, he sat down directly on the floor. The Chinese nearby spread a handkerchief and a newspaper on the floor to sit on. During the time waiting for the plane, both of them wondered the dirty way the opposite chose in sitting.

Chapter 2

Haptics (touch)

Haptics is the use of touch as a form of communication. It is the study of how touch is used to communicate with others, whether it is in an intercultural setting or among individuals that share a common bond culturally.

Touch is an extremely important sense for humans as well as providing information about surfaces and textures. It is a component of nonverbal communication in interpersonal relationships, and vital in conveying physical intimacy. It can be both sexual (such as kissing) and platonic (such as hugging or tickling).

Touch is the earliest sense to mature. It comes into its own in the embryonic stage long before eyes, ears, and the higher brain centers begin to work. Soon after birth, infants begin to employ their other senses to interpret reality.

During the same period, they are highly involved with touch: They are being nuzzled, cuddled, cleaned, patted, kissed, and in many cases breast-fed. Human babies have been observed to have enormous difficulty surviving if they do not possess a sense of touch, even if they retain sight and hearing. Babies who can perceive through touch, even without sight and hearing, tend to fare much better. Touch can be thought of as a basic sense in that most life forms have a response to being touched, while only a subset have sight and hearing. As we move from infancy into childhood, we learn the rules of touching. We are taught whom to touch and where they may be touched. By the time we reach adolescence, our culture has taught us how to communicate with touch. Striking, pushing, pulling, pinching, kicking, strangling and hand-to-hand fighting are forms of touch in the context of physical abuse. In a sentence like "I never touched him/her" or "Don't you dare to touch him/her," the term "touch" may be meant as a euphemism for either physical abuse or sexual touching.

Touching is treated differently from one country to another. Whether or not someone will be offended by being touched during a conversation depends on their culture. Socially acceptable levels of touching vary from one culture to another.

For example, the French and Italians love to continually touch as they talk, while the British prefer not to touch at any time unless it's on a sports field in front of a large audience. Intimate embracing by British, Australian and New Zealand sportsmen is copied from South American and Continental sportsmen who embrace and kiss each other after a goal is scored and continue this intimate behavior in the changing rooms. The moment the Aussies, Brits and Kiwis leave the field, it reverts to the "hands off — or else" policy.

In the Thai culture, touching someone's head may be thought rude. For to many Asians, the head has a religious meaning. Many Asians believe the head houses the soul. Therefore, when another person touches their heads, it places them in jeopardy. It is prudent for outsiders to avoid touching the heads and upper torsos of Asians. Many African Americans are also annoyed if a white person pats them on the top of their heads. They believe it carries the same meaning as being told, in a condescending manner, that they are a good little boy or girl.

Men in much of Eastern Europe, Spain, Italy, Portugal, and the Arab world will kiss when they meet their friends. There is also much more same-sex touching in Mexico. Men will greet each other with an embrace. In much of South-East Asia, people not only avoid touching when meeting, but also have very little physical contact during the course of the conversation. In Japan, there is no word for "kiss," so "kissu" is used. If a man in Saudi Arabia holds another man's hand, it means they respect each other, but not in Australia, America or England.

Section 1 Kissing

A kiss may be used to express sentiments of love, passion, affection, respect, greeting, friendship, and good luck, among many others. The word came from Old English *cyssan* "to kiss," in turn from *coss* "a kiss." The act of kissing has become a common expression of affection

among many cultures worldwide. Yet in certain cultures, kissing was introduced only through European settlement; prior to this, kissing was not a routine occurrence. Examples of this include certain indigenous peoples of Australia, the Tahitians, and many tribes in Africa. Cultural connotations of kissing vary widely.

In modern Western culture, kissing is most commonly an expression of affection. Between people of close acquaintance, a reciprocal kiss often is offered as a greeting or farewell. This kind of kiss is typically made by brief contact of puckered lips to the skin of the cheek or no contact at all and merely performed in the air near the cheek with the cheeks touching. People may kiss children on the forehead to comfort them or the cheek to show affection, and vice versa.

In Slavic cultures until recent times, kissing between two men on the lips as a greeting or a farewell was not uncommon and not considered sexual. Symbolic kissing is frequent in Western cultures. A kiss can be "blown" to another by kissing the fingertips and then blowing the fingertips, pointing them in the direction of the recipient. This is used to convey affection, usually when parting or when the partners are physically distant but can view each other. Blown kisses are also used when a person wishes to convey affection to a large crowd or audience. The term *flying kiss* is used in India to describe a blown kiss. In written correspondence a kiss has been represented by the letter "X" since at least 1763. A stage or screen kiss may be performed by actually kissing, or faked by using the thumbs as a barrier for the lips and turning so the audience is unable to fully see the act.

In some Western cultures it is considered good luck to kiss someone on Christmas or on New Year's Eve, especially beneath a sprig of mistletoe.

Kissing in traditional Islamic cultures is not accepted between two members of the opposite sex who are not married or closely related by blood or marriage. Kisses on the cheek are a very common form of greeting among members of the same sex in most Islamic countries, following the Mediterranean pattern.

Case study Kissing as greeting

Wang Jun was in charge of foreign affairs at a Chinese university. A number of specialists from Scandinavia, France, Australia, Belgium, Germany, Britain and Japan were visiting the university. When he held a party for them, at the start there was a little embarrassing. The Scandinavian met the Belgian and

kissed him once, but the Belgian leaped forward and hugged and kissed him, while the Scandinavian turned away. When the German shook hands with the American, he just shook hands once and wanted to turn to another person, but the American held his hand and kept shaking it.

Questions:

1. Why is the incident embarrassing?
2. If you were Wang Jun, what would you have done before the party?

Case analysis:

The conflict in the case is their unaware of the differences of the kissing culture and shaking hands culture. The best way is to subdue to the opposite culture.

In this case, we basically know some differences of kissing culture in some European countries. When it comes to greeting with a cheek kiss, the Scandinavians are happy with a single kiss, the French mostly prefer a double, while the Dutch, Belgians and Arabs go for a triple kiss. The Australians, New Zealanders and Americans are continually confused about greeting kisses and bump noses as they fumble their way through a single peck. To most British people, they will show their firm resolution and retreat one pace and refuse the greeting of kissing.

If you learn the proper way to greet someone in another culture, including understanding body language, you may be pleasantly surprised at how well you will be received when traveling to another country. Greetings are often people's first impressions of one another, so learning how to greet someone appropriately is important in making a good first impression.

Case for students' practice:

John, an American teacher, teaches in one university in China. He always found many couples walking side by side and keeping a certain distance. He wondered whether their relationship was intimate or not. They didn't kiss each other and hug each other. Even sometimes husband or wife would blame the opposite in the public.

Section 2 Touching

We can communicate anger, interest, trust, tenderness, warmth, and a variety of other emotions very potently through touching. Touch can communicate many different things, such as affection, playfulness, hospitality and urgency.

There are four universal recognized aspects of touch:

(1) The professional touch, used, for example, by business people, between a professor and his/her students or two people meeting at the first time.

(2) The ocial/polite touch, used by acquaintances who wish to convey friendly but slightly detached appreciation and affection.

(3) The friendly touch, which could be used by close friends or close business people and colleagues congratulating one another on an accomplishment.

(4) Intimate touch, which is usually reserved for couples expressing love and affection.

People differ in their willingness to touch and be touched. Some people give out nonverbal body signals that say they do not want to be touched, and there are other people who describe themselves and are described by others as "touch freely." There are many taboos associated with this form of communication. Many misunderstandings and much discomfort can arise from a situation that places two people from dramatically different cultures together.

Case study Fondling babies

Sophie, her husband and their baby came to visit her Chinese friend's family from England. The Chinese family invited them to have dinner outside. Since it was an open restaurant with clear air, many people liked enjoying their dinner there. Lucy, the baby, was very beautiful and healthy. She attracted the attention of many people nearby. One elderly woman at the next table came directly to the baby and smiled to her and wanted to hug the baby. Sophie was frightened and angry with that and held the baby

tightly. She refused the elderly woman very impolitely. The elderly woman felt embarrassed. Sophie's Chinese friend explained to her about this aspect of Chinese culture. Sophie was a little reassured.

Discussion:

1. What do you think of the elderly woman's behavior? Is it very common in China?
2. How do you understand Sophie's reaction?

Case analysis:

In this case, the main conflict is whether the baby can be held by strangers. In China, it is very common for a stranger to hold a baby because it means the baby is very lovely. But in England, people don't like strangers to be close to their babies.

In China, people often fondle their own babies and very small children or fondle those of their relatives, friends, and sometimes strangers. Such behavior — whether touching, patting, hugging or kissing — is merely a sign of affection and friendliness. Children and their parents will not mind at all. But in England, or other Western countries, such action in their own culture would be considered rude, intrusive, and offensive unless it was that of their most intimate relatives. The children themselves dislike being touched by others, even to the extent that they cry, or push the person away. Therefore fondling the children of other countries' people would be unwise.

Case for students' practice:

Alfred, a man from the United States, was on a crowded bus trip. Five children were seated on a bench for three people, and three adults shared two seats. Since there was a long way to go, a man nearby who sat on a seat signed to him to sit close to him so that they could share the seat. Alfred refused and felt offended. The Chinese man wondered why this foreigner did not accept his kind offer.

Chapter 3

Appearance and dress

Appearance and dress refer to various kinds of articrafts with communicative functions, such as cosmetics, adornments, dress, grooming, smell and furniture, etc. which can send nonverbal communications and display the user's personality and cultural characteristics. There are three elements that affect communicator's first and long-lasting impression: dress, make up and smell.

How you groom and dress is not only an individual statement, it is part of your image created in the eyes of others.

It is an expression of your personality and a reflection of your attitude, focus, stature and status. The attention to detail spent on personal care, knowing what to wear, how to wear it, and when to wear it has a direct effect on influencing people, positively or negatively.

Concern with how one appears is universal. We often make judgments on personal appearance, dress, and the type of objects carried around or placed on the body. When deciding whether or not to strike up a conversation with a total stranger, we are influenced by the way they look.

Though our physical attributes are respected we can change our appearance to suit the occasion.

In the United States, people tend to value the appearance of tall, slender women. In Japan, diminutive petite females are deemed the most attractive.

And China has its own unique standards for evaluating what is often referred to as the "feminine mystique." In former times, women kept their hairstyle simple and made little attempt to draw attention to themselves through personal adornment such as colorful scarves, jewelry, or makeup.

But as a result of greater contact with western cultures, the orient has changed their perception of what is considered "attractive." Regarding to makeup, Chinese women now often use it for formal occasions. Young women have a tendency to apply it more liberally than the older generation who adhere to more conventional wisdom, "all things in moderation."

On the other hand, in the U.S., it is not uncommon to see women wear make-up and earrings not only for formal occasions, but for leisure activities as well. The younger generation is more inclined to apply makeup lightly and the older, perhaps less secure in their own natural attributes, have a tendency to increase makeup in an effort to conceal their age. As with the shade of the clothes they wear, the makeup at daytime is lighter than at night.

Due to the different cultural norm, Chinese people will be puzzled at seeing an elderly American women wearing a colorful dress and heavy makeup since this less than subdued public display is reserved for the young, or what sometimes is euphemistically referred to as "working women." The reigning Queen of England often wears colorful dresses and extravagant hats in the tradition of English monarchs. However, this would be out of place in Chinese society.

Furthermore, the custom of wearing hats is also different. It is not common for Chinese women, as well as men, the exception of older men who wear a hat for the sake of keeping warm. Once they put it on, they will have a tendency to wear it indoors or outdoors. Conversely, Westerners sometimes wear hats in formal occasions, such as wedding ceremonies, and other social events. However, social etiquettes require that they take off their hats when indoors, and with the exception of a country western bars this is considered extremely impolite. Why this anomaly is considered socially acceptable only for cowboys has as much to do with their pride in unconventional behavior as it has to do with their pride in their oversized hats.

Clothing is also a reflection of a culture's orientation. For example, Muslim girls usually use scarves (hijab) to cover their heads and are not allowed to participate in coed swimming classes because of religious prohibitions against exposing their bodies. The requirement of wearing a hijab is not limited strictly to Muslim nations, but to immigrants in the west. Recently in France and the Netherlands where this requirement was imposed on children in public schools, it has been challenged in the courts. German men are stereotyped as extremely conservative and the way they dress is no exception.

Male business attire often consists of an impeccably pressed, dark suit and tie with a plain, white shirt and dark shoes and socks. (White socks with this outfit would be considered an unforgivable fashion *faux pas*). This highly fashionable, officious look, commonly associated with government workers and secret agents was popularized in the recent blockbuster, *Men in Black*.

In many Arab countries people wear traditional garments such as a long loose robe called a dishdasha, or thobe, a headpiece, and a white cloth banded by a black egal to fasten it.

There is an international acceptable principle of appropriate dress known as the Time-Place-Object Principle (TPO).

That is to say, the dress should be consistent with time and season. It should be in agreement with place and occasion and varied according to the communicator and topics so as to achieve the objective and make a good impression.

Case 1 Suits or casual dress?

Jun Chen works in one American company that has formal dress code. And his boss is a kind man, whose name is Brown. Being unaware of this, when Jun Chen went to the company for registration, he wore a jeans and a T-shirt. His fellow employees were surprised at his lack of discretion. The boss told him in the future he would wear suits.

The next weekend the boss invited him to his house for dinner. Jun Chen remembered how embarrassed he had been previously, and so to insure that it would not happen again, he wore formal suit to the dinner. But to his surprise he found the boss wearing a pair of jeans and a T-shirt. The boss was of course a little puzzled why Jun Chen chose to wear a suit instead of casual clothing.

Discussion:

1. Why was everybody astonished at seeing Jun Chen wear casual clothes at their company?

2. Why was the boss also astonished at finding Jun Chen wearing a suit to his home?

Case analysis:

The conflict of the case involves a misunderstanding of what is and is not appropriate clothing to wear in the situation given. It is a fairly common misunderstanding and to one degree or another, we have all experienced the feeling of being inappropriately dressed. For Jun Chen, what clothing to wear was not an important consideration. His "work ethic" was the only thing that he considered to be important.

And to many people who work for the companies in China, what you wear is considered irrelevant. It is what you do, how hard you work, and what you are able to personally contribute to a company that is the only concern.

But to Jun Chen's boss and his colleagues how one dresses in the workplace is a demonstration of respect towards the company that they work for. But how one dresses when outside of the work environment is a matter of personal taste.

Once upon a time in the western countries, traveling by airplane, going out to eat, or staying at a hotel was regarded as an important occasion, and people dressed accordingly. It was "an experience" and invariably you will see it portrayed in the old movies where people are "decked out" for what is now considered a common, day to day routine.

But vacationers have now become more casual in the way they dress. They would prefer wearing shorts and T-shirts to something less comfortable. Sandals or running shoes are much more common than leather-shoes. Their reasoning is that they are on vacation and not out to impress anyone. Therefore comfort is their first priority.

With respect to the tag on the sleeves of suit jackets, Westerners invariably remove the tag. Leaving it on would be considered quite gauche, a sign of being extremely unsophisticated. In common slang one might characterize that type of person as being a "rube."

Chinese people, especially those traveling abroad, chose dressing formally on such occasions. It is not uncommon to see a Chinese man wearing a suit at a tourist attraction. They tend to overdress when they first go abroad because they simply assume that a suit is the proper thing to wear in the west. This may be attributed to both the influence of TV and a desire to create a good first impression.

In order to help people plan on how to dress, some invitations to social function and even business meetings will offer advice such as black tie, business formal, business casual, casual resort wear, or even country and western.

Normally while attending the formal meeting or dinner, both the man and woman are expected to wear suits. For men it is fashionable to wear dark, solid color suits and matching socks. For the women, pansuits is in vogue, particularly since Secretary of State Hillary Clinton had the habit of wearing them to state functions. Also a midlength skirt is quite fashionable. Shorts, mini-skirts, halter tops and other types of a casual dress are inappropriate for the women to wear in a formal situation.

In America men are expected to wear clean shirt every day. If a man wears the same shirt more than two days in a row he may be regarded a bit tasteless, even "tacky," particularly if the shirt is dirty. Above all perspiration odor is socially reprehensible.

The distinction and expectation are important and sometimes rather subtle. It can all be very confusing. The only solution is to remember others are confused too, and then ask. Another case should be mentioned in that in Chinese campuses, some girls like wearing T-shirts without caring about the English words or sentences on it. Some foreign teachers mention that there are some dirty words on it.

These distinctions and expectations are important and sometimes from one culture to another are sometimes rather subtle and confusing. But usually cleanness, neatness, and modesty are never out of style.

Case 2 Your skin is very white!

Calgary is the largest city in the Province of Alberta, Canada. The winter of here is very long. On an average year ice covers the ground from October to May. If they have the time and money Canadians enjoy going to exotic locations to "work on their suntan," that is to say that they associate a dark tan with prestige, being part leisure class that has time to vacation. Ironically this is just the opposite of some people with darker skin pigmentation who associate white skin with prestige; being part of the leisure class that does not have to work outdoors.

Yang Lin isn't aware of this western custom. In the office, he praised one of his colleagues, "Your skin is very white!" After hearing this, his colleague felt a bit deflated and apologized that he had no time to travel and that was why his skin was so white.

Discussion:

1. What are your personal feelings about the different perceptions concerning to

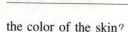

the color of the skin?

2. Why did Yang Lin's colleague apologize for the color of his skin?

 Case analysis:

For Chinese, white is the color of beauty. So Yang Lin thought his colleague was very beautiful. But to his colleague, white means no vacation, no money. The different perceptions of the skin color caused the conflict.

In many tourist destinations, Chinese people use umbrellas to avoid exposure to the sun. But foreigners prefer being suntanned. Because being bronzed is not only considered more attractive and healthy, it is considered a status symbol. Many foreigners wondered whether Chinese girls like opening umbrellas just in case it rains.

Opinions on the matters are, however, changing with more public awareness of the harmful effects of long term exposure to UV rays. Fewer people now intentionally expose themselves to the sun. It is well publicized that the exposure to UV rays causes skin cancer and premature aging. For that reason beach umbrellas and sunblock are common accessories for a day at the beach.

Another common phenomenon associated with people "wanting what they don't have" involves the dying of hair. It is popular among Chinese men and women to dye their hair blond and conversely for American natural blonds to dye their hair black. The perception of the beauty is what defines it and the psychological impact of feeling "deficient" or "inadequate" fuels most of industries that market products which change our appearance.

 Case for students' practice:

Jane was a tourist in China and spent some time staying with a Chinese friend at her home. They watched a children's programe while having breakfast one morning. A young man, the host of the program, gave instruction of a game to a few children, and then joined them running in a circle.

"My, he's wearing a tie and running crazy with the children!" Jane exclaimed. The Chinese friend shrugged, "Is this very unusual?"

Chapter

4

Olfactics (smell and taste)

People naturally concern certain smells with different feelings and emotions. This sense is powerful at triggering our memory, with certain fragrances being tied to different emotions, people or events.

Olfactics are also one of the most common parts of body language, with perfumes, colognes, fragrances, and deodorants being very important, especially in America and Europe. Differences in use of smell can create misunderstandings when people from different cultures communicate.

The way people use or accept body odors varies greatly between cultures. Saudi Arabians welcome them and use them in the interpretation of health. In a typical Arab conversation, it is common for the parties involved to touch hands and get so close to one another that they share the same breath.

Saudi Arabian males often use the scent of each other's breath to gauge their health; if the scent of the breath is unpleasant, men often communicate to their partners that they may be unhealthy.

In some rural Middle Eastern areas, when Arab intermediaries make a call to inspect a prospective bride for a relative, they sometimes ask to smell her. The purpose is not to make sure she is clean; ostensibly they sniff her to make a character evaluation. If there is any lingering "odor" of anger or discontent they believe that they detect it.

Similar practices are found in Arab countries where breathing on people as you speak to them signals friendship and goodwill — and to "deny" someone your breath-smell conveys a personal affront.

In India, the traditional affectionate greeting — equivalent of the Western hug or kiss — is to smell someone's head. An ancient Indian text declares "I will smell thee on the head, which is the greatest sign of tender love."

In contrast, Americans seem to maintain their distance and suppress their sense of smell.

Some of the cultural variations in grooming practices result from physical differences between races. Whereas many Asian men have little facial hair, Westerners have a lot. As a result, most American men spend some time each day shaving or grooming their facial hair. Beards and mustaches are common sights in America, although their popularity changes from generation to generation. Most American men who wear facial hair try to keep it nicely trimmed. American women, on the other hand, generally prefer not to be hairy at all. Many of them regularly shave their legs and armpits.

Communication is not just the act of talking but behavior that is influenced by all of one's senses. Research shows that pleasant scents generally have a positive effect on mood and memory while unpleasant chemical odors produced a negative effect. The use of pleasant smells, like perfumes and colognes, may have positive impacts on people, making them feel happier and may elicit the remembrance of good memories.

Taste is one of the traditional five senses. It refers to the ability to detect the flavor of substances such as food, certain minerals and poisons.

With humans and all vertebrates the sense of taste partners with the sense of smell, constitutes the brain's perception of flavor. In the West, experts traditionally identified four taste sensations: sweet, salty, sour, and bitter. In the East something being "spicy hot" is a type of pungence specific to the sense of taste. And savoriness (also known as umami) has been traditionally identified as basic tastes as well.

The Chinese focus on color, fragrance, taste and form in food, with a priority placed upon refined food vessels, and the elegance of the dining environment. Hence from time immemorial the Chinese advocated the philosophy of the "five tastes in harmony."

The Chinese invented ways to adjust blended ingredients and spices for a wide variety of tastes. Revolving around the "five tastes," which are sourness, sweetness, bitterness, pungency and saltiness, dishes can evolve into more than 500 different flavors. Of the "five tastes," saltiness is the principal taste in China. It is the most simplistic and most crucial. But to the Westerners, they do not like putting too much salt in the food.

By comparison, seasonings are used more sparingly in the western cooking. As a result western foods are not palatable to Chinese tastes.

Part IV *Case Analyses in Intercultural Nonverbal Communication* 121

Case 1 What a smell!

Garlic is Fang Yu's favorite. He works in a Canadian company and likes eating garlic every day. Once after dinner, without brushing his teeth, he rushed to the elevator that was full of other Canadians there. They were crowded together for a few awkward minutes when one Canadian girl blurted out, "What a smell!" Fang Yu felt embarrassed and held his breath for the remainder of the ride.

Discussion:

1. What caused Fang Yu to be embarrassed?
2. After this conflict, what do you think Fang Yu should do?

Case analysis:

The main conflict of the case is the odor awareness of different cultures. Chinese people usually are not concerned about the breath odor after eating and they are not aware of the importance that Westerners attach to having fresh breath and no discernable odors when communicating with others. For that reason Westerners have the habit of using mouthwash and colones before going out.

The first impression of one's appearance is his or her cleanliness. Americans generally bathe daily and use deodorant. Many consider body odor of any kind to be extremely unpleasant.

Some foreigners complain that Chinese people's so called "garlic breath" is a personal affront. Often Westerners are amazed at some of the foods that Chinese people would consider delicacies, such as bean curd, fried chicken feet, and duck head. In the West, these body parts are discarded as waste, or used to feed livestock, and never served as a main course in a restaurant. But now gradually Chinese people try to avoid such things, for example, the policemen in Shanghai, the Expo 2010 are suggested not to eat garlic before being on guard.

It is much like Chinese attitudes to the varieties of cheese that Westerners enjoy.

Different cultures have different tastes. So to be on the safe side, it is better not to send your own favorite food to others without considering the cultural differences. Also, out of courtesy, reserve your opinions of others' diet, as you would expect them to do to you.

Case 2　Different tastes for drinking coffee!

While studying in the United States, Lin Jun made a few American friends. One day he invited two of them to his apartment and cooked them a meal. When his friends said they would like some coffee, he started boiling some water. Without asking them any questions, he made three cups of coffee, the way he usually took it.

Both friends tasted the coffee and frowned. One said she always took coffee black; the other said he preferred to have less sugar in his coffee. They also told him that the spoon was for stirring the coffee. Lin Jun was embarrassed. He had thought that everyone drank coffee the same way he did.

Discussion:

1. Do you often drink coffee? How do you serve coffee for others?
2. How can you explain the serving procedures of tea for foreign guests?

Case analysis:

In this case, the conflict lies in the misunderstanding of the coffee preparation. Chinese people usually put milk and sugar into the coffee because it is more tasteful. But for the Americans, they like to put things according to their own tastes. Sometimes they prefer some original coffee. Sometimes they like coffee with cream alone, some with sugar alone, and some with cream and sugar. For that reason it is always served black and the guest is given the option of adding other ingredients in the amount that they prefer. In the same way an American would have difficulties preparing a cup of tea exactly to the preferred tastes of their Chinese guests. The proper thing to do would be to serve the tea plain and allow their guests to add ingredients according to their own personal preferences.

Coffee is not a traditional drink in China. It is relatively new in the market. When it was introduced to China, it was known to go with milk and sugar.

Since it is regularly consumed by the majority of people, few are concerned about the nuances of how much, or how little cream and sugar is in it. They usually don't drink enough coffee to develop their own personal preferences for how it is served. And like many other Chinese, Lin Jun had thought the coffee spoon was for drinking purpose rather than for stirring.

Although not every North American drinks coffee, most do and they often begin as students. There is a wide range of coffee brands, different ways of roasting the beans, different flavors, and different ways of preparing coffee. Sometimes there is a choice of different types of sugar as well as toppings such as cinnamon, cocoa, or nutmeg. They may ask to have a flavored syrup added as well.

When serving coffee, people are usually asked, "How do you take your coffee?" rather than serving everyone the same way.

In Arab countries, if a guest is invited to drink coffee with the family, the guest should show his gratitude and response accordingly.

While tasting the coffee, he should give compliment in the same way that one may compliment their host on a final meal. And following the ritual, he should not clear his mouth with fresh water but "savor" the taste for as long as possible.

Case for students' practice:

Mr Wu invited Fabrice and his family to his home for a meal to show his thanks to their kindness for help. A large number of delicious dishes were put in front of them by Mrs. Wu. Without too much difficulty, Fabrice's family consumed everything. Then, to their surprise the same number of different but equally delicious dishes appeared in front of them. Although they had eaten a lot, they felt it would be impolite to leave food on the table, so they again managed to consume everything. Then their mouths fell open as more dishes appeared in front of them. They looked at each other and said, "Come on, we must try. They will be offended if we don't eat everything." They just managed to do so but this time was on the verge of collapse. Then suddenly even more dishes arrived! They threw up their hands in defeat, "We can't eat any more," they protested. "Oh, we thought you were still hungry because each time you finished everything," said Mr Wu. They all had a good laugh.

Chapter
5

Proxemics (body space)

The term proxemics, also referred to as our use of space, is the study of the distance between or among people who are engaging in an interaction and the factors that determine the size of distance. It was introduced by the anthropologist Edward T. Hall in 1966. In general, it studies how people use physical  space in an interpersonal interaction and the functions culture plays in it.

Like animals, human beings also have their own personal portable "air bubble," which they carry around with them; the size of which, to a large extent, is determined by the population density in the place where they grow up. Personal space is therefore cultural-specific. Some cultures, such as the Japanese, are getting used to crowding; others prefer a wider personal space and like people to keep their distances.

People who feel close will tend to be close, though the actual distances in different cultures are quite different. Generally speaking, Europeans don't need as much personal space; French have special emphasis on outside and public space; Arabians prefer high ceilings, out of normal line of vision, and an unobstructed view; Asians place higher focus on functional space. Americans recognize four main categories of distance: "intimate" distance, ranging from direct contact to about 45 centimeters, stands for the closest relationships such as those between husband and wife; "personal" distance is the most usual one maintained for conversations between friends and relatives, which is usually between 45 and 80 centimeters; "social" distance, varying from 1.3 to 2 meters, is applicable to people who work together or are meeting at social gatherings; the last type is "public" distance, the typical example of which is that between a lecturer and his listeners.

Different opinions on the distance in a conversation have been observed in other cultures. People in Arabian culture usually stand closely to each other, but that would be the last thing the Americans will do — they simply don't want to take the risk of exchanging breath with other people. People in China may stand closer than those in U. K. or U. S. A. Furthermore, North Americans and Latin Americans have diametrically different ideas on the proxemic system. North Americans usually keep a distance from one another; Latin Americans, however, stay very close to each other. From the simple fact, we can know much about these people's different concepts of privacy.

Proxemics means a lot in the cross-cultural communications and people can get something insightful from it. We may meet serious problems in communications if we don't pay enough attention to it.

In the following part we will take Chinese and Americans as examples to illustrate that culture says something in the human use of space.

Americans value more about privacy than their Chinese counterparts when it comes to the use of space

While standing in line, Chinese always stay very close to each other. As for Americans, space could always be found between people. In China, when accidents happen in streets, you can find a large crowd of people around the site. Some may be out of curiosity; others think that they can offer some help if necessary. But if American people are under the same circumstance, they are most likely to stand away from the site because they feel that is better. The reason why Chinese like to stay together and Americans don't is that American people want to be independent and dislike to be interfered by others while Chinese believe that people staying together could help each other and become more powerful.

Americans value more space among one another while Chinese people's attitude toward it is more flexible

It is said that Americans always like to have more space because they want more freedom, so they choose to keep distance from other people in public. While Chinese people have more conception on being together even with strangers, so they would like to feel it okay with strangers standing besides them.

When facing the violation of personal space, Americans may react unconsciously or consciously while Chinese people will try to ignore it or bear it

When their personal space is violated, Americans may move away, put up a personal barrier, change their body position unconsciously, or they may deliberately react to it by spreading out, turning around, asking the other person to move away, or even using verbal warning. However, most people tend to prefer passive measures to active measures when their personal space is violated, because reclaiming personal space directly is too intimidating and aggressive.

While violation of personal space happens to Chinese people, most of them will choose to ignore it or wait until the other part withdraws. Because people think that it is impolite to react in such situation even in today's China. Some of them may react automatically by moving away or changing body position, but those actions would be regarded as being unfriendly. To avoid feeling uncomfortable when our personal space is invaded, we may avoid eye contact with the other party. That is the reaction most Chinese people will do.

People handle with space differently. Their opinions of it are largely determined by the culture in which they are born. Therefore, one's use of space conveys special information about one's culture.

Generally speaking, there are three fundamental elements involved in proxemics: namely *space*, *distance*, and *territory*.

Section 1　Space

To put it simply, personal space refers to an area with invisible boundaries surrounding a person's body, into which other people may not intrude. The size of the area differs from one culture to another. For example, the British prefer larger size of personal space than the French. When  personal space is violated, people will take some defensive gestures, such as shifting posture, attempting to move away and so on.

Scholars have identified three types of space: *fixed-feature*, *semi-fixed feature*, and *informal space*.

Fixed-feature space refers to the actual space in which things are organized. For example, cities, buildings, houses, rooms, etc. are organized spatially.

Semi-fixed feature space is very significant for interpersonal communication, because meanings can be conveyed by it in many different ways. Semi-fixed feature space can be further divided into two types: socio-petal space and socio-fugal space. The former refers to those which link people together and encourage participation, while the latter separates and promotes withdrawal.

Part IV *Case Analyses in Intercultural Nonverbal Communication*

The importance of *informal space* lies in that it includes the distances people unconsciously maintain when they are together. Though the bounds of informal spatial patterns are distinct, and significance is implicit, we should by no means ignore or misunderstand it. If we do ignore or misunderstand it, disasters will happen, because they are an essential part of culture.

Case 1 Is he gentleman-like?

Xiaomei, a summer student from China, is studying in the University of Nottingham. She used to major in English in one Chinese university and is a middle school English teacher in Shanghai. She has a good command of English and has learned a lot about English culture, especially British culture.

One day when she was visiting Newstead Abbey, she came across a British man at a narrow stair. The stair is very narrow and only allows one person to go comfortably. If two persons walk on it simultaneously, they can not avoid hustling. Xiaomei was at the footstep and about to go upstairs while that man was about to go downstairs. Xiaomei stepped on the stair after thinking twice, and the man stood at the other side waiting for her to pass. She was impressed by the man's gentility, and said "thank you" while passing him. After coming back from the visiting, she told this to her British teacher as an impressive experience. But to her surprise, her teacher just smiled and said nothing. Xiaomei was confused, and then she remembered the strange expression on the man when she looked up. Is he gentleman-like or not?

Discussion:

1. Why did the man wait until Xiaomei went upstairs? Do you think that man just wanted to be a gentleman?

2. How do you think Xiaomei's foreign teacher smiled?

Case analysis:

The conflict in the above story was caused by the misunderstanding of keeping a space or being a gengtleman. Actually, the reason why the man stands there waiting for Xiaomei to pass is that he doesn't want others to invade his personal space. However, Xiaomei interprets it as a behavior of a gentleman. In fact the man may feel it annoying to meet a person in such a narrow stair. But Xiaomei knows nothing about it, so her "thank you" seems to be funny.

For Chinese people, meeting another people in a narrow stair is nothing awkward. When it happens, they usually choose to hustle through. But as for British people, hustling through a narrow stair with another person is considered a violation of personal space. In order to avoid awkwardness, most of them tend to let others go through first. In this way, they can keep away from others.

Case 2 Can you stand away from me?

Pierre had stayed in the United States for over ten years without returning home in France. His trip home ten years later was really hard because he had forgotten a lot of his native language and spent most of his time translating everything in his mind first before he could say it in proper French. But what was even worse for him is going to a post office. People crowded around the teller rather than waited in a line. There were many people around him, and it seemed that those people didn't know how to behave properly in public, because they stayed very closely to each other without respecting the rules of personal space, to which Pierre had been accustomed in the United States. All these made Pierre very angry.

Discussion:

1. Do those people around him in the post office want to peep at what he was writing? Why did Pierre feel so angry with so many people around him?

2. What do you think is the different perception of the personal space in this case?

Case analysis:

Again the conflict in this case was also caused by the different perception of the

Part IV *Case Analyses in Intercultural Nonverbal Communication* 129

personal space. Pierre, who has been accustomed to the American system of personal space, could not bear people staying too close to him. However, French people are more bearable about the crowded phenomenon, especially in public places.

Americans and French have different requirements on the personal space. Americans ask for more personal space than French people. For example, in America, children can have their own rooms from very young at home, and in schools every student has his own lockers to stock his private things. In public places, they keep distance from others and avoid physical contact with other people, which are considered as good manners.

Different from Americans, French people require not as much personal space, especially in public. They stand closer while talking and are less sensitive about the violation of personal space in crowded public places.

 Case for students' practice:

Before coming back to work in China, Jia He had lived in the United States for seven years. She had become accustomed to the social habits in North America and is dissatisfied with some behaviors in China, which cause her some discomfort. For example, one day when she was waiting in a queue to use an ATM, she noticed that people stayed very close to each other. In fact, the person behind her could even see her entering the PIN of ATM card. To make people be aware of the discomfort, Jia He deliberately kept distance from the person in front of her. However, the people behind her pushed her to move forward.

Section 2   Distance

Distance is a relational concept, referring to how far one individual is from the other. As we have mentioned at the beginning of this chapter, there are four types of distances, namely *intimate distance*, *personal distance*, *social distance*, and *public distance*.

Intimate distance: (0 – 18 inches) between close friends, family members; show affection, give comfort or protect;

Personal distance: (1½ – 4 feet) most conversations;
Social distance: (4 – 12 feet) less personal situations, in business, workplaces;
Public distance: (>12 feet) lectures, churches, public gatherings.

People from different cultures have different opinions on space. For instance, when someone does not keep the proper distance from them, people in North America may feel uncomfortable. And the situation may be even worse if the two persons are of the opposite sex. Evidence about this can be found from their language. Expressions like "get your face out of mine" and "he shook his fist in my face" reveal how important body boundaries are for Americans. The expression "I don't bite" Costa Rican language shows that people from this culture feel uncomfortable when others are too far from them. The Arabs also prefer a shorter personal space. In Arabian countries, it is normal for people to stay close to and touch strangers and their distance from others in ordinary social conversations is equal to that of intimate conversations of Westerners. However, in North America and Britain if you touch a stranger, you must offer an excuse.

According to researchers, cultures such as Arabs, Latin Americans, Greeks, Turks, French, and Italians, who usually keep small distances among themselves belong to high-contact cultures; while cultures such as Chinese, Japanese, Thai, Germans, Dutch, and North Americans, who "stand further apart," belong to low-contact cultures.

Case 1   Oh, my God! So many homosexuals in China!

Rose, an American girl, came to China in 1992 as a foreign teacher in one university. At that time she was only 20 and knew little about China. Yang Mei, a middle-aged woman teacher, was assigned by the university to meet Rose at the airport. Out of hospitality and warm-heartedness, she invited Rose to her house for a dinner after helping her settled. Rose felt ill every time Yang Mei touched her while Yang Mei failed to notice it. At the dinner, Rose tried to escape from sitting by Yang Mei, but failed. When Yang Mei found Rose trembling, she patted Rose in order to comfort her, which led to more tremble. At last, the dinner turned out to be a disaster for both of them.

After having stayed in China for two months, Rose decided to quit the job and returned to America. It was from the letter left by Rose Yang Mei knew the reasons why she continuously trembled at that dinner and why she quitted the job. Rose thought Yang Mei was homosexual because Yang Mei always tried touching her. And then in her stay in China, most female teachers had physical contact with her which shocked her to death by thinking "so many homosexuals in China." She could not bear it, so she chose to quit the job and China.

Discussion:

1. Are there so many homosexuals in China as Rose thought?
2. Why do you think Rose felt so nervous when other females touched her?
3. What are the different conceptions on the distance between people in this situation?

Case analysis:

The conflict in this case was the consequence of being innocent of the different perception of the distance between cultures. Patting or touching another person of the same gender, in China, is a way of expressing one's concern or friendliness, while in America, without doubt, it will be understood as a homosexual signal.

In China, distance only exists between or among strangers or rivals. People who are familiar with each other (sometimes even they have been familiar with each other for a few minutes) will completely ignore the distance. It's common, in China, for people of the same gender to walk hand in hand, or touch each other, even to sleep in the same bed, but it is immoral for people of different genders to do so unless they are dating or married (sometimes even lovers are not expected to show intimacy in public). No one will consider it as a homosexual sign if your friend of the same sex touches you. On the contrary, we feel comfortable and intimate because that means we are good friends.

The situation in America is diametrically different from that in China. It is unbelievable to see two Americans of the same gender — gays and lesbians are exceptions — to walk hand in hand or touch each other, not to mention sleep in the same bed. The very thought of it will make ordinary people feel disgusted. But it is acceptable for two Americans of different genders to live together, even when they are school students. So in some American universities, girls and boys are allowed to live in the same dormitory, which is something impossible in China.

From the above analysis, we know that the dilemma in the above case is completely due to Yang Mei's and Rose's innocence of the different views of space between the two cultures, especially that of the same sex. If they had known more about the cultural differences in understanding and perceiving the personal distance, their problems would have been solved.

Case 2 Americans are cold!

Eva, who is studying in an American college, comes from Peru. She wanted to improve her English, so she chose to live with an American family. The foreign student office of her college found the Larsen family for her to live with. Eva spoke with Mrs. Larsen on the telephone. Mrs. Larsen sounded very friendly. Eva was very happy about it.

Eva arrived the next day with all her luggage. She was excited to meet the Larsens. A tall, blonde woman answered the door with a big smile. She said, "Oh, you must be Eva! I'm so glad you're here! Let me help you with your bags. Come on in. I'm Hilda Larsen."

When they got inside, Mrs. Larsen put the bag down and stood across from Eva about 3 feet away, she crossed her arms in front of her and asked Eva, "Tell me about the trip. I'd love to go to Peru someday."

Just then, her teenaged son walked in, hands in his pockets. "Jimmy, meet Eva. Maybe she can help you with your Spanish this semester," said his mother.

Jimmy said, "Hi, glad to meet you." His hands stayed in his pockets while he nodded his head.

Eva didn't know what to do with her hands. She felt uncomfortable. But she smiled and said, "Hi, nice to meet you."

The Larsens showed Eva her new room. Then they left her alone to unpack. Eva felt a little disappointed, but she did not know exactly why. She thought Mrs. Larsen seemed so friendly on the phone, but now she wasn't sure. Jimmy also seemed a little bit cold.

Eva tried to find what was wrong, but failed. She thought to herself. If an American girl came to stay with me in Peru, she would get a warmer welcome than that. My mother would give her a big kiss, instead of just standing there, on the other side of the room. And my brother would give her a proper greeting. Well, people told me that Americans were cold. I guess they're right.

Discussion:

1. Are the Larsens unfriendly to Eva? Why did not they give Eva a warm welcome as Eva expected?

2. Do you think Eva is right in saying "Americans are cold." just because of her first day?

3. What is the different understanding of the distance between people in this case?

Case analysis:

The conflict in this case was caused by their different understanding of the distance in different cultures. Eva felt she was not welcome in a warm way because in her country, people stand closer when greeting each other, within 46 centimetres. And when they greet each other, they may have physical touch, such as a hug, a kiss, or a handshaking which shows respect for others. While for Americans, the distance within 45 centimetres is regarded as intimate distance. Mrs. Larsen viewed Eva as a stranger, so it is impossible for her to stand so close. Eva thought she was not accepted by the family, but in fact the Larsens gave a warm welcome in American culture.

While greeting, American culture focuses more on language than actions. They may choose to stand 3 feet away to show respect for other people's personal space. In American culture, everyone needs his own space. No one likes the personal space being violated. Therefore, to be friendly with a stranger means to stand away from him and wear a smile, greeting by talking.

While in Peru, standing away from others means being cold to others. It is polite for people to be closer than those in America while talking with each other. And physical touch is seen as a warm and friendly way of welcoming a friend. When it comes to a stranger, it means accepting the stranger as one of their friends.

Case for students' practice:

Teresa is a Chinese American teaching English temporarily at a Chinese university. She is very easy-going, and soon the students get to know her well enough to invite her out regularly.

Crossing the very busy and wide streets in the city was a scary experience for Teresa, and she complained of it repeatedly. As a result, the female students began to try to help her by taking her hand or grasping her arm while the male students seemed to be shy about protecting her.

Teresa was uncomfortable with her female students touching her, and told them they didn't need to do it. Her female students thought she was being polite and continued to take care of her in the same way. Teresa became so uncomfortable that she tried to move away from her female students whenever they had to cross the road.

Section 3　Territory

The word "territory" originates from the word "terra," which means "land." Territory usually refers to an area — both land and waters — possessed by an individual or a group of individuals. The study of territory has significant implications for communication.

There are four types of territories, namely *public territory, home territory, interaction territory and body territory*. Public territories are public places, such as libraries, or restaurants, where all people enter; home territories refer to the area confined to family members, such as brothers and sisters; interaction territories or areas are where people meet informally such as a lounge or the local gym; and body territories refer to the space used by ourselves. As it's known to all, people, like animals, claim territories to protect themselves from invasion. For example, in class, each student has his own table and chair, the space centering on the table and chair is his body territory. At home, the father usually has a fixed place at the table, and other family members are not expected to sit there.

Generally, there are two ways to delimit territories. One is to place personal property on or around the area; the other is to use it frequently. Students may go so far by throwing a book on the table and the tiger marks its territory by leaving pee on the trees it usually passes by. In the past, people in China seldom claimed their territories in public places, but now, Chinese people become increasingly aware of the importance of claiming territory. For example, people who do not know each other do not mind sitting at one table in a restaurant in the past, because there are usually not enough tables in restaurants. However, today people are not likely to sit together with strangers when eating out in a restaurant because they do not want to be disturbed by others.

Case 1   Am I a good teacher?

Sarah is from Manchester, U. K. She works as a teacher in Xi'an. When she is teaching, she finds students continuously note down what she says in class. In order to let her students relax, she tries to make friends with them, so she invites them to her apartment. She wants to talk with them, but most of the students keep silent. Then she sees one of the students walk into her study without asking her permission and sit in her favorite chair on which she puts her favorite novel. She feels annoyed, but does not know how to tell the boy. Before she can find a way to tell him, he opens the book and reads it. Sarah can not bear it, so she says to the boy, "Excuse me. You should ask my permission if you would like to read my book." The boy is very awkward and closes the book at once. Sarah feels depressed, doubts whether she is a good teacher and begins to think about quitting the job since she can not succeed in teaching these students.

 Discussion:

1. Why does Sarah feel annoyed when she sees the boy walk into her study without asking her permission and sit in her favorite chair?

2. What is the different thinking about territory between Sarah and the boy in this situation?

3. Do you think Sarah is right in thinking she can not succeed in teaching just because of the boy's behavior and the students' silence?

Case analysis:

The conflict in this case was caused by the different understanding of territory. In Sarah's opinion, her apartment is her territory. She invites the students into her sitting room, but it doesn't mean that they can go into her study and read her book. As for the boy, he obviously does not know the British way of being a guest. In China, if you are invited into others' house, it means you are permitted into any rooms with an open door without asking for permission. To search through the house is impolite, but to read the book on the desk seems acceptable. But for Sarah, that is her private thing. Anyone who would like to touch it should get her permission.

The significance and understanding of territory differs from one culture to another. In China, when being invited to a house, friends are permitted into rooms with an open door and to touch things on the table or sofa. If some room is considered inappropriate to let guests in, the host may close it or even lock it. The things that the host does not want his or her guest to touch will be put away before the guest comes. Things that are not locked mean no secrets.

As for British, the house is one's territory, without permission, no one can enter others' room, no matter whether it's open or not. And without asking for permission, one is also not expected to touch others' possessions, even though they are placed by your hand. Generally speaking, Westerners have a stronger sense of claiming territory and protecting privacy.

Because Sarah and the boy have different views about territory, so misunderstanding arises, which even leads Sarah's thought of quitting the job. Maybe she believes that the students do not respect her and her teaching. The fact is that the boy just does something he usually does in his friend's house. So from this case we know how important the right understanding of the territory is.

Case 2 That's my woods!

Mr. Chen and his wife went to America to visit their son, who had settled there. Once their son drove them to a countryside house to stay for a short period of time.

One day after lunch, Mr. Chen and his wife walked around and were attracted by one beautiful

woods. They went directly into it and picked some nuts fallen from the trees. Then the barking of a dog could be heard. They did not care too much because they knew pets were often kept in the houses. They went deeper and the louder the barking was. The host of the house was woken up and took a gun. When he found them, he began to shoot at them while shouting, "Freeze! It's my woods!"

Mr. Chen wanted to leave quickly but his wife knew a little English and held him and said, "He asked us not to move. We just followed his order."

Mr. Chen was angry and said, "It is like a joke. We did nothing and just walked in the woods. How can he treat us like that?"

Then the man came close to them and listened to Mr. Chen's wife explaining to him. He telephoned to Mr. Chen's son and the son drove there quickly and apologized to the host.

Discussion:

1. Do you think it is a shocking experience?
2. Why did the host prepare to shoot at them? Do you think that he had the right?

Case analysis:

The conflict of the case lies in the territory protection in different countries.

In China, people always regard the woods as a public territory because large population will rarely let people own one woods of their own. Even if one woods belongs to a person, it is always permitted to visit.

There is a western proverb, "Wind may come in, rain may come in, but the king may not," which is to say that even a poor person living in a slum has his own inviolable rights. In America, if anyone enters others' house or courts without being permitted, no matter whether he is a robber or not, the host of the house has the right to shoot at him. Before shooting, the host will always give warning of course. The law of America endows the power for every citizen to do that. But in China, people do not have the right to own guns. The law does not give the host such a right and it is suggested to turn to the policemen for help. A tragedy happened in the 1990s to a Japanese overseas student who entered an American house by mistake and heard "freeze." Since she didn't know the meaning of the word and still ran, she was shot dead and the host was pronounced no guilt by the American court.

 Case for students' practice:

Andy came from Britain and taught in one Chinese university. When being asked any requirement to the arrangement of his classroom, he said that he just needed a classroom with moveable chairs and desks. But since all the classrooms are fixed with chairs and desks, it was hard to meet his demand. Feeling very upset, Andy often had to take his students out and sit on the grassland in circle instead, which made the teaching affairs office leader feel confused and not happy.

Chapter

6

Chronemics (time)

Chronemics is an important concept in nonverbal communication. And it is defined as the study of the use of time. In other words, it refers to the ways how we understand time, organize time and react to time. People's perceptions of time vary  from culture to culture in the process of nonverbal communication. Time perceptions cover punctuality, willingness to wait, and interactions. The ways how we use time, to a large extent, determine our ways of living, daily schedules, speech speeds, swings of movements and durations of listening to others.

Time is regarded as circular in some cultures, so people in those cultures are worried about the future and have no pressure. However, most cultures, such as North Americans and Asians, believe that time runs in a linear way. Generally, cultures that regard time as linear value punctuality more than others. In these cultures, being on time is thought as a good manner. If you promise to arrive at 8 o'clock, you should arrive at 8. In Britain or North America, being late within 5 minutes for an appointment is considered acceptable, but you should never be late for fifteen minutes. As for business, Americans are expected to arrive at meetings on time and even earlier, while for parties and dances, they may arrive late. People in Latin America are known for their desultoriness. You can never expect them to be on time, because in their culture arriving earlier or on time is considered rude. Time is of critical importance in American workplaces. North Americans and western Europeans are clock-bound while Africans, Latin Americans and some Asian-Pacific cultures are obviously not. In European and American societies, during communications, it is man who generally controls the use of time, talks more rather than woman.

Considering the use of time, we divide people into two categories: monochronic time people (M-time) and polychronic time people (P-time). North Americans and North Europeans are M-time people, who consider time as linear and focus on schedule. Latin Americans and Africans belong to P-time people, who usually handle several things simultaneously and focus on people's participation. The differences between the two categories can be concluded as follows:

Monochronic People	Polychronic People
do one thing at a time	do many things simultaneously
concentrate on a job	are highly distractible and subject to interruptions
be serious about time commitments	consider an objective to be achieved, if possible
are low-context and need information	are high-context and already have information
committed to the job	are committed to people and human relationships
adhere religiously to plans	change plans often and easily
are concerned about not disturbing others; follow rules of privacy and consideration	are more concerned with those who are closely related than with privacy
show great respect for private property; seldom borrow or lend	borrow and lend things often and easily
emphasize promptness	base promptness on the relationship
are accustomed to short-term relationships	have strong tendency to build lifetime relationships

There are many differences between monochronic time system and polychronic time system as we can see from the above table. However, the following four points should be specially emphasized.

1. *The focus of M-time people is on schedule while P-time people on people*

In the view of M-time people, only their time system is the scientific way to use time. While for P-time people, focusing only on the schedule and ignoring the people involved will affect the relationship among people. M-time people focus on one at a time, while P-time people think that doing many things within the same period is the best way to deal with time.

2. *M-time people plan things ahead and always adhere to plans while P-time people change plans frequently*

Nowadays, time means a lot for everyone, especially for those political leaders and businessmen. So they usually have a careful plan of their time and prepare schedules ahead. However, in P-time people value relationship between people more than schedules. They always invite people to an activity at a short notice and consider it a good way.

3. People's understanding of punctuality is different, even they are of the same time system

Though the significance of being on time is accepted by most people now, the meaning of punctuality varies from culture to culture. For example, when being invited to a formal appointment, British and Americans are required to be on time while in Arabic countries, to be 15 minutes late is normal. As for parties, being late for 10 minutes is acceptable in English-speaking countries, but it is impolite to arrive early or on time. While in China, arriving earlier for a party is believed to be a good manner, because guests can arrive earlier to see if the organizer needs help.

4. Views about duration of an activity are also different between or among cultures

How long an activity lasts is proper? The answer depends on the nature of the activity and the culture in which the activity is organized. Generally speaking, for a formal activity with an opening ceremony and a closing ceremony, it will, no doubt, last for a long time. In western countries, dinner parties may last three to four hours and even longer for young people. The time of dinners in Arabic countries and Latin America may last longer than that in the U. K. or the U. S. A. If duration of the party is too short, it means that people are not hospitable. In Spain or Portugal, it is acceptable for parties to continue even after the midnight. In China, formal dinners usually last two hours or so, no more than three hours. Chinese people do not have as many parties as in western countries. But they usually invite relatives or friends to their home to celebrate some traditional Chinese festivals. The duration of the celebrations varies from region to region, and from family to family.

To learn Chronemics can help people understand the use of time in other cultures, which in turn can make it easier for them to avoid misunderstanding and achieve successful communication.

Section 1   Monochronic time

Monochronic concepts:
- concentrating on one thing at a time is the best;

- taking time commitments, deadlines or schedules seriously;
- always sticking to plans.

Under M-time system, one only does one thing at a fixed period of time. And time, which is scheduled, organized and controlled, is segmented into precise, small units.

For Americans, time is precious and should not be wasted. This saying is taken from studies of Colorado State University: "We buy time, save time, spend time and make time. Our time can be broken down into years, months, days, hours, minutes, seconds and even milliseconds. We use time to structure both our daily lives and events that we are planning for the future. We have schedules that we must follow: appointments that we must go to at a certain time, classes that start and end at certain times, work schedules that start and end at certain times, and even our favorite TV shows, that start and end at a certain time."

In the views of monochronic cultures, time is regarded as something tangible, something like a commodity. That is why they say "time is money." Countries like Germany, Canada, Switzerland, the United States, and Scandinavia, etc. belong to monochronic culture, so people in those countries place a paramount value on schedules.

Case study　Sorry, I have a plan this weekend

Simon is from America. He is a teacher of one Chinese university in a southern small town of China. In the first month, Simon always felt bored in the weekend because he had no classes and no other activities, so he complained about that to the co-teacher Xiao Wang who was assigned to help him in the teaching. When the  department knew about it from Xiao Wang, it planned a journey to the nearby mountain. When Xiao Wang informed this to Simon one day before, she thought Simon would be excited about it, but she was disappointed to hear "Sorry, I have a plan this weekend. I will go to my friend's university." Because he always felt lonely in the weekend, Simon began to plan his weekend and design different activities for every weekend in that semester. Xiao Wang could not understand it. She felt these foreigners were really hard to deal with and it was difficult to meet their needs. And

Part IV *Case Analyses in Intercultural Nonverbal Communication*   143

she was criticized by her leader because of this. She felt angry, and even did not want to see Simon again.

1. Is Simon hard to deal with? Does he mean to hurt Xiao Wang?
2. Why do you think Simon refuse to take part in the journey?
3. What is the different understanding about planning ahead in the situation? What is the misunderstanding?

The problem in the above case obviously is caused by the different conceptions of planning ahead. In Simon's view, if the department wants to organize a journey, they should inform him at least one week earlier. As for Xiao Wang, she did report Simon's complaints to the department, but without getting notice from her leader, she could not inform him to avoid the possible clash of the plans. And in her view, informing a journey to Simon one day before leaving will give him enough time to prepare.

The secret of the conflict lies in that although Chinese culture is also a monochronic culture, the time Chinese plan things ahead is shorter than Americans. It is common for Chinese to inform an activity a day before, or even several hours before, especially for something emergency. In addition, their dealing with scheduled plans is more flexible than their American counterparts.

Chinese people are known for their hospitality. To satisfy guests' need is an important way of showing our hospitality. Though complaints of our own people may be ignored, but guests' complaints will be taken into serious consideration. In order to make guests feel at home, we will set aside other things, even our jobs, to accompany them, organize activities for them. If guests feel unhappy, that means we did not do a good job, then we need to find a way to make them happy. That's why Xiao Wang reported Simon's complaint at once to her leader and that's why the department planned a journey. In fact, to organize a journey is not easy for them. As for Simon, he told Xiao Wang his boring weekends, just because he regarded Xiao Wang as his friend and he could tell her something unhappy, but he did not take that as a problem, which should be solved by others. In fact, he could manage it.

Some foreigners think Chinese people want to please them just because they are from other countries. Actually, Chinese people will try to make all guests feel happy, no matter whether he is from home or abroad. But the definition of guest is changing with situations. Between relatives and friends, friends and people from other parts of the country, fellowmen and foreigners, the latter group is regarded as guests, while the former group is not. For example, when relatives and friends come to one's home simultaneously, friends are treated more like guests. In China, guests from afar are the most distinguished, just as Confucius said, "Isn't it delightful to have friends from afar?" So the fact is that we pay more attention to foreigners not because they are foreigners, but because they are guests from places further away. That's Chinese culture.

As for American culture, things are planned ahead longer than in China. And Americans' attitude towards scheduled plans is rigid; they won't change their plans without a good reason.

In order to achieve success during intercultural communication, people should first know more about their partners' culture; second, when conflicts happen, deal with it flexibly, not trying to impose your own logic on others.

Case for students' practice:

Sam, one teacher from England, asked his student Ma Hui whether he was free for teaching him Chinese next Saturday.

Ma Hui answered, "Maybe."

Then Sam asked again, "Are you sure?"

"Yes!"

"How about meeting at the gate of the park?"

"Maybe."

"Are you sure?"

"Yes."

"How about 8 o'clock?"

"Maybe."

"Are you sure?"

"Yes!"

Part IV *Case Analyses in Intercultural Nonverbal Communication*   145

Section 2 Polychronicity

Polychronic concepts:
- doing many things simultaneously;
- distractions/interruptions are acceptable;
- valuing relationships more than time;
- changing plans often and easily.

Under the polychronic time system, several things can be done at the same time. The ways of scheduling time are more flexible than those of M-time system. As Raymond Cohen notes, polychronic cultures are deeply steeped in tradition rather than in tasks — a clear difference from their monochronic counterparts. Traditional societies have all the time in the world. The arbitrary divisions of the clock face have little saliency in cultures grounded in the cycle of the seasons, the invariant pattern of rural life, and the calendar of religious festivities.

Latin American countries, Arabic countries and many African countries belong to this time system. People in those countries focus more on relationship between people rather than watching the clock. They do not bother about being late for an appointment if they are with family or friends because their relationship is what really counts. Therefore, polychronic cultures have less formal perception of time. They often schedule multiple appointments simultaneously so keeping on schedule is impossible.

Case 1 The meeting begins at 3 o'clock!

Christina is from South Africa. She is also a teacher in a Chinese university. She likes going for a walk after supper and talking with her students. She is a good teacher and very serious about her teaching plan.

One day, she was informed by Li Mei to take part in a meeting at 3 o'clock in the office building. When every one was seated before 3, she was not there. Then Li Mei called her and was told that she was about to set out. The leader asked Li Mei whether she informed Christina the right time. Li Mei felt very sad and said yes. But half an hour passed, Christina still did not get to the meeting room. Li Mei called Christina again and was told that she was on the way. It was only 5 minutes by walking from her apartment to the office building. Another half an hour passed, Christina arrived and smiled to every one present. What upset Li Mei most was Christina even did not apologize for being late. The leader was angry with Li Mei because the meeting was postponed to 4 o'clock for that while Christina knew nothing about it.

Discussion:

1. Why was Christina late for the meeting? Does she mean to upset Li Mei?
2. Why do you think Li Mei felt Christina should apologize?
3. What is the different understanding of time in this case?

Case analysis:

The conflict in this case was caused by the different perception of punctuality. Obviously, Christina did not think being late for a meeting as something serious. In Li Mei's and her leader's view, a meeting is not a party, one is not expected to be late. In addition, Christina kept them waiting for an hour but even without apology. It's no wonder that Li Mei and her leader felt angry.

South Africa belongs to the polychronic time system. As mentioned above, polychronic has no pressure about time. People in this culture system are known for their desultoriness about time, and they do not stick closely to the principle of punctuality. And because they value relationship more than punctuality, they do not think being late for a meeting is something serious, so they needn't apologize for it.

Different from South Africa, China belongs to monochronic culture system. Under this culture system, people adhere to punctuality religiously, especially in workplace. If the meeting is said to start at 3 o'clock, it will start exactly at 3 o'clock, and everyone is expected to arrive earlier. Being late for a meeting, even arriving precisely is regarded as a bad manner and not polite. Being late for a meeting for one hour is unbearable. Because Christina is a guest, the leader would not be angry with her. Li Mei, however, is an employee of the department, so the leader was angry with her. For Li Mei, she had done her duty, so she did not think she was the one to blame. The problem lies in the different understanding of "on time."

Part IV *Case Analyses in Intercultural Nonverbal Communication*   147

Though the use of time seems a minor problem, if one knows nothing about the difference of time system in another culture, conflicts are easy to happen in the process of intercultural communications. Therefore, people in intercultural communications should pay attention to differences of time systems between cultures.

Case 2　Does the invitation say the dinner begins at 7?

Harry is a U. S. manager who intended to negotiate a contract with a Mexican firm. On his first trip to Mexico, he was invited to a dinner party by his Mexican counterpart. Since the invitation indicated that cocktails would begin at 7 p. m., Harry arrived promptly at that time. His host seemed so surprised, and no one else had arrived. Harry felt very embarrassed. People began arriving about 8 p. m. Harry knew he had read the invitation correctly but felt he had gotten off a bad start.

 Discussion:

1. Why was there no one, except Harry, who arrived on time?
2. What do you think is the problem in this case? What advice would you have to give Harry?

 Case analysis:

This is another example of conflicts caused by the different perception of the use of time. From the case above, we can see that Harry's on-time arrival surprised his Mexican partner. Obviously, in the view of Harry's Mexican counterpart, Harry needn't be on time for an activity since they are friends. To be on time or early for a party in Mexico is even considered as impolite.

In American culture people believe that time can be measured or divided, so they always carefully schedule what they are going to do. They concentrate on one thing within a certain period and value efficiency, so they are always on time for any scheduled activity. That's why Harry felt it was natural to arrive on time for the dinner party since the invitation says it begins at 7 p.m.

However, Mexico belongs to a polychronic culture, in which time is not regarded as tangible as in monochronic culture. People emphasize more on completing human transactions than on sticking to schedules. To be late for a dinner party is not only acceptable, but something normal and natural.

 Case for students' practice:

Jack, an American businessman, went to an Asian country for the negotiation of a business. He and the CEO of the Chinese company made an appointment to meet at twelve o'clock and had a meal later. Jack arrived at the designated place punctually and waited for almost half an hour. But Mr. Li didn't come on time. Jack felt offended and angry and left without having the meal. Ten minutes later, Mr. Li went to the restaurant normally, just as usual. He also felt astonished he didn't see Jack. Jack thought Mr. Li's behavior impolite when he returned to the hotel and called his own company to get the business over with Mr. Li. Yet, Li was puzzled to Jack's behaviour.

Chapter 7

Paralanguage

Paralanguage refers to elements directly accompanying our verbal communication. It is not the phrases and sentences with clear meanings. It is to transform information by sound, such as "Ouch," which displays encountering an unexpected pain. Chinese "哇噻" shows astonishment. Besides, the pitch of
tone and loudness or quietness of voice also belong to paralanguage.

Those factors are of great importance in communication or intercultural communication. They are used to help articulate meanings and express emotions. Sometimes those factors are applied by the speaker intentionally, while in most cases they are used unconsciously.

Paralanguage cues are very helpful. From them, we can infer information of our partners, such as emotional state, socioeconomic states, age, intelligence, race, regional background, educational level and so on.

In America, African Americans and white Americans often encounter communication difficulties because their perceptions of the use of paralanguage are different. Such African Americans become serious, sensible in their expressions. Volume and pitch which vary much aren't inherently good nor inherently bad, however, to some extent, their practices about language are useless. Many white Americans think African Americans are aggressive, loud, etc. in view of being out of dominance. However, most of African Americans also regard white people as too formal and lack of their ideas.

Paralanguage consists of voice qualities and vocalizations. Voice qualities cover factors such as pitch, range, resonance, lip control, and articulation control.

Vocalizations involve three kinds, namely vocal characterizers (laughing, crying, yelling, moaning, whining, belching, yawning), vocal qualifiers (volume, rhythm, tempo, tone) and vocal segregates ("uh," "humm," etc.). Except for voice qualities and vocalizations, silence, pause, and turn-taking are also included in the study of paralanguage.

Section 1 Silence

Silence is defined as the absence of sound in speech or conversation, such as acting silently or pause. Silence itself sometimes contains important message for communication.

By providing an interval and time for participants of ongoing interactions to check what has been said, to adjust emotion, to give a proper response, or to start another line of thought, silence plays a significant role in successful communication. Silence also helps provide feedback, informing both sender and receiver about clarity of an idea or its significance in the overall interpersonal exchange.

Silence is emphasized differently between Chinese and American cultures. According to researchers, Chinese culture belongs to high-context cultures, in which meanings are not expressed explicitly, and many things are left unsaid, letting the culture explain. While American culture belongs to a low-context culture, in which meanings are expressed clearly by words. It is agreed that silence plays a more important role in high-context culture.

Case study Silence in the classroom

Professor Johnson was invited to give a guest lecture at a Chinese university in the early 1990s. He could tell that the students were very attentive. They applauded warmly when the lecture came to an end. However, professor Johnson was disappointed when no one asked any questions, even after they were encouraged to do so.

In fact, most students avoided eye contact with him as he tried to communicate with them.

Part IV *Case Analyses in Intercultural Nonverbal Communication*   151

 Discussion:

1. Do you think it is a common phenomenon in the classrooms in China?
2. What suggestions can you give to improve such a thing?

 Case analysis:

What happened to Professor Johnson is common in Chinese classrooms, because, traditional students were not encouraged to ask questions in China. Asking the teacher questions might be regarded as challenging the authority of the teacher on the one hand. Or it might suggest the student is slow and is not clever enough to understand the lecture on the other hand. As a result of those bad implications, Chinese students will listen to lectures attentively but seldom raise questions or attempt to engage in discussion.

The situations are very common in Chinese universities, while Western Universities are considered as places where students are expected to challenge conventional wisdom and exchange ideas. An important part of students' education is to engage in a lively give-and-take of opinions. If a student asks the professor questions, that means he is interested in what the professor has explained and wants to know more about the topic. Different opinions are not just tolerable, but are often encouraged.

Another reason why Chinese students usually keep silent is that in the Eastern tradition, the value of silence is highly emphasized, just as the old saying goes, "Silence is gold." Especially for those who believe in Buddhism, they believe that words can contaminate experience, and the inner peace and wisdom come only through silence. Therefore in China silence sometimes is regarded as a sign of politeness and maturity, not only acceptable but also being highly valued. On the contrary, Americans don't like keeping silent, they value voice more, as being exemplified in the idiom "voice or vanish."

 Case for students' practice:

Susan, an African woman, was seeing a film. It was a funny story and she enjoyed very much with a noisy laugh. A white man sat next to her turned to her and

said, "You are really outrageous!" Susan felt uncomfortable by his words and asked why. The man answered, "Your voice is too loud." But Susan said, "I mean. Come on! It's interesting." Susan felt strange about this. After thinking about it she decided the man required her to feel the laughter instead of expressing it.

Section 2   Turn-taking

Turn-taking is an important mechanism in conversations, it includes two aspects: the simplest systematics and the high-involvement style. In different cultures and languages, the conventions of turn-taking are different; therefore, learners of a foreign language may find it difficult to take their turns naturally and properly while speaking a foreign language. So turn-taking should receive more attention in intercultural communication studies. Generally speaking, western people lay great emphasis on vocal cues of the turn-taking when speaking or conversing:

(1) Giving feedback (e.g. Oh, I see.);

(2) Interrupting (e.g. Excuse me, but I have a question.);

(3) Asking for focused repetition (e.g. Could you say that last part again?);

(4) Asking for meaning (e.g. Excuse me, what does it mean?);

(5) Checking bits of information (e.g. So you mean...?);

(6) Holding your turn (e.g. Let me think...);

(7) Correcting misunderstandings (e.g. Well...actually...);

(8) Summarizing (e.g. Okay. So...).

So while having a conversation with Americans, we should take advantage of those rules and skills of turn-taking. If you want to have a successful communication with Westerners, please pay attention to the following suggestions.

(1) Always gives vocal feedback instead of making no response;

(2) Do not hesitate to ask what you are unsure about;

(3) State out any disapproval but using a polite way;

(4) Avoid making vague reply;

(5) Interrupting when necessary is acceptable, but it should accompany by an apology like "Excuse me, but..." or "I'm sorry, but...";

(6) Ask for repetition by saying "Pardon?" or "I beg your pardon?";

(7) Don't forget to show your interest in the topic by making eye contact;

(8) *Pay attention to one cultural difference: Chinese people like to make the sound.*

Case study Um...Um...!

Xiao Wang invited his American friend Peter to have dinner. When she ordered mushroom, she asked Peter whether he liked it. Peter seemed a little uncomfortable and hesitated to say, "Um... If you like it, please!" Xiao Wang did not understand his meaning and ordered the dish. During the dinner, she found that Peter did not touch mushroom at all.

Case analysis:

In the above case, Xiao Wang may interpret the meaning of "Um" as "okay." In fact, Peter disliked mushroom, but it was impolite for him to deny the order, so he used "um" as a signal of turn-taking. Unfortunately, Xiao Wang didn't get the implication correctly.

Case for students' practice:

John's friend asked to stay in his home for a few weeks. But he has always come late, affecting John's rest. In order to show his dissatisfaction and also keep friendship between them, John says to him like that:

Mmmm...just a...we've been kind a...Mmmm...well...we go to bed kind an early around here. We were wondering if ah...if it would...if you wouldn't mind... and if you could manage to come home a little bit earlier.

Part V

Typical Cases in Intercultural Business Communication

International business has more and more important impact on the world economy. In the last twenty years, international trade has multiplied twenty fold. The world has been becoming a global village, and firms of all sizes must search the world for customers and suppliers. With the increase of international trade and cooperation, business negotiations among people from different countries and cultures have become more and more frequent. Intercultural business negotiations are becoming a very important part of life for most globalizing firms.

International negotiation is naturally a cultural interaction, as it is carried out by negotiators from a certain culture or cultures. International negotiations cross not only national boundaries, but also cultures. Culture shapes how people think, communicate and behave. Different cultures have different values, attitudes, morals, behaviors and linguistic styles, all of which can greatly affect the process and outcome of negotiations.

Culture also affects negotiating styles. The way one negotiates is colored by his own cultural assumptions and is largely operating at an unconscious level. The negotiating style one uses so effectively at home can be ineffective and inappropriate when dealing with people from another cultural background. Because there are no longer shared values, interests, goals, ethical principles or cultural assumptions between the negotiating parties. Making assumptions about another is often counterproductive since it can lead to misunderstandings. In fact, its use can often result in more harm than gain. So it is essential for success in international business negotiations to gain an ability to assess cultural differences and properly handle the consequences.

Generally speaking, culture impacts negotiations in four ways: by conditioning one's perception of the reality; by blocking out information inconsistent or unfamiliar with the culturally grounded assumption; by projecting meanings into the other party's words and actions; and by impelling the ethnocentric observer to an incorrect attribution of motives.

To be more specific, culture influences international business negotiations in the four aspects: ***people's perception of negotiation***, ***negotiating goals***, ***methods of communication*** and ***negotiating style***.

Chapter

1

Value perception conflict

People acquire communicative competence during the process of socialization; they gradually form their own value systems. Value systems are peculiar to different nations. People could be instructed by value systems that what is good or what is bad; what is kind or what is evil; what should be praised or what should be punished, etc.  Indeed, it forms moral criteria, behavioral principles, and living philosophies.

Values fundamentally influences people's behavior in society. They do not only describe how people act in a culture but dictate what people ought or ought not to do. People make all the decisions on the basis of values and evaluate their own and others' actions on the standards of values. Thus a value can be defined as a conception, explicit or implicit, distinctive of an individual or characteristic of a group, of the desirable which influences the selection from available modes, means, and ends of action.

The core of cross-cultural communication is value orientation. In some sense, most cross-cultural barriers result from the differences in value orientation. People from different cultures behave differently according to their own value systems which could decide how a person communicates with others within his or her culture as well as across his or her culture.

Eastern and western worlds have different value systems. In English speaking countries, people greatly respect and value independence, individualism, and privacy. They specially emphasize individual elements, self-fulfilling and self-help. They treat every member as equal regardless of his or her social status or education background. Individual is the most important unit in any social setting and the uniqueness of each individual is of paramount value. The "I" consciousness prevails: Competition rather than cooperation is encouraged; personal goals take precedence over group goals; and every individual has the right to his or her properties, thoughts, and opinions. This kind of culture stresses individual initiative and achievement.

Chinese respect cooperation, loyalty and collectivism. Collectivism is characterized by a rigid social framework that distinguishes between in-groups and out-groups. The "we" consciousness prevails and individual emotionally depends on groups.

In the intercultural business negotiation, buyers and sellers must negotiate in order to create their own values in the business trade. The negotiation must be on the basis of the customer orientation, in which buyers can customize the products they want, and sellers can recommend and negotiate these products with a selling policy. The customers can get their personal values or preferences from a decision model, and then use the generated utility function to negotiate with sellers.

Case 1 Why are they so silent in the meeting?

Alan Richardson was assigned to head up the relatively new marketing treatment of his company's off-shore office in Mexico City. He was very excited about this career opportunity and the chance to use his fluent Spanish. His overall responsibility was to increase marketing's visibility and role and bring new personnel  on as well. With increasing competition in Mexico, U.S. headquarters communicated to Alan that he was to bring the department in line with those in other international offices.

Alan called his first meeting in his office on Friday afternoon with the men who had been handling markets and working with all support staff. After everyone arrived, he greeted them briefly and promptly began the meeting. The first item on his agenda was to ask for suggestions as to how they might increase sales by using promotional campaigns. After a short discussion, he then proposed that the two primary marketing researchers, Eduardo and Miguel, look into a marketing research system, thinking that whoever proved to be the better researcher would be promoted to manager. He concluded the meeting by thanking them for their time and saying that the group would meet again next week to share information.

The group sat silently until Alan said in his fluent Spanish that he had been speaking all day, "That's all for now, guys. Have a good weekend."

Part V *Typical Cases in Intercultural Business Communication*   159

Next week at the follow-up meeting, he was surprised to find that no one in the group had anything to suggest or report on.

1. Why did the group sit silently when Alan was having the meeting?
2. Why did no one in the group have anything to suggest or report on?
3. If you were Alan, what would you do to fulfill your responsibility there?

 Case analysis:

An important feature of group culture is that the members seek group harmony and consistency and nobody is willing to make a showy display of his abilities to take the initiative or pursue priority. Mexico advocates group culture. Alan had been playing his own show throughout the meeting while his Mexican colleagues present kept silent, reluctant to suggest anything because "Common fame is seldom to blame." Mexican culture is utterly different from the culture Alan belongs to, the latter encourages suggestions and individual prominence. Therefore, Alan was surprised to find nobody made a suggestion. The second reason for the difference is the differences in degree of avoidance of uncertainties. Mexicans are anxious of uncertainties and ambiguity and will make a suggestion only when they are sure that it's absolutely true and precise. They are afraid of being scolded or blamed for unreasonable or unfeasible ideas so that they keep silent to avoid mistakes. From the perspective of Alan, all constructive suggestions are to be encouraged and collective minds lead to more valuable ideas. The third reason is the differences in attitudes towards superiors and authorities. Mexican staff treated Alan, the marketing supervisor assigned by the headquarters, as their superior, so they kept silent to show respect, otherwise, they would think the superior was offended. In Alan's culture, the division of superior and inferior is minimized and the concept of equality extends to work environment where there is no difference between the superior and inferior but only differences in jobs. While equal communication is the most important.

This case shows that in a different culture, one has to master cultural differences and adopt corresponding measures and tactics so that individual advantages and abilities can be exerted. Thus business and management are not impeded by cultural differences or conflicts.

Case 2 Private or public?

Mark was a native English speaker from Britain. As a teacher of English, first he had chances to work in some Asian countries such as Singapore and Japan. In 2001, he was offered to work in Shanghai as a senior trainer. He was glad to accept the offer and was full of confidence to develop the huge potential market. He left for Shanghai with an expectation that he would start a brand new life, for he believed that he had known a lot about oriental culture to communicate with local people.

Just as what he had expected, he received a warm welcome from the hospitable Chinese colleagues when he arrived in Shanghai. With the help of the Chinese colleagues, he was able to open three new training centers downtown during the first several months. When he received a large bonus, he treated his Chinese colleagues to show his gratitude for their cooperation and hard work. At the dinner, he was thrilled with excitement and ambition.

Cooperative and hardworking as they were, the Chinese colleagues annoyed Mark in several ways. First, they seemed to care too much about his private life. Several days after they met, they began to ask private questions while chatting, including age, family and marriage. When they knew he was still single now and then they introduced girl friends to him in spite of his opposition. He was quite embarrassed on such occasions.

Another offence was unexpected arrangement of off-work entertainment. The Chinese colleagues seemed to arrange things on pulse and informed him at last minute of going karaoke or outgoing. At such a moment, he was at the edge of breaking down to rearrange his timetable to narrowly leave time for it since he did not want them to lose face. However, seeing there was no hope for them to respect his personal schedule, Mark chose to refuse unexpected invitations.

Mark sensed that the relationship between them had undergone a subtle change, for his Chinese colleagues began to treat him in a deliberately polite way. When he entered the office, they nodded with a routine smile. They did not invite him to dinner or karaoke any longer. At office, they gathered together and whispered in Chinese. Mark sometimes felt lonely and intended to break the ice between them but

Part V *Typical Cases in Intercultural Business Communication*   161

he did not know how to start.

Mark indulged himself in work and tried to neglect the tense atmosphere in office. However, one day he broke the tension by a burst of anger.

It was a tradition that the staff took medical examination every year, and they just had it two weeks before. The personnel manager put a notice on the bulletin that the medical report had come out. Mark got his report with the doctor's comment that there was something wrong with his stomach and he would better eat more vegetables and drink less wine.

To his astonishment, every one in the office seemed to know his situation and asked him to take good care of himself and even recommended him to take Chinese herbal medicine. To make things worse, they volunteered to help him with his curriculum design and teaching materials. Surrounded by them like a fool, Mark could not bear it any more and stormed into the personnel department for an explanation.

"How can they have my medical report?"

Stunned at his fury, the personnel manager stammered that this was a usual practice to put the medical reports on the table of the reference room. Suddenly he didn't know what to say but stared at his Chinese colleagues who came to see what had happened.

At that moment, he wished he had never been here at all.

He asked to transfer to another country. After he left, his Chinese colleagues commented that Mark was too arrogant and far from maturity. Till now, they did not understand why he lost his temper at such a trifle thing.

 Discussion:

1. Why did his Chinese colleagues arrange entertainment without notification beforehand? Do you think it is acceptable in British culture?

2. Do you think it is proper for Mark to lose temper to his colleagues? If not, what is the proper way in this situation?

3. If you were the personnel manager, what would you do to harmonize the conflict between overseas employees and local employees?

Case analysis:

This case tells the contradictions and conflicts between the foreign staff and the local staff in a multinational company. The contradictions are tiny but lead to the leaving of the foreign staff and dissatisfaction of the local staff. Mark's privacy conflicts with the passion and hospitality of the local staff.

Chinese people are famous for hospitality. The local staff show much consideration and caring for Mark, the foreign young man, however, this type of caring means too much for Mark from a different culture and even offends his private life. Therefore, he takes negative measures to avoid contact with the local staff as much as possible. Nevertheless, this approach obviously harms the feelings of the local staff who gradually keep away from Mark. This type of obstructed communication finally leads to the intensification of contradictions so that Mark becomes furious about his medical report while the local staff do not understand his action.

Chinese culture is quite different from the British one and the scope of individual communication is totally different between the two cultures. In China and many other Asian countries, many interpersonal relationships are overlapped, for example, colleagues may be friends and family members may be colleagues and friends at the same time. Such overlapped relationships make people establish intimate colleague relationship in the office, thus they can talk about private subjects besides work. However, in British culture, individual relationship circle is relatively closed. Colleagues are only limited to cooperation at work and they have no right to ask private questions. The Chinese colleagues of Mark obviously ignore such cultural differences so that they ask about his private life. It severely offends his privacy and makes him embarrassed. To protect his privacy, Mark has to narrow his individual relationship circle and tries not to overlap with other relationship circle, so his colleagues think he is reluctant to make friends with them.

The arrangement of off-work entertainment is the second contradiction. Chinese colleagues complain Mark makes them lose face, but to Mark, they do not respect his personal schedule. Chinese culture puts much emphasis on face. Some British understand the issue of face in Chinese culture to some degree but do not fully understand the importance of face. It's unacceptable for his Chinese colleagues that Mark straightly refused the invitation of his colleagues many times.

It's a reflection of harmonious colleague relationship to care about others' health in Chinese culture, so the Chinese colleagues of Mark cannot understand his intense response on the issue of medical report. It is quite common in China that leadership and colleagues go to the hospital to visit sick employees while it is considered cold and unreasonable that a colleague does not care about the health of others. In British culture, individual health and medical report are absolutely private and the doctor should keep the patient's condition confidential except for the patient himself or herself. If the condition is exposed without permission, the patient has the right to take legal actions against the responsible party. Therefore, it is understandable that Mark is furious about the exposure of his medical report.

In this case Mark keeps taking negative attitude and avoiding the contradictions with his Chinese colleagues, which results in escalation of the contradictions. Even under such circumstances, he fails to take measures to tackle the problem but chooses to leave instead.

Mark shall take the initiative in the conversation and try to avoid topics he is unwilling to mention. He'd better skillfully avoid questions concerning privacy instead of being always passive.

Mark can reject some entertainments but not all of them and can arrange some activities to invite his colleagues to participate. Or he can politely suggest his colleagues to give him an early notice for activities in future. By such means, the face of his colleagues is kept so is his own schedule.

People shall be calm in conflicts. Getting angry in the public is a taboo in Chinese culture because this is a manifestation of poor character. Chinese people pay particular attention to harmony and try to solve conflicts in the minimum scope. For example, Mark can talk with the personnel manager to solve similar problems between the two of them instead of magnifying the conflicts.

Chinese staff shall avoid centering on Chinese culture in cross-cultural communication. Individual privacy should be paid attention to, the counterpart's culture shall be fully respected and certain distance shall be kept if necessary.

Case 3 To leave or not to leave

The New Enterprise Group was set up 7 years ago, providing a range of accounting and auditing services to growing entrepreneurial companies with gross annual revenues of between $5 and $100 million. It also acted as principal business advisors in the areas of corporate finance*, tax consulting, problems of acquisition and divestiture, etc.

The New Enterprise Group was a division of Jame-Williams located in Toronto, one of the 6 largest public accounting firms in Canada, with 400 partners practicing in 30 Canadian cities. The New Enterprise Group was organized as a collegial system of partners who managed their own clients and activities within the performance objectives established by James-Williams, and under the general supervision of the Practice Director who was also a partner. Staff members below the partner level were organized on the staff system. A staff usually consisted of one or two senior staff accountants and several intermediate or junior staff under a manager. A partner would have one, two or three managers and several staff reporting to him or her.

Staff would be hired out of business school as junior staff accountants for a two-year period while they studied for their chartered accountant examinations. At the beginning of their second year, they were promoted to intermediate staff accountants until they passed the CA exams. If they passed, they were promoted to senior staff accountants. If they did not pass, they still have another year to prepare for a final chance at the exams.

The normal promotion process at James-Williams was for staff to remain as senior staff accountants for two years while they developed a consulting specially of their choice. Then they might be promoted to manager and supervise six to nine staff. Most partners were selected from the ranks of the managers after they had been with the firm for ten to eleven years.

Bob Chen's background at James-Williams

Bob Chen was born in Hong Kong and came to Toronto as a high school student for Grade 13. He graduated with a bachelor of commerce from Queen's University in Kingston. James-Williams offered Bob a job so that he could obtain landed immigrant status in Canada. So Bob felt very loyal to the company. In September after graduation, Bob started with James-Williams in the New Enterprise Group as a junior staff accountant, doing accounting work and studying for his chartered accountant exams which were scheduled for two years hence. In the following fall he was promoted to intermediate staff accountant as was standard for all second-year staff at James-Williams. During his first two years with the New Enterprise Group, Bob worked under the supervision of several managers including Tak Li and a partner named Lara Witmer. Due to turnover of staff in the New Enterprise Group during those years, Bob was attached for various jobs to a number of managers and partners. About the time that Bob was scheduled to write his CA exams, he learned that Lara

Part V *Typical Cases in Intercultural Business Communication*

Witmer had been asked to leave the firm. Bob would be assigned to work for Jane Klinck under the project supervision of Erin Cole.

In the New Enterprise Group Bob was seen as quiet and soft-spoken. One of his managers described him as "shy and accommodating." He does what he is asked to do and a bit more. Casual requests get immediate results. He was also a very private person whose politeness often meant not saying exactly what he wanted out of a situation or from another person. His civility may have masked from his colleagues his strongly felt desire for success and strongly held views about his possible contribution to the firm.

Bob was well liked by the people around him. Some partners and staff thought that Bob was fairly outgoing and had much better oral communication skills than previous staff from Hong Kong hired by the company. His colleagues believed that Bob had good potential with James-Williams.

The problem

Bob's willingness is to specialize as a tax consultant. Before he passed the CA exam, he met formally with David Shorter and expressed his interest in becoming a tax specialist. David reviewed his performance appraisal, and Bob thought he would get the tax assignment during his preparation of the exam, but no such assignments materialized.

After he got the news that he passed the exam in December, David Shorter called him in for an interview during which David gave his congratulations and told Bob he had to work as a senior auditor because his auditing skills were not strong enough. And he also asked Bob to consider the idea of specializing in Hong Kong. Bob said he would think about it.

Bob was aware that the New Enterprise Group had a shortage of senior auditors. He felt that he was being asked not to pursue his career interests because of this shortage and not because of any weakness he had as an auditor. Bob was also aware that he had a reputation for doing what he was told. He tried to anticipate the needs of his supervisors and his clients, and he worked extra hard to accommodate their wishes. Partly, this was his natural tendency, but he also felt a strong loyalty to the firm for hiring him and thereby providing a way for him to stay in Canada. Now he wondered if David once more, and after extensive discussion got David to compromise to send Bob on a three-year tax-training program. But this program taught no tax and becoming a tax consultant required hands-on experience and the opportunity to deal with the tax problems of real companies in real situations.

Again and again, this process went on and on, Bob got refused to do the tax consulting. And the last straw is a meeting, the purpose of which Bob felt was to coerce him into taking on a Softdisk audit. Even though finally he said he would do the job out of pressure, Bob felt he had been unfairly treated.

 Discussion:

1. What's the cultural implication of Bob's working behaviors? Why could such behaviors be a great hindrance to his career potential?

2. From the cultural perspective, why did the partners and managers exert a concerning management style on Bob?

 Case analysis:

In this case, the biggest conflict is the work assignment of Bob Chen. At James-Williams Company, there is a set of formal procedures for staff development in the company. It usually recruits staff from the business school as they just join the company as junior accountants, and then prepare for the CPA exam during the next two years. If they pass the exam, they will become senior accountants, otherwise they would be given yet another year of preparation time. The formal process goes like this: After being a senior accountant for two years, the employees can choose their own areas of focus, then they may be promoted to manager, managing 6-9 staff, and then select a partner from the managers who have stayed in the company as long as 10 to 11 years. Bob is now in the second stage, where he has passed the CPA exam, and is ready to choose his favorite field for further specializing. He chooses to do tax consulting while his manager and director try to make Bob continue to do the auditing instead of his own areas of interest. Even after repeated consultations, the issue remains unresolved.

The reason in the first place is that New Enterprise Group where Bob stays is lacking a senior auditor, thus in great need of a person like Bob who has passed the CPA to keep auditing for the company. So the task of taxing is not assigned to Bob not because Bob has poor skills and needs further training, as its Business Director David claims. In this way, the company's arrangement for employees is in conflict with their own will. This is the problem which occurs in all cultures, but in this case, both sides show their cultural identities in the exchange.

At work, Bob tries hard to accomplish or exceed the mandate entrusted to him, and he tries to guess the needs of his leadership and customers, in the greatest efforts to fulfill their aspirations. This feature is part of his character, but there are other cultural factors. Because James Williams gives him the job so he can emigrate to Canada, he is very loyal to the company. Chinese culture always emphasizes collectivism rather than individualism, and great importance is attached to the loyalty to organization where the individuals belong, with a kind of "Gratitude Return" complex. Bob usually does not openly express his views, which characterizes the Chinese modesty and their philosophy of maintaining harmony with everything. That is why he gives others the impression of being amiable and accommodating, willing to do everything assigned by his boss. Bob's managers start with an attitude of reluctance and stalling to achieve their own working arrangements.

On the other hand, Bob comes to Toronto ever since his study at high school and his cultural values have changed after receiving the Western higher education. Rather than simply following the traditional Chinese cultural values, and making self-sacrifice to meet the requirements of the company, he pursues his personal career development and makes his career decisions based on his own interests and wishes, which is typical of the spirit of individualism. Therefore, he would discuss the matter of taxing consulting with David again and again, and he would still stick to his ideas even after repeated failures. His insistence eventually prompts a meeting by his superiors, so that Bob feels that the sole purpose of the meeting is to force him to continue to do the auditing. He feels like he has been treated unfairly, and decides that he should not be so loyal to a company which is dishonest to him.

From the point of view of New Enterprise Group's directors and managers, they do not communicate well with Bob, and do not quite understand that beneath his gentle humility he also cherishes a strong desire for success and his potential contributions to the company. Therefore, during negotiations with Bob, they just think he is a shy and easy-going guy, and take a perfunctory attitude. Even afterwards they also take a high-handed and forceful attitude, which makes the staff feel the unfair treatment, thus reducing their loyalty to the company.

Personnel arrangements should always take into account the company's needs and the wishes of the staff themselves, and both sides need to consult each other. Especially in the atmosphere of James Williams, the staff's will can be reflected through their own efforts and arrangements of their superiors, which requires the directors and managers to take a more moderate alternative way and communicate frankly with Bob in handling the issue of his work assignment, in a bid to adopt a mutually acceptable solution. From the standing point of Bob, he should often express his own ideas in front of superiors and colleagues. It would not have led him to such an extent as to encounter much more resistance than others do in making career choices.

Cases for students' practice:

Case 1

Age and status

A manager in a data-processing company was having difficulty dealing with a conflict between a young, ambitious French Canadian male and his co-worker, an older Chinese woman who was on a special visa from China. She had recently become uncooperative and had made it clear to the manager that she would not be willing to travel to the capital with her co-worker to hold discussions with legislators about a new product with great enthusiasm.

When the manager asked her what the problem was, he received no clear explanation. When he asked her co-worker, the young man had no insight to offer. The young French Canadian was clearly annoyed, however, that the Chinese woman was refusing to share her data with him. That meant he couldn't make the presentation to the key data on her computer disks.

The manager's repeated questions to her "problem" got nowhere. So he changed his approach. He began explaining his concerns. As manager and spokesperson of the company, about the upcoming meeting with legislators, his explanation about his position was unemotional. In that climate she then felt she could explain her position. She revealed she felt that as an older, and to her mind, more senior person, she should not be sent to the capital with a younger employee who would do the presentation of material she had worked hard to develop. That would diminish her status, she felt. Therefore, the general manager knew the root of his headache.

Discussion:

1. What do you think caused the conflict?

2. What would you do to resolve the conflict if you were the general manager?

Case 2

Praising Japanese in public workplaces

American: Mr. Sugimoto, I have noticed that you are doing an excellent job on the assembly line. I hope that the other workers notice how it should be done.

Japanese: (He is uneasy) Praise is not necessary. I am only doing my job. (He hopes other Japanese workers do not hear.)

American: You are the finest, most excellent, dedicated worker we have ever had at the Jones Corporation.

Japanese: (He blushes and nods his head several times, and keeps working.)

American: Well, are you going to say "thank you," Mr. Sugimoto, or just remain silent?

Japanese: Excuse me, Mr. Jones... may I take leave for five minutes?

American: Sure. (He is annoyed and watches Sugimoto exit.) I can't believe how rude some Japanese workers are. They seem to be disturbed by praise and don't answer you... just silent.

Discussion:

1. Why was the conversation between Mr. Jones and Mr. Sugimoto not so pleasant?

2. Why did they have such different reactions towards praising in public workplaces?

Case 3

Being straightforward or reserved

Ted Washington is a manager of sales department of an American company. Recently he rejected two proposals about selling their products. One was proposed by an American employee Dell, the other was proposed by a Japanese one Gaoqiao Xiufu. These two proposals were quite different, and the two employees were both optimistic and extremely hoped that their suggestions could be accepted by their manager. So when getting rejected, they almost broke down.

After that, Dell talked about his opinion with Ted. It seemed that there was a conflict between them. Dell stated the problem and disputed it with his manager, he also used a variety of methods, such as expressing facts, listing figures and drawing charts, to illustrate his plan.

In contrast, Gaoqiao was so shocked by such a direct rejection that he considered the conflicts as distrust. Actually he planned to resign as soon as possible.

Discussion:

1. What were the reactions of these two employees toward the rejection? What were the differences? Why?

2. What would you do if you were the person whose proposal was rejected?

Chapter 2

Corporate culture matters

Culture typically includes socially transmitted behaviors, beliefs, attitudes, human thoughts and creations. It affects every aspect of people's lives — the way we look at things, the way we act and react and the way we express our feelings.

Culture also influences business practices and organizational behaviors. National cultures and values shape human progress and influence economic prosperity.

In spite of the pervasive influence of national culture, within each nation exist different types of organizational cultures, because the personality and philosophy of the founder or leader may also shape the culture of each corporation.

It is the leader's job to provide the vision for the group. A good executive must have a dream and the ability to get the company to support that dream. But it is not enough to only have the dream. The leader must also provide the framework by which the people in that organization can help achieve the dream. This is called corporate culture.

Generally, corporate culture refers to the prevailing implicit values, attitudes and ways of doing things in a company. It often reflects the personality, philosophy and the ethnic-cultural background of the founder or the leader. Corporate culture dictates how the company runs and how people are promoted.

Leaders and managers need to understand how different types of corporate cultures may either facilitate or inhibit organizational efforts to improve performance and increase productivity. They also need to have the necessary competency to foster corporate culture change. It is important to transform organizational culture in order to adapt to changing times. They have developed an assessment instrument to identify four types of cultures, namely, market culture, advocacy culture, clan culture, and hierarchy culture.

2.1 Toxic corporate culture

In terms of relationships and adjustment to changing times, the following corporate cultures are described as toxic. They undermine the social/spiritual capital, poison the work climate and contribute to organizational decline.

2.1.1 Authoritarian-hierarchical culture

The big boss alone makes all the major decisions behind closed doors. Even when the decisions are harmful to the company, no one dares to challenge the boss. The standard mode of operandum is commanded and controlled, with no regard to the well-being of employees or the future of the company.

In this kind of culture, employees are to be controlled, manipulated and occasionally pacified like the children. Workers are motivated by fear rather than love for company or passion for the work. They are expected to do what they are told without questioning. The main criterion for promotion is loyalty to the boss, rather than competence and commitment. As a result, star performers who dare to question some of the administration's decisions are sidelined or let go, while those who obey the boss blindly and who are willing to be hatchet men get the nod for promotion.

Hierarchies are not necessarily bad in and of themselves. Some sort of hierarchy in terms of decision-making and responsibility is always inevitable. However, when hierarchies are used to control and abuse workers, problems inevitably occur. Hierarchies without accountability tend to have a corrupting influence on ambitious, autocratic leaders. When the boss is dysfunctional and has the power to impose his selfish, irrational decisions on others, the entire company suffers.

2.1.2 Competing-conflictive culture

There is always some sort of power struggle going on. Leaders are plotting against each other and stabbing each other on the back. Different units and even different individuals within a unit are undercutting, backstabbing each other to gain some competitive advantage. There is a lack of trust and cooperation. People often hide important information from each other and even sabotage each other's efforts to ensure that only they will come up on top.

There is no regard for the larger picture and the overall goal of the company.

Both management and workers are obsessed with their own survival and self-interests. As a consequence, the organization is fragmented and there is a lot of valuable resources because of duplications and sabotage. Such tense competition within the company creates divisiveness, conflicts and mistrust.

2.1.3 Laissez faire culture

There is a vacuum at the top, either because the leader is incompetent and ignorant, or because he is too preoccupied with his personal affairs to pay much attention to the company. Consequently, there is an absence of directions, standards and expectations. When there is an absence of effective leadership, each department, in fact, each individual does whatever they want. The leadership void will also tempt ambitious individuals to seize power to benefit themselves. Chaos and confusion are the order of the day. No one has a clear sense where the company is going. Often, employees receive conflicting directions and signals. Often, they are made in the morning only to be nullified in the afternoon. Given the lack of direction, oversight and accountability would be all cross-the-board, and productivity would decline. In this kind of culture, the company either disintegrates or becomes an easy target for a hostile takeover.

2.1.4 Dishonest-corrupt culture

In this culture, greed is good and money is God. People have little concern for ethnics or for law. Such attitudes permeate the whole company from the top down to individual workers. Bribery, cheating, and fraudulent practices are widespread. Creative accounting and misleading profit reports are a matter of routine. Denial, rationalization and reputation management are blinded by greed and ambition, their judgment becomes distorted and their decisions seriously flawed; as a result, they often cross the line without being aware of it.

2.1.5 Rigid-traditional culture

There is a strong resistance to any kind of change. The leadership clings to outdated methods and traditions, unwilling to adapt to the changes in the market place. They live in past glory. Change threatens their deeply entrenched values and their sense of security. Workers are discouraged or even reprimanded for suggesting innovative ideas. Their accounting, marketing and delivery systems are no longer competitive with the fast-paced technology-driven market place. Their products and services have not responded to changing market demands. Their mantra is "We have always done things this way." As a result, the world passes them by, and eventually they are left with an empty shell of the former self.

The above five types of toxic cultures are not mutually exclusive. A corporation may be both authoritarian and traditional. Similarly, a corporation can be both authoritarian and corrupt. When a company suffers from a multiple of diseases, drastic operations are needed to save it from demise. Unfortunately, not so many managers are competent in the diagnosis and treatment of toxic corporate culture.

2.2 Healthy corporate cultures

2.2.1 Progressive-adaptive culture

There is openness to new ideas and a willingness to take risk and adopt innovations. It is a culture that adjusts quickly to shifting market conditions. It values the certainty of remaining the same; the company is future-oriented and innovative. It is confident in catching and riding the waves of change.

It is a culture compared with the enterprising spirit of creativity, boldness and taking ownership. The management strives to be the cutting edge, and encourages continuous development of workers. There is a pervasive, restless creative energy, constantly seeking and creating new ideas and new markets. The company celebrates every innovation, and every discovery. Excitement is in the air. Employees are all caught up in the adventure. This culture is the opposite of the rigid-traditional culture.

2.2.2 Purpose-driven culture

The leadership articulates and crystallizes the purpose of the company effectively, so there is a common purpose, a shared vision for all the workers. Everyone knows what the core values and priorities are, and everyone knows where the company is going. Workers are highly motivated, because they are committed to the same set of core values. More importantly, the overarching purpose tends to go beyond the bottom line. All great companies endure because they serve a higher purpose.

One example is Anita Roddick, founder of the Body Shop. She has a clear vision, a higher purpose for her company: The Body Shop will be an ethical, caring company, which will care about the environment, human rights, animal protection and the community. This vision is incorporated into all respects of her corporate goals and practices.

2.2.3 Community-oriented culture

There is a strong emphasis on collectivity and cooperation. The leadership attempts to build a community where people respect, support each other, and enjoy working together.

A community-oriented culture goes beyond team building and aspires to create an authentic community in which every worker is treated as a valuable member. Community building is more extensive than team building. Members from different work groups treat one another in a positive, supportive way in order to boost morale. Such a community requires collaboration and communication throughout the organization. Management involves and empowers all staff members in a combined effort to improve efficiency and productivity, such as required by Total Quality Management.

For teamwork to be effective, team building training becomes an important part of personnel development. Typically in team building, groups are created in each work area and group members interact and work together to identify and resolve issues that affect individual and group performance. Team members work together in mutually supportive atmosphere. Team members know the role they play in the achievement of the end goal.

To create a sense of community, management need to provide a trusting and safe environment, in which workers are free to express their ideas rather than try to "fit in" and please the managers. The emphasis on community building also creates a climate of cooperative problem solving and a willingness to share information and expertise. In such a company, there is a healthy acceptance of diversity and a willingness to listen to and to learn from others. A community-oriented culture is just the opposite of a competing-conflictive culture.

2.2.4 People-centred culture

There is a genuine caring for each worker in the organization. Everyone is valued and validated, regardless of their positions in the company. The organization cares for the whole person — body, soul and mind in terms of recognizing workers' basic needs for learning and growth, for belonging and being connected, as well as the need and spirituality. Each worker is encouraged to develop his or her full potentials, personally and professionally. Such a culture will create a climate of mutual respect and genuine civility.

Organizational care for employees is based on organization's deep-seated core values and practices. It involves meeting workers' needs, promoting their best interests, valuing their contributions, setting up the necessary infrustructure to facilitate care-giving, such as providing support systems, employee assistance and development programs.

People-centred organizations which embrace the core ideology of caring may have different ways of expressing their core values, nevertherless, caring needs to be implemented on a consistant basis.

The above four cultures are positive, because they create a positive work climate, which is conducive to productivity and job satisfaction. They contribute to high performance explicitly linking reward to performance. The ideal company should possess the attributes of all four types of healthy corporate cultures.

(*Lessons from the Enron Debacle*: *Corporate Culture Matters*! Paul T. P. Wong, PhD, C. Psych.)

Case 1 How to realize cultural synergy in south Korea?

In early 1990s, Motorola South Korean Company, as one of huge producers in the production of semi-conductors and integrated circuits in the world, was managed inappropriately, and after careful analysis, Motorola headquarters decided to take a suggestion that the corporate culture of Motorola South Korean Company be transformed to establish a new leadership behavior.

Donald Jerome from America became the new president and general manager of Motorola South Korean Company. He believed that the establishment of a new leadership way or management culture in a specific country or business culture might conflict with local cultures. In other words, the company shouldn't change the values or behaviors of the people outside the company in life, and simply require the local employees to observe the new "leadership way or management culture" in the organization.

Guided by this thought, Jerome established a complete senior-level team, and further developed a new mode that would respect the South Korean culture and combine the characteristics of Korean cultures and those of American cultures to become a unique corporate culture of Motorola South Korean Company with the aim of improving the business efficiency through setting up a high-efficient team.

Part V *Typical Cases in Intercultural Business Communication*

Many differences between two national cultures may result in some difficulties for the company. For instance, pay rise and promotion in South Korea depend on seniority while in America they rely on achievements; South Koreans strictly follow the orders while Americans ask for more clear explanation. However, the transformation of the team doesn't focus on these differences but emphasizes commonalities. Most people hope to do their job well and their contributions would be recognized. They anticipate to be trusted and be given opportunities to do better, but they wouldn't like to be criticized in public, hoping to be treated fairly. Based on commonalities, Motorola South Korean Company put forward ten leadership principles.

It's known to us all that it's always one ball that decides the final result during one match. It's heartbroken if such a good opportunity is missed.

In South Korea, it's a virtue that the young respect the elder; it is also a social norm and value. However, in Hiddink's view, such a "virtue" has become a hindrance for the football team in world competition.

Here is what Hiddink does, firstly. He asked five players in the team who were over 27 years old to empower those young players that in case of the final shooting, the five elder players unanimously agreed to pass the ball to other young players in a better position for shooting. Secondly, young players are allowed to call the names of elder players directly so that the sense of equality among team players will be enhanced.

 Discussion:

1. What is the typical South Korean culture?
2. What is the key of the success of Motorola South Korean Company in establishing a new corporate culture?
3. What can you learn from Hiddink's transforming South Korean national football team?

 Case analysis:

For both Donald Jerome, General Manager of Motorola South Korean Company and Hiddink, their common dilemma is how to combine their own cultural characteristics with the local culture to develop acceptable leadership methods and how to better absorb the advantages of both cultures and seek the conjunction point for the concerted effect of both cultures.

Facts show that Jerome and Hiddink both successfully addressed cultural integration problems. In this sense, they are experienced inter-cultural managers. Jerome is from the United States and Hiddink comes from Holland. They are representatives of the European American culture. While the South Korean style is a typical Asian culture. The clashes between the two cultures are inevitable.

Thanks to the large power distance displayed in an organization or enterprise in South Korea, the organization or enterprise has a distinct hierarchy. The leaders prefer the top-down decision-making mode and the subordinates strictly abide by their superiors' instructions. The power distance in Motorola that embodies the American culture, however, is small. The organizational structure tends to be flat. The leaders opt for the bottom-up decision-making mode and readily accept the subordinates' opinions. In addition, the subordinates are willing and have the courage to raise suggestions or doubts. In case of ambiguity, they will approach their superiors for inquiry. To rebuild the corporate culture, the Motorola South Korean Company changes the leadership methods to respect the authority of superiors and works out new leadership principles to encourage the inferiors to freely express their views, creating a participating, innovative, and cooperative working environment.

Salutation is another representation of power distance. In the case, the young South Korean players do not directly call the elder players by names and should use courtesy titles instead. Having realized this, Hiddink does not forcibly require the players to change their established habits. Instead, he seeks common grounds between his own culture and the South Korean culture. He demands changes only on the football court and makes no attempt to touch upon the values and behavior regulations of the players, making the solution much easier.

South Korea is deeply rooted in the Confucian culture. Confucian norms include respecting the old and cherishing the young, and the hierarchy of nobility and humbleness. It is widely recognized as social virtues. This is even displayed on the football area. It makes sense why a young player passes the ball to an elder player rather than another young player at a better shooting position. Hiddink gets to the point and takes advantage of the value system for respect of the elders in the Korean culture. He asks the elder players to empower young players to pass the ball to other young players in a better position for shooting by sticking to the common objective of scoring and winning. Hiddink successfully implants the equality concept in the

Holland culture to enhance the mutual respect and trust among players.

Jerome and Hiddink set up a good example for people to become inter-cultural managers that take advantage of different cultures. When it comes to conflicts in cultural integration, people should not always succumb to the local culture, give up the advantages of our own culture to blindly adapt to the local culture, or attempt to change the culture or behaviors of the local people. Instead, people should set up a core organizational or corporate culture by giving into play the advantages of different cultures. The core culture is like a toolkit that hosts different cultural tools and allows immediate usage when required. Apart from understanding one's own cultural principles, people should also grasp cultural equilibrium and flexibility principles to adapt to the local conditions in different scenarios.

Case 2   To ask or not to ask

The Annual Group Supply Chain Management Conference held at the Headquarters was bouncing along. The Headquarters Director of the Supply Chain Management Division had just declared the planned stock turnover to be achieved by all the regional headquarters the next year. Whispers swept the conference hall when Mr. Hatcher, the newly appointed North America Supply Chain Management Director proposed a question demanding the ground on which the planned stock turnover was based.

Much to his surprise, the Headquarters Director pulled a long face on this, and all the Japanese at the conference seemed greatly disturbed, lowering their heads and resuming silence. The conference hall was suddenly frozen. On seeing Mr. Hatcher's puzzled face, Mr. Ando, sent from the Headquarters to France 12 years ago to work there till now, stood up and explained, "What Mr. Hatcher wants to say, I guess, is that a thorough understanding of the background information of the planned turnover is essential for a better performance. For instance, the new planned turnover may be based on the study carried out by the Headquarters on the collected data of our competitors or the analysis on the present situation of the corporation." "Yes, that's right," Mr. Hatcher echoed, "As a district principal, I deem it my responsibility to assign my team a job clearly. I will assign the task and see it be appropriately carried out on each step of the process if the planned turnover comes out of well-grounded data, and take some measures if it doesn't. Lack of information is dangerous for the process of the job." On these words, most of the Japanese relaxed and murmured to each other while the Headquarters Director's face softened a bit. The host seized this opportunity and said, "As the time is limited, we'll provide more detailed communication on this later. Thanks." Thereafter the meeting continued, just as usual.

At the break of the meeting, the host came to Hatcher and explained to him and other Japanese nearby the background information of the new assignment. Soon, his explanation reached every attendant at the conference.

Discussion:

1. Why did the Head Director's face turn blue on Mr. Hatcher's question?
2. Why did the Japanese people at the conference lower their heads and keep silent?

Case analysis:

The Headquarters Director throws out new task indicators at the conference. Apart from Mr. Hatcher, many participating Japanese also have doubts about the task background. In the presence of a big crowd, however, Hatcher raises his question. This violates against the "heart-to-heart" rule and is considered as a challenge to the Director. So it makes the Director embarrassed.

Japanese companies generally have strict regulations and distinct relations between superiors, predecessors, and inferiors. The superiors have authorities and require unconditional submission of the inferiors without any objection. This mode features unified and concerted internal actions and high efficiency but the severe seniority system makes subordinates bear heavy pressure.

An implicit rule in the Japanese corporate culture is that the subordinates should follow their superiors. Although no explicit remarks are made, the subordinates are supposed to understand their superiors' intentions. This is generally referred to as "heart-to-heart."

As far as the Americans are concerned, direct and simple communication with their superiors is always preferred. They would like to raise their doubts to their superiors and directly express their own opinions in case of disagreement with the superiors' practices. They may also work together with their superiors to seek better solutions. As superiors, they consider themselves being responsible to clearly express tasks assigned to the inferiors so as to better complete the task.

It can be concluded that the face problem is not only important in China but also in Japan. On the management level, managers should adapt to different cultural backgrounds and follow the inter-cultural management requirements at MNCs.

Case 3　Is he a responsible engineer?

A Chinese electronic engineer, Mr. Xue, of Sony Corporation (BKK) Ltd. told his own experience. One day, he saw a broken PCBA, which was a circuit board for the multimedia computer. He picked it up and found there were many expensive components on it. As an engineer, he thought it was his duty to repair it. Otherwise, it would be discarded as useless. It took him two hours before he finally fixed it, and it worked perfectly when tested. As he felt so proud of what he had done, he signed his name on the card that was tied to the PCBA.

About an hour later, the PCBA was rejected by the QC Department, and he was called to the General Manager's office. When he arrived there, he was so surprised to find that Mr. Tsuyoshi Kondo, the Japanese general manager, and Mr. Frank, QC Manager from France, looked so cold.

"It is he who put the damaged PCBA on the production line," said the QC Manager to the GM with an aggressive voice. "Why did you repair that damaged PCBA and put it on the line?" Mr. Kondo asked him suspiciously.

"It's not a defected piece any more. I'm sure it works well," he answered with a confident gesture. "In order to save money for the company, I have done a hard but excellent job. It is good for the company. Why do you call me here and ask me in such a serious way?" He looked directly into the managers' eyes.

Instead of answering his question, the QC manager asked him a direct question. "Do you want to buy a multimedia computer with this seriously broken but well repaired PCBA inside?"

Suddenly, the Chinese engineer came to realize something — if he were a consumer, he definitely would not buy a computer like this one. However, there was something that pushed him to try to find some reason that he was not in the wrong. He remembered that when he was very young, his parents often told him that it would be a good habit to save everything and make use of it as much as possible. And he also remembered his teacher often taught him to "use something for three years when it looks new. When it looks old, it should be used for another three years. When it is broken or worn, have it repaired or mended, and then use it for another three years."

He suddenly understood there was a cultural difference between the GM, the QC Manger and him. So he said in an apologetic way, "Yes, well, Mr. Londo and Mr. Frank. Saving the thing when it still has some value is our Chinese way. But from this case I understand what quality means to us now. It's true that if I were the consumer, I wouldn't buy a computer in a good working condition but with a broken PCBA inside it."

"It is a reasonable explanation, and that's a cultural difference," Mr. Kondo said with a satisfied expression on his face, and Mr. Frank's face also changed from cold to warm.

"You know, Mr. Xue. You tried to save 1,000 US dollars for Sony, but the goodwill of Sony is priceless. If the repaired broken PCBA passed our checks and went to the consumer, it would be a disaster for Sony's goodwill. And that's why we must throw away those seriously defected PCBAs." Mr. Frank said to him with a smile.

Discussion:

1. Is Mr. Xue a responsible engineer? How does the manager think of him?
2. How do Chinese and Japanese differ in perceiving responsibility?

Case analysis:

In this case, Mr. Xue voluntarily repaired a disqualified expensive PCBA circuit board to help the company to save costs. The circuit board, however, failed to pass the inspection of the QC department. Although the repaired circuit board could function normally, the Sony manager believed that it was irresponsible to apply the circuit board that used to have severe problems to the product and concluded that this practice would hurt Sony's reputation.

The Japanese electrical appliances manufacturing industry attaches importance to product quality and corporate reputation whereas the traditional Chinese values advocate conservation. Mr. Xue's encounter at Sony shows the conflict between the Sony operation philosophy and the traditional Chinese virtue.

Conservation is one of the traditional virtues for the Chinese. Born in 1970s when China was in a tough situation and the general public led an impoverished life, Mr. Xue's generation formed the habit of diligence and frugality. They try to save anything that can be saved. There is an old Chinese saying, "Use something for three years when it looks new. When it looks old, it should be used for another three years. When it is broken or worn, have it repaired or mended, and then use it for another three years." This is the vivid representation of the education that Mr. Xue and his generation received. The Chinese media also continue to promote typical cases of corporate conservation. Influenced by the traditional Chinese education, Mr. Xue naturally concludes that he has done a good deed for Sony by voluntarily repairing an expensive disqualified PCBA circuit board. This means that he is a responsible engineer. Sony, on the other hand, maintains that the company has to be first responsible for clients. Sony believes that using a circuit board that used to have severe problems on the product hurts the corporate reputation, and it is unfair for clients and irresponsible on its own part. It can be learnt that both parties differ in understanding the responsibilities that they emphasize. Mr. Xue believes that his duty is to help the company to lower costs whereas Sony assumes customer satisfaction as its responsibility. As an engineer, Mr. Xue is not as broad as the manager in terms of horizons. Mr. Xue realizes the importance of cost reduction in his duty but fails to understand the impact of this minor conservation on the corporate reputation that has been built for many years and the huge losses that may occur.

In the 1940s and 1950s, the Japanese used to have severe quality problems for the Japanese goods. To get rid of this bad reputation, the Japanese government proposed the strategy of "quality salvation." The quality of Japanese products is now in the front ranks of the world. A company is recognized by clients only with good qualities. This is the path for long-run prosperity of Sony. The loss of client trust due to inferior quality is the largest loss of Sony.

Japan is small in area and has limited resources. The Japanese thus also attach great importance to conservation. Japan hosts TV programs, newspapers and magazines to specially promote conservation and organizes conservation competitions to reinforce the conservation awareness of people. In this case, however, the Sony manager did not criticize Mr. Xue for his conservation awareness but for his omission of client interests while pursuing the corporate interest.

Mr. Xue finally realized the root cause of the problem and provided the general manager with a proper explanation. Both concluded that this is more of a cultural difference that indicates the differences of corporate operation philosophies between the Chinese and the Japanese. How to reduce this difference and make all employees in the company understand and uphold the corporate philosophies?

First, praise Mr. Xue for voluntarily repairing the PCBA circuit board to lower costs but also explain why such activities may impair client interests, clarifying any doubts and misunderstanding among the Chinese employees.

In addition, Sony may set up training courses on quality management to implant the quality oriented philosophy to all employees and take the opportunity to promote Sony's responsible attitudes for clients.

Case 4 Rules-sticking or face-giving?

Since 1984, Intel has begun to establish the office of general manager in China. From 1993, Intel entered Chinese market on a large scale and set up two limited companies IADL and "Intel Technology."

Born in China, Tang Fei began to work in Intel after graduation in America, and has been living in America for eight years. In 1993, he was sent back to China, and then worked for a period of time until he again was assigned as a marketing director in Beijing, directly reporting to the president of Intel in Chinese market. It is obvious that he is caught between western and traditional Chinese management style; motivating employees based on small rewards and on seniority, he is both a foreign assigned manager and a local person. Arriving in Beijing, he made an analysis of the whole working process and assignments, and found some assignments were not consistent with the direction of company development. For instance, a client manager named Liu Yong was compiling a client manual which was unrelated to the company strategy. Thus, Tang Fei decided to call off the project.

Liu Yong is a client manager with many years of working experience in Intel. He is very committed to working, showing great concern with clients' satisfaction and developing good relationships with many important clients. To meet their needs, Liu

Yong began to compile a client manual which he supposed to be thin but turned out to be as thick as a college textbook. This compiling took up a large amount of time and money. After Tang Fei took office, before long, he asked his assistant, Chen Chen, to inform him to cancel this project. However, in a great fury, Liu Yong refused to accept the decision.

In face of such a dilemma, Tang Fei needs to decide how to cope with it. On the one hand, he doesn't want to lose Liu Yong, for he is very important for company's future development; on the other hand, he needs to safeguard his authority, and this is the first important decision he ought to make since he took office. What shall he do next?

Discussion:

1. Why was Liu Yong so angry when he was informed of calling off his project?
2. Can you imagine what Tang Fei would react when he knew this situation?
3. What are the deep-rooted reasons that can explain the conflict between Tang Fei and Liu Yong?

Case analysis:

As a marketing director dispatched to the Beijing representative office by Intel, Tang Fei introduced the empathetic western management style and wished to build up and maintain his authority within the shortest time. As for Liu Yong, the client manager with senior experiences in the Chinese market, the compilation of the client manual based on his market understanding played an important role in maintaining and developing customer relations to promote corporate development. His full intent gave into full play his dedication to the project. The newly appointed director, however, notified him to stop the project because it was inconsistent with the corporate development strategy. This western management method of Tang Fei made Liu Yong lose his "face."

Influenced by their traditions, the Chinese and the American corporate cultures differ in several aspects. As one of the most successful American MNCs, Intel inevitably represents the characteristics of the American corporate culture. Shortly after taking office, Tang Fei, who has received his education and worked for a few years in the United States, starts to promote the western management model that he is familiar with. He gains a full understanding about the work procedures at the Beijing office and drastically cuts off projects that do not comply with the corporate development strategy.

Based on years of experiences with clients, Liu Yong realizes the significance of sound customer relations to service development. Therefore, he is fully committed to compiling the client manual, a practice that conforms to his values of dealing with people shown as one of his persistent styles. When Tang Fei cuts off the project, Liu Yong boldly rejects. This is because Liu relates the project to his face, a distinct feature in the relation-oriented Chinese culture that respects another person's face. The face indicates one's dignity that can either be work related or not. The act that Tang Fei asks his assistant to inform Liu Yong of his opinion already makes Liu Yong uncomfortable. In view of Chen Chen's inferiority status, Liu Yong feels at ease to make a fury in Chen's presence. On a subconscious level, Liu also wants Chen to report to Tang Fei his attitudes and stance. That is, he is not the easy target for a newly appointed leader. As far as Tang Fei is concerned, the decision to cancel the project is solely based on the corporate strategy. He has no selfish motives and no intention of making things difficult for any one. This is clearly the American "business is business" principle. This principle happens to violate against the human-oriented relation in the Chinese corporate culture. The Chinese corporate culture is permeated with too many unsystematic factors such as people governance and relation governance. Even in foreign enterprises like Intel, the values of the Chinese employees are more or less involved. This case demonstrates the human-oriented value system of Liu Yong.

The core concept of Intel is "Disagree, Commit." It can be seen that Intel allows different opinions and tolerates uncertain changes. It encourages employees to take an active role in policies and plans and gives into full play the democratic styles. The behavior of Tang Fei in this case represents his business is business principle but fails to incorporate democracy into the western management style. He should listen to Liu's opinions rather than making a decision based on his subjective determination. This case shows his own conflict. Familiar with the Intel management style as he is, he is not completely independent of the Chinese management method. This is exactly the conflict trigger.

In such a thorny and intricate situation, what should Tang Fei do as a director? First, Liu Yong is a senior employee in the company and has set up several sound client relations. If Tang decides to stick to the original decision and leaves alone Liu's feelings, Liu will feel that he loses his face. This brings down his enthusiasm and may even lead him to quit and join the competitor, resulting in severe losses of Intel. If Tang cancels his decision, he will lose face himself and render his authority doubtful. If Tang covertly supports Liu's project, this will promote money spending on questionable projects by employees. Therefore, to maintain the face of both parties and uphold the values committed by Intel, Tang should directly communicate with Liu, make an apology for his precarious decision, and seek the opinions of Liu and other colleagues to make a final decision. In this manner, the superior and subordinate relations become harmonious and mutual trust can be built up.

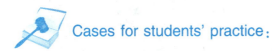

Cases for students' practice:

Case 1

Haier's tactics in marketing

On April 30, 1999, Haier established its industrial park in South California of the United States, covering 0.47 km² with annual production capacity of 500,000 sets. In 2000, manufacturing of home appliances started on a large scale, and Haier cracked into the American market with its quality products and individualistic design.

The new U.S. headquarters and Camden facilities are examples of Haier America's commitment to the U.S. market. The consummate attention of the American consumers' wants and needs along with the aggressive pursuit of quality assurance poise Haier America for its continued achievements in the U.S.

Haier makes its product highly localized. Haier has many information centers and design sections abroad. These centers and sections develop the products that suit for the locals. This will improve the competitiveness of its products. Even Haier's advertisements are localized. The advertisement in America is "What the world comes home to." And the ad in Europe is "Haier and higher!"

In addition, Haier outstrips the demands of the customers instead of only satisfying them. High quality is not enough. Haier does higher than what the customers want, for example, Haier developed a kind of refrigerator that can save 50% of energy and has no chlorofluorocarbons, so it can protect the environment. It can save energy, so it is very cheap to use it. In Germany, government even gives subsidies to customers who buy this kind of refrigerator, in order to encourage people to buy this environment-friendly home appliance.

Discussion:

1. How does Haier carry out its localization strategy in the U. S. ?
2. What can we learn from the success of Haier in America?

Case 2

Disneyland is not always successful!

For years, the Disney Theme Park Empire was built upon three crown jewels located in California, Florida, and Japan. Combining the familiar, family-friendly characters and images upon which the Disney reputation was built, with clean and well-operated theme parks helped Disney set new standards for efficient, friendly customer service in the theme park industry, with its parks becoming major international tourist attractions. When Disney expanded its theme park empire across the Atlantic, many expected Disney winning streak would continue.

However, when Euro Disney opened in Paris in 1992, the standard model of Disney theme parks, long considered to be a recipe for guaranteed financial success, soon ran into trouble. Tackling the many problems faced by Euro Disney operations has posed many new challenges to Disney, forcing them to reconsider their cookie-cutter standard model for success. For the Euro Disney theme park to survive, Disney must find ways to adapt their theme park model in a manner which preserves the best of Disney while more closely fitting the needs of the European market.

Staffing problems upsets the balance of power in the new Magic Kingdom. The staff of nearly 3,000 cast members was still not large enough to meet the needs of a Disney-run property. The employees also faced language and cultural barriers from American management.

Customer service, the hallmark of all things Disney, was sorely lacking in the European theme park. Park guests, accustomed to world-class treatment at the parks in Florida, California and Tokyo, complained that the cast members were apathetic, and cast members complained about what they considered to be Disney's unrealistic customer service expectations. The employees did not subscribe to the Disney philosophy of complete guest satisfaction, which broke down the illusion necessary to create Disney magic. This left park guests, especially Americans, feeling cheated out

Part V *Typical Cases in Intercultural Business Communication*

of the Disney experience.

Unlike Disneyland Tokyo, which had been locally owned and operated, Euro Disney was owned largely by foreign investors. U.S.-based Disney still held a 49 percent share of the park and maintained management from afar. The distance management approach was a recipe for disaster. The park suffered as operations decisions were made by a management team with little understanding of the European culture or market.

Discussion:

1. Can you find the problems in the management of the Disneyland in Europe?

2. Can you put forward any suggestions about the building of the Disneyland in Shanghai?

Chapter

3

Corporation system and management

Institutional culture consists of system concept, system values, system management standards, system implementation and system and such a material form. System culture is a part of corporation culture in certain economic and cultural environment, production system and management practices operated in the formation of consensus. Cultural conflicts in this section focus on two main aspects of the differences in

the system level between the East and the West. In terms of management contract approach, it is the rule of law or the rule of man (universalism or particularism).

Corporation management and contract concept (Man-governing vs. Law-governing)

People from the West emphasize the law and pay close attention to the concept of contract, which has penetrated into all aspects of society. With the supremacy of the Constitution, the judge may cancel the provisions of the legislature. They despise authority and compassion, and insist that comply to the personal status or authority is the challenge of the rule of law. Everyone has a strong awareness of their rights under the law. But the Eastern traditional ethics thinking focuses on friendship with weak legal concepts. Chinese pursue psychological identity and harmony, as to the laws and rules, they always feel impersonal. During the initial negotiations, the U. S. side always takes their lawyers, in order to avoid future disputes. But Chinese think this is the lack of sincerity and unfriendly expression. In Chinese eyes, less than a last resort and the two sides are unwilling to use the legal tools to rigidly dispute resolution. Such differences often result in international business communication problems, misunderstandings, and conflicts.

Fons Trompennaars and Hampden-Turner in "Riding the Waves of Culture" presented the concept of universalism and particularism. Universalism's behavior is usually concrete, in accordance with certain practices and rules not allowing the destruction. As social behaviors are based on the established rules, once they are damaged, the system will be weakened and the entire social system will collapse.

Western culture emphasizes rational thinking and fair performance in the social system, which is based on the law-governing country, and in business, system management is based on its establishment and perfection. On the one hand, the product of rational thinking system is the results of comprehensive analysis on business and management; on the other hand, because of the system, rules and regulations should be objective and fair. The guiding ideology of Confucian philosophy is essencial to traditional Chinese legal thinking. The Chinese law ruling spirit emphasizes the role of human, moral role, and the emotional factors, which should be in line with "human." When encountering difficulties in the management of enterprises, management and employees often think of how the relationship or acquaintance can solve the issues, so that people work tirelessly to establish personal relationships.

In international business, the contract is a very important aspect of its commitment provided the two sides concerned. However, the cultural differences and traditions, people's attitudes towards contracts are different, and some rules-oriented, while some relationship-oriented (Rule-oriented vs. Relation-oriented). Western culture is a contract culture, so they attach great importance to the accuracy of contract. The contract should be settled specificly in accordance with the details. They also focus on the authority of the contract. Once in force it will be strictly enforced. But in the Eastern culture and tradition, the contract is only the beginning of the negotiations, as negotiations proceed, the contract is changeable to their business depending on the relationship of the two sides, and they focus more on credibility. Based on the large number of Chinese and Western trade contract disputes, the differences of China and the West contract fall into the four aspects: The first is the interpretation of the applicable law; the second is to make the contract requirements, the third is economic cooperation projects need government approval issues; the fourth is the contract terms or heavy government or the competent department of red tape or regulations. Behind these differences are re-regulation and heavy human, rule orientation or relational orientation differences.

Rules and different cultures on the relationship can be reflected in the following cases.

Case 1 Why is Mr. Green so angry?

A Chinese software company wanted to cooperate with an American software company, so they invited the American company to China to have a negotiation. The latter was very interested in this invitation because they all knew that nowadays China was the largest potential market in the world. Therefore the American company sent three persons to China, of whom Mr. Green was in charge of this matter for this Chinese company.

When finally Mr. Wang saw Mr. Green at the airport, he smiled, "You must be very tired!" Mr. Green was somewhat puzzled, but he did not pay much attention to that. Then, when they arrived at the hotel, Mr. Wang treated Mr. Green with a big dinner. Mr. Green was at a loss when he saw that so much food was served. "That is impossible to eat all that food," said Mr. Green. But Mr. Wang said, "I'm very sorry that we've just prepared some poor food. I hope you don't mind about it." Mr. Green was totally puzzled, "Who says that China is a developing country and Chinese are poor? If the poor live in this way, there must be no God!" He also considered Mr. Wang as an insincere guy apologizing for this big dinner.

The next day when Mr. Green suggested that they should begin the negotiation, Mr. Wang just laughed, "There is no need to hurry after all, and you come to China for the first time, so just see around our city for several days. First enjoy yourselves, and then talk about business. Would that be all right?"

But Mr. Green was a little unpleasant, "If we don't begin our negotiation, what on earth did we come to China?"

"I know that our business is negotiation, but we also hope that you can enjoy yourselves. We can start our negotiation several days later," said Mr. Wang.

"Business is business. We really appreciate your good will, but we came to China not for ourselves but for the company," said Mr. Green.

Mr. Wang was a little embarrassed hearing this, but finally they began their negotiation. When they were all seated, Mr. Green felt very strange. He just couldn't understand why the Chinese company sent so many persons to this negotiation. After all, this was just a business negotiation, not a big fight.

After Mr. Wang introduced all his members to Mr. Green, the latter finally found out that these persons included sales manager, technicians and some other concerned people. "I can't see why these people come," thought Mr. Green. Then he introduced his members to Mr. Wang, "This is my secretary, and this is the lawyer of our company." When hearing the word "lawyer," all Chinese people present felt somewhat disappointed and angry. Mr. Wang frowned and totally got no idea what to say. "Why lawyer? It's just like calculating family property in preparation for a divorce at a time when we are just beginning to fall in love," thought Mr. Wang.

During the negotiation, Mr. Green recommended several articles, but each time Mr. Wang would just say, "Oh, that is very good, but I have to talk to my boss." Mr. Green was very unpleasant, for he couldn't understand why the company sent Mr. Wang if he couldn't make any decision. What is worse, sometimes Mr. Wang would give some puzzling answers, like "I fully understand this, but I am afraid there are many problems about this. It's very complex."

"Then what are the problems?" asked Mr. Green. This made Mr. Wang embarrassed and he just kept silent.

At last, Mr. Green couldn't help losing his temper, "I don't think that your company really wanted to cooperate with our company!"

Mr. Wang also felt angry, but he just said, "Take it easy. In fact, we do want to cooperate with you, but you can see that things are complex."

Mr. Green was so angry to these cloudy words that he accidentally fell back onto the seat. All the Chinese people present laughed and asked, "Are you OK?" Mr. Green said nothing and left the room for he thought he was not respected.

The next day, he left China with his members.

Discussion:

1. Why did Mr. Green feel kind of puzzled when he heard Mr. Wang say "you must be very tired" at the airport?

2. Why did Chinese serve their counterparts such a big dinner? What did Mr. Green think of it?

3. When Mr. Green introduced his lawyer at the negotiation table, why did the Chinese feel very uncomfortable?

4. Why did Mr. Green think that the Chinese company was unwilling to cooperate with his company?

Case analysis:

This case presents to people the huge differences of negotiation styles and interpersonal communications between the Chinese and the Americans. The Chinese, as represented by Mr. Wang, consider the American culture as impatient, straightforward, and interest-oriented. On the other hand, the Americans, as represented by Mr. Green, conclude that the Chinese are too sloppy, cautious, reserved, and are involved in complex relations. It thus makes sense that the negotiation started unpleasantly and ended up in vain.

The negotiation failure appears for the following reasons:

Different negotiation styles

The contrast of the American task-oriented and the Chinese relation-oriented negotiations is the first reason. The United States is the cradle of target management and the cause-and-effect thinking plays a dominant role in the American culture. In business activities, the Americans first try to identify their objectives and then work out strategies to achieve these objectives. During the process, the Americans want to closely follow the progress so as to get first-hand information about their project completion. In this case, Mr. Green and his delegation considered their Chinese trip only as a business activity and concluded that their top priority was to negotiate matters concerning the cooperation. This is why they were impatient and doubtful when the Chinese delegation extended a warm reception and arranged relaxation activities to tour around the city. They made it clear that the business trip was not a holiday and asked the Chinese delegation when the negotiation would start. When Mr. Wang indicated that he could not give any immediate responses to the clauses proposed by Mr. Green, Mr. Green concluded that the Chinese were not willing to cooperate with his company. This was because such uncertainty took time and added costs to task completion. Green had no knowledge about the Chinese relation-oriented negotiation style and so did Mr. Wang to the American task-oriented style. In a relation-oriented culture, maintaining sound relations is a key step in business trade. This mutual trust relation can ensure the expected results of a negotiation. The successful contract signing is based on the earlier sound relations and only such relations can ensure the implementation of a contract.

This type of culture attaches no importance to the results but to the methods to achieve the goals. In this case, Mr. Wang spent lots of efforts, time, and money, such as preparing for the welcome banquet and arranging visits in an effort to set up sound relations with the American delegation. His purpose was to lay a foundation for further cooperation. Even if this cooperation fails to turn out as expected, the joint efforts of both parties in the cooperation can still strengthen the mutual relation that may lead to more fruitful achievements in the future cooperation. This task or relation style also matches the embankment point of the Hofstra individualism and collectivism.

Individualism vs. collectivism

The Americans cherish individualism. They generally act on their own and are unwilling to request instructions from their superiors all the time. It is considered as incapable and not good for one's own achievements. Unless specially specified and restricted, they can make their own decisions based on the actual conditions. Therefore, Mr. Green was surprised and bewildered to find out the participation of so many Chinese delegates in the negotiation. His team consisted of only three people, himself, his secretary, and a lawyer. In China, the collectivism culture prevails. People are group members rather than individuals. Every Chinese belongs to one of the four basic communities of working unit, family, school, and neighborhood, and is to some extent restricted by the community. A Chinese is responsible for the community and considers himself as a member, lacking social or geographical mobility. In the west, however, people do not experience such work restrictions and thus have great difficulty in understanding that the Chinese are given limited choices when it comes to make decisions to change the current situation or take independent actions. For example, Mr. Green couldn't understand why Mr. Wang insisted on requesting his superior's opinions every time a decision is required.

Legal regulation vs. relations

The American legal system is complete and citizens have high legal consciousness. To avoid unnecessary disputes in the future cooperation, they prefer to write down all matters into the legally binding contract before the cooperation. The contract would be a strong evidence in case of any dispute. Chinese still have no sophisticated legal systems, relations are the primary factor in business. Trust building seems to be an easy task when one does business with relatives and friends. The presence of a lawyer in the negotiation signifies distrust and disrespect for the Chinese. As a result, the Chinese delegation had difficulty in accepting Green's gesture. It was thus not so difficult to understand why Mr. Wang claimed that the lawyer was there to help two people who just fell into love how to divide their common properties when they divorced. It should be noted that with the entry to the

WTO, many Chinese practices are integrated into the International standards. The Chinese businessmen have gained better legal and contract consciousness.

Straightforward and reserved

The Americans believe that time is money and life. They do not want to waste any time in their pursuit to make as much money as possible through diligence, speed, opportunities, and power. Their business decisions are generally not affected by emotions. Therefore, the Americans are quite frank and sincere in negotiations but lack of patience. Mr. Green showed great unwillingness when Mr. Wang suggested them enjoying themselves for a few days and instead, demanded to kick off the negotiation soon. On the other hand, the Chinese are very reserved and focus more on building sound and mutual trust relations before the formal negotiation. This was why Mr. Wang asked whether Green was tired after the trip and prepared fancy meals and travelling plans for the American party. To Mr. Green, however, these activities were a complete waste of time and money.

In addition, the Chinese do not easily express their emotions and avoid direct confrontation even if in the case of no consent to another person's views. This was why Mr. Wang, who tried his best to set up sound relations with the American delegation, was caught in a dilemma when Mr. Green declared that they came to China for business not for fun in front of Mr. Wang.

The eventual unhappy breakup of the negotiation is not anticipated for both the Chinese and American delegations.

Both parties are responsible for the negotiation failure. If either party had some understanding about the other culture, they would have been more tolerant of the "mistakes" (only to people in a foreign culture. Due to differences in thinking patterns, a commonplace thing in one country may seem unacceptable to people in another country) when a dispute arose.

On the one hand, the Chinese should strengthen their legal consciousness during business activities with foreigners to protect their own legal rights, better cooperate with foreigners, and build up good images on the international market. On the other hand, the Americans should drop their attitudes and stop being centered around their own culture. They should try to learn and understand other cultures during intercultural business negotiations.

Case 2 Personal luxury or family loyalty

Joe was a native of Ganzpoor, a mega city in the developing nation of Chompu. Joe entered this life as the first of five children of an impoverished cloth peddle. Against all odds, by means of sheer guts, hard work and ability, Joe has brought himself to the United States and managed to earn a prestigious degree in engineering from Cornford University. Motorola snapped him in a week after graduation, and during the next five years gave him challenging assignments in Florida, Phoenix, Scotland and Mexico.

Meanwhile, Motorola's business in Chompu began taking off. The Chompu Group was eager for more engineers. But the HR office was having difficulty finding candidates willing to accept assignment to Ganzpoor. The news reached Joe, who soon began a vigorous campaign for a transfer. HR saw him as a guy good to be true: qualified both professionally and culturally, Joe got his transfer.

Upon his assignment to Ganzpoor, Joe was informed in writing that he was expected to reside in a safe and seemly residence of his choice, and would be reimbursed for the actual cost of his rent and servants, up to a maximum of $2,000 per month. "Joe, just give us your landlord's receipts and servants' receipts, and we'll get you promptly reimbursed," explained Pierre Picard, a French Motorola assigned as financial controller for Motorola/Chompu.

Joe found a place to live, but even months later, other motorolans were not sure exactly where it was because he never seemed to entertain.

Each month Joe would send Pierre a bill for $2,000, accompanied by a rental and service receipt for exactly that amount, duly signed by his landlord. Each month Pierre would reimburse Joe accordingly. This went on for several months, until one day, a traditionally dressed Chompunese man came to see Pierre. He complained bitterly that Joe was his Master and that Master had cheated him of his servant's wages for the past three months. At this point Pierre, despite his personal regard for Joe, had no alternative but to check into the facts of Joe's lining arrangements.

Pierre and the local HR manager, Harry Hanks, had trouble getting the facts of the case, so finally they got a car and driver and went looking for Joe's address. It took almost two hours. The address turned out to be on the edge of a slum area of Ganzpoor, where houses were poorly marked.

Their first concern was for Joe's safety. Also, they felt, Joe's unseemly residence was hardly good for Motorola's image. Aside from these considerations, though, was the fundamental matter of simple integrity.

Harry felt he had no choice but to report the case to the regional HR director, who had no choice but to order a full-scale investigation.

When Joe learned that he was under investigation, he exploded in a fury. He complained that his right of personal privacy was being invaded. Further, he argued that his receipts were legitimate, despite the fact that the investigation revealed that rent plus service in so humble a dwelling could not possibly cost Joe more than $400 a month, and probably cost much less.

Joe finally explained, "Yes, it was true that he actually paid less than $2,000 a month." But, he argued, just because he was willing to "make sacrifices" should not Motorolans receive. To clinch his defense, Joe argued, "Look, I'm a Chompusnese as well as a Motorolan and in Chompu this kind of things happens all the time."

The hearings officer pressed further. Finally Joe, near tears, explained that all four of his younger siblings were now of college or high school age, and he was putting all four of them through school with the reimbursements he received from Motorola, plus a fact that most Westerners wouldn't believe his poverty even if they saw it. This money can mean the difference between hope and despair for all of them. "For me to do anything less for my family would be to defile the honor of my late father. Can't you understand?"

A week later, Joe was asked to step into the director's office to learn his fate.

Discussion:

1. Could Joe have achieved his end in an ethically acceptable way? If so, how?

2. Is Motorola's policy on housing, servants, and reimbursement in Chompu a reasonable and defensible one?

3. Is there a better policy that Motorola might adopt? If yes, what would it be? If not, should Motorola take measures to prevent other cases like Joe's?

Part V *Typical Cases in Intercultural Business Communication*

 Case analysis:

This case describes the story of a Motorola employee called Joe from Chompu. To receive more corporate subsidies, he misrepresents his housing expenditure and violates against the Uncompromising Integrity regulation of Motorola. This regulation requires that all Motorola employees be honest, just, and do the right thing, even if in difficulty.

As a corporate benefit, Motorola reimburses the housing and servant expenditures of employees during their working at Chompu and stipulates the maximum amount is $2,000 per month. Joe submits a receipt of $2,000 for reimbursement every month until one day his servant complains that Joe has not paid his wages for three months. A corporate investigation reveals that Joe lives near the slum area where the monthly rent is about only $400 and Joe has made a false report on his reimbursement receipts.

Joe explains to Motorola about his poor family and his responsibility to save money for his four siblings to finish school. In the eyes of Joe, he should be responsible for his family. Family plays a more important role in his values. To make his family lead a better life, he would rather live in poor conditions and even dare to violate against the basic philosophy of integrity required by Motorola. His behavior indeed benefits his family but the company requires that every employee be honest in every deed. Other employees also cannot accept the fact that Joe misrepresents his actual housing expenditures or understand his practice of lying to the company for the sake of his family.

Since the security situation in Chompu does not look optimistic and Motorola may sometimes require employees to work over time, Motorola wishes the employees to live at comfortable and secure places to ensure their safety. Living comfortably also helps to enhance labor efficiency. Therefore, Motorola is justified to provide the $2,000 monthly subsidy for housing and servant services. But Motorola also specifies that this expenditure is reimbursed on an actual basis and the upper limit every month is $2,000. In this case, Joe spends only $400 but reimburses $2,000 from the company through fake receipts, clearly in violation against the company regulations. Although Joe believes that he is responsible for his young brothers and sisters, he is also obliged to observe basic corporate philosophies as a Motorola employee.

Joe also maintains that the secret investigation on his housing conditions violates against his personal privacy. But the investigation is made because of his servant's complaint to Motorola. The company is entitled to investigate into such matters that have an impact upon the corporate image and the reputation of employees. Joe argues that he is entitled to demand the same reimbursement since other employees also get $2,000 for their housing subsidies. The key in this case is that the reimbursement amount submitted by Joe is fake. This is not a matter of equal rights with other employees but a matter of his honesty.

In the presence of strong defenses by Joe, will Motorola forgive him? How can both parties properly settle this problem?

First, Motorola should make it clear to Joe that he must truthfully report his housing expenditure and Motorola only reimburses the actual amount.

Second, Joe can suggest the HR department setting up scholarships for the family members of Motorola employees that attend local schools. In this manner, Joe's brothers and sisters may be granted with extra educational grants. Of course, this measure should be applicable to all Motorola employees.

In the end, Joe should be punished for being dishonest. Should he continue to submit false receipts to obtain extra incomes, the company should fire him. Still, Joe is proven valuable to Motorola and the company should properly handle this problem.

Case 3 A deadline in the contract

A mansion construction project was a RMB 800 million worth investment. A company in charge of the project asked for a bank loan abroad with a native branch bank as a guarantee for the investment. Mr. X was sent to work in Beijing as a project manager from a bank in North Europe, a leading bank for other banks involved in the overseas investment. Mr. X, a forty years old former lawyer, was precise in his daily work with the Chinese. Whenever he had a negotiation with the guarantee, he carried with him  all the contracts and documents for reference. He was a hypercritical person by the guarantee. Once he had a clash with the guarantee and the construction company involved in the investment, because the completion of the construction was postponed for two months. As a representative of the leading bank, he declared the construction project a violation of the deadline in the contract. As a result, the company couldn't draw out the loan needed until redress of the violation was made. The company had an excuse for the postponement of the construction. Since the project was big and complex, deferment in the completion of a mansion was quite natural. Mr. X insisted on his decision no matter what the guarantee said to him, leading to a series of conflicts between the guarantee and the leading bank, including taking legal proceedings against each other.

Discussion:

1. What is the role of contract in U. S. and Japanese business?
2. Is it possible that the two parties would cooperate better without the contract? Why or why not?

Case analysis:

This case reflects the different attitudes towards time between the Chinese and the Western cultures, and the differences of valuing contracts and laws, especially the latter. These differences led to the Chinese company's failure to complete the project on time and get the bank loans as expected, so far as to go to the court. It can be seen from this case that without due attention, the cultural differences will reappear and lead to the same kind of problems, thus directly affecting economic and trade cooperation between China and foreign countries.

Firstly, there is the different understanding of the contract between China and Western countries. Although the contract in China is nothing new, but the Chinese people, to a certain extent, pay not enough attention to the contract, failing to recognize that the contract is a promise and failing to fulfill it will involve the legal responsibility. In practice, many of the disputes between China and the West are caused by it, and even such disputes often arise among the Chinese. Many Chinese people do not have a careful study of the contract before signing it, and only after the disputes arise will they begin to realize. This defect in the understanding of contracts is not conducive to China's social stability and economic development. China is a high-context country, stressing first the establishment of a broad social atmosphere of trust, which is built on good interpersonal relationships. For example, the mutual trust between friends and relatives is absolute. Chinese people think that these good relations are worthy of trust, and if you sign the contract with friends and relatives, it would be a negligence of human nature and loss of face. Westerners are very much different from the Chinese people in this respect. The West is a low-context society, emphasizing the facts more than human feelings, and contract is their final certificate. So contract is a very common behavior in the West, even among friends and relatives. This does not mean they do not trust others, but a dispute-avoiding behavior, which should be a model conduct to be learned by the Chinese people. Mr. X in the case, who always carries with him the relevant contracts and documents while negotiating, would be considered by Chinese people as a fault-finding and oversensitive. Chinese people do not like this behavior, and regard it as distrust and suspicion to them. In fact, in the opinion of Mr. X, it is a respect to each other, and can prevent the contract dispute from spoiling their future cooperation.

Secondly, there are huge differences in the understanding of the law between Chinese and Western cultures. China is a society of human sensibilities which focuses on human feelings and ignores the facts. There is sometimes a conflict between the rule of law and the rule of morality in China. If a conflict arises between the Chinese people, the first choice of the solution is not to use the law, but with human feelings, including some of the principles of good public morals and social ethics. While China is working to improve the legal system and the rule of law, the role of human feelings in real life is often greater than the law. It can be said that some Chinese people have not accustomed themselves to the legal means to resolve disputes, and even regard it a disgrace to appear at the court. This is the embodiment of the Chinese people deeply affected by the traditional rule of morality. Meanwhile the Chinese put much emphasis on building a harmonious society and good relationships, try to avoid all conflicts, thus reducing more opportunities to use the law. So there is still a long way to go for the penetration of law in China. In the West, law is the best way to find a civilized settlement of disputes. In order to better use the law, they emphasize the importance of facts, hence the importance of the contract. They choose their partner not based on human feelings but on interests. Perhaps the Western attitude and way of life are too cruel in the eyes of the Chinese people, but it has avoided a lot of arguments and estrangements among friends and relatives.

In addition, the Chinese people focus more on process and objective factors, while Westerners focus more on results and subjective factors. In the case above, the Chinese side first tried to find many reasonable explanations after the delay in the project, to find the objective factors rather than analyzing the subjective reasons. Chinese people are very receptive to these explanations, but the Westerners think that

Part V *Typical Cases in Intercultural Business Communication*

the content of the contract is your commitment and should be strictly honored; and the breach is the subjective fault regardless of the objective factors. There is no use explaining. In this case Mr. X ignores any explanation on the complexity, and believes that the difficulties should have been recognized clearly before signing the contract, so the construction company should bear the corresponding legal responsibility for its breach of contract.

Moreover, there exists a very different concept of time between China and Western countries. The Chinese people pay more attention to quality than time, because they believe "soft fire makes sweet malt," as a similar Chinese proverb goes. According to the Chinese, the human can adapt to time, and time is linear and a cycle, irrelevant to the people or things. The circular time is not a scarce resource, and it seems endless and easy to obtain. For example, drinking tea while reading the newspaper is often the case in Chinese offices. As long as the work is completed, no emphasis is placed on efficiency, and a time limit would not be deliberately set to complete the given task. In addition, a meeting in China can always be postponed if someone has not arrived yet. These are intolerable in the West, where people have a very strong sense of time. Every day, they have a timetable for them to strictly abide by. They like the efficient way of doing things, and dislike work delays and unpunctuality. In the profit-oriented society, time is a precious and even rare commodity, and time is money. They think that such acts are disrespect to them and even a waste of their life, so they think it is not worth working in cooperation with those people. The case above reflects a strong sense of time of the Westerners. A two-month delay in completion by the construction companies was in violation of the contract deadline, so Mr. X was very dissatisfied and cancelled the loan. Of course there are many cases where the Chinese quite value time. For example, China and Germany reportedly signed a major project, and the Chinese side completed it two months ahead of deadline by working overtime. However, the German side thought that there were only two possibilities: They cut corners with low quality standards or the original timetable for the project was wrong. So they insisted on rework, resulting in heavy losses for China.

As there is a big difference in our understanding of the law and time, it is quite common for the conflicts to arise in daily interactions. However, in order to better cooperate and promote each other, we should make great efforts to prevent similar cases from happening. It is not desirable for Chinese people to pay so little attention to the efficiency. To integrate into the wave of globalization, we must enhance the sense of time and improve work efficiency. In the communication with the West, we should bear in mind the sense of time, and we must know that punctuality is actually one of the traditional Chinese virtues.

We must understand that contract is the provisions of rights and obligations, which is mutually beneficial to both parties. Before signing the contract, we must carefully read it, and understand the relevant provisions of the rights and obligations of both sides to avoid future disputes.

We should vigorously strengthen legal education, making the law become a standard to measure behavior in people's minds. We must look seriously at the role of the law, and change the traditional concept that a lawsuit means a loss of face. We must realize the importance of commitment. Maybe your accidental kind words will be interpreted by people as sincere invitation. Do not mind the Westerners' serious attitude towards the contract, but regard it as an act of mutual benefit. If we heed all these aspects, there should be even less conflicts in our communication with the West.

 Cases for students' practice:

Case 1

Geddy's Dilemma

Mr. Geddy Teok, an American-Chinese (Second generation) emloyee of a large New Jersey pharmaceutical firm, was based in Tokyo, Japan. His main aim was to get a major joint venture going with one of the largest Japanese pharmaceutical manufaturers. After four years of negotiating, the supreme moment had come for signing the contract. Obviously the lawyers from HQ in the New Jersey were well prepared and sent the contract to Geddy one week before the "ceremony."

After four years of Japanese experience, Geddy was shocked when he received the document from the USA. He told us, "I could not even count the number of pages. There were too many. But I remember the number of inches it measured when laying it on the table. I would guess that with every inch one of the Japanese would leave the room in despair. I hope they will sign the contract, but you should not take it too far."

Geddy Teok decided to call HQ and ask for some help. The legal department said that the relationship was so complex that the contract needed to cover many possible instances. Moreover, a consultancy firm there advised them regularly said that Asians

Part V Typical Cases in Intercultural Business Communication

in general and Japanese in particular had a reputation of being quite loose in defining what was developed by them and what came from the USA, "We'd better have some pain now and be clear in the terms of our relationship, than to turn into problems later because of miscommunication. If they sign it at least they show they are serious."

Geddy was in despair, but he only had a day to decide what to do. The meeting was tomorrow. Should he perhaps call the Japanese CEO, with whom he had built quite a relationship? Or should he just go for it? Geddy framed his dilemma quite clearly to us, "Whatever I would do, it would hurt my career. If I insist in the Japanese partners signing the contract they will see it as proof of how little trust has been developed over the years of negotiation. This might mean a postponement of discussions and in the worst case the end of the deal. If I reduce the contract to a couple of pages and present it as a 'letter of intent,' HQ in general and even worse the whole legal department will jump on me, jeopardizing my career."

If you were Geddy, what would you do?

Case 2

Wenzhou shoe makers in Spain

In the evening of September 16th, 2004, at about 7 o'clock p. m., when a large number of Chinese containers just arrived at the Chinese shoe city in Arch, a small city in the southeast of Spain, more than four hundred Spainish people who were holding a demonstration right in the city rushed to the containers and burned the goods. In the troops of demonstration, someone shouted angrily, "They (the Chinese people) have no fixed opening time. They work for 24 hours a day. They should work the same as us." The owners of the containers were merchants from Wenzhou city of China. Many of their holds and warehouses have been burned. And the lost has been come up to more than one million European dollars.

Before this vicious event, Wenzhou people had already been more and more boycotted in Europe. There were many conflicts between Chinese people and Spainish or even European people. In the street of Arch city, there were always people dispatching handbills requiring the Chinese shoe merchants to leave the Spainish market. And two days before this event, there were already a lot of slogans encouraging the residents of Arch city to take part in the demonstration around the Chinese shoe city. Also, after this, on September 23rd, Arch city again burst out a demonstration against Chinese merchants. The demonstrations openly threatened that *they would hold on a demonstration every week.*

There were more incidents against Chinese merchants especially for Wenzhou shoe sales, for example, from August 2001 to January 2002. Chinese shoe merchants including those of Wenzhou Dongyi Compamy were detained in Russia. The loss came up to almost 3 billion RMB. At the beginning of 2003, in Paris, the government workers of 11 regions walked out more than once lodging a protest against Chinese textile wholesalers because the wholesalers were considered to be untidy and not taking care of the environments. In the winter of 2003, the products of more than 29 Wenzhou shoe companies were burned in Rome, Italy. The loss is not clear.

Chapter 4

Cross-cultural negotiating style

No country can provide all the necessities by itself. Most corporations are becoming more culturally sensitive and globally minded because of foreign competition and the need to trade more effectively overseas. As a result, effective intercultural communication in the business negotiation is very important. In the normal  business, most agreements are signed through the employment of business negotiations.

Negotiation is a process in which two or more entities discuss common and conflicting interests in order to reach an agreement of mutual benefit. In international business negotiations, the differences in negotiation process from culture to culture include language, culture conditioning, negotiating style, approaches to problem solving, implicit assumptions, gestures and facial expressions, and the role of ceremony and formality.

For international negotiations to produce long term synergy, and not just short-term solutions, individuals involved in the negotiations must be aware of the multicultural facets in the process. The negotiator must understand the cultural space of his or her counterparts. Negotiating is a skill and it can be improved, and this section addresses some of the cultural variables and considerations of negotiations.

Differences in negotiation styles

International business negotiation deals not only cross borders, also cultures. Culture definitely influences how people think, communicate and behave. It also affects the negotiation style in business transactions.

Negotiating goal: contract versus relationship

Chinese business negotiators are apt to place more emphasis on establishing a sustainable business relationship rather than a contract. They think a negotiation is not a signed contract but rather the creation of a relationship between the two sides.

For Americans, signing a contract is closing a deal; however, for Chinese, signing a contract might more appropriately be called opening a relationship.

The different negotiating style in negotiation goal also leads to different attitudes towards the process of negotiation. Chinese negotiators, who value long-term relationship than contract, extend much more time on pre-negotiation stage. Chinese spend most of the time engaging in activities that build trust and friendship between members of each team and discussing broad objectives, such as the intent of the parties to work together and mutual long-term interests.

Personal style: informal versus formal

Personal style relates to how negotiators interact with counterparts at the negotiating table. A negotiator with a formal style insists on addressing counterparts by their titles, avoids personal anecdotes, and refrains from questions touching on private or family life of members of the other negotiating team. An informal style negotiator tries to start the discussion on a first-name basis, quickly seeks to develop a personal, friendly relationship with the other team, and may take off his jacket and roll up his sleeves when deal making begins in earnest.

China has a high concern for protocol; hence Chinese negotiators will adhere to strict and detailed rules that govern personal and professional conduct, negotiating procedures, etc. They address their counterpart with their job-related titles, titles of educational levels if one does not have a former title or family name during the negotiation. Seating arrangement also reflects how strict and formal Chinese negotiators are. Individual should take his or her seat according to his or her social status.

For American negotiators, egalitarian enables them to treat people equally, and contributes to their informal behavior. They also have relatively low concern for protocol, thus they prefer a much loose defined set of rules. They are not restricted by the difference in rank, seniority, experience, family background, connections, race, gender, etc. and they strive for power equalization and justice, at the same time they tend to express themselves freely and openly, and sit casually to make themselves comfortable.

Communication: direct versus indirect

People from certain cultures tend to adopt direct and simple methods of communication, such as Americans; while people from other cultures tend to rely on indirect, more complex methods, such as Chinese. The differences in communication style, to a certain degree, also refers to how much people rely on nonverbal cues to convey and interpret intentions and information in a dialogue. In business practices, what is actually said carries only part of the meaning of a message.

Nonverbal cues, such as facial expressions, eye contact, gestures, movement, touching patterns, silence, seating, use of space, etc. can provide additional meanings. A frequently quoted example to support his or her argument is the ambiguity of Chinese way of saying "Yes" and reluctance of saying "no." Indicators such as "maybe," "difficult," "I'll try" all carry implicit meaning of "no" in Chinese context.

Silence is another weapon often used by Chinese negotiators. Silence cues may be interpreted either as evidence of agreement or disagreement, comprehension or incomprehension. It can also be interpreted as demonstrating seriousness and sincerity in considering the matter. It can also be understood as evidence of lack of interest, showing disagreement without directly expressing a negative opinion, injured feelings or contempt.

Emotionalism: high versus low

The factor of emotionalism is related to the different views between cultures as to the appropriateness of displaying emotions, as these differing cultural norms may be brought to the negotiation table.

Chinese negotiators obviously are more conservative compared with American negotiators. The cultural value of Confucian plays an important role in shaping Chinese norm regarding emotionalism. As in a highly hierarchical society, each person has a fixed place in the social order with corresponding obligations and responsibilities. People should operate by the rule of respecting the hierarchy and being polite. Chinese negotiators are expected to be cool-headed, steady, calm and self-composed; those who easily reveals their feelings are thought to be superficial and immature, thus are deemed not ready for important tasks.

American negotiators, coming from legalitarian and individualist society, are emotionally independent, self-motivated, self-expressive and self-fulfilled. They are open-minded, straightforward, and easy-going. They have rich facial expressions, revealing to some extent whether they are happy or unhappy, and whether they have done their business well or not. They can more easily say "no" and are more likely to show their frustrations and anger when things are not going well.

Case 1　Why France?

Because of a shortage of paper supplies in China, the Hebei government in the early 1990s had approved funds for purchasing a set of advanced papermaking equipment from abroad, and a paper mill in Hebei Province was looking for a supplier.

Mr. Johnson, the president of a papermaking machinery factory in the American Midwest, learned of the opportunity through his local Chamber of Commerce and responded immediately to the Chinese paper mill with the relevant data and specifications. A month later, Johnson was invited to visit the paper mill, and he and his senior engineer, Mr. Smith, left for China, enthusiastic about a potential contract that could generate $15 million to $20 million in sales.

When they arrived in China, they were met by Mr. Wang himself, who was the mill's general manager. They were escorted to a nice hotel and a banquet that evening. At the banquet, the American visitors were warmly welcomed by several officials of the Hebei Provincial Government and Mr. Wang, as well as some others from the mill. One of the officials toasted for "friendship and long-term working relationship" between the Chinese and their American guests. Both Johnson and Smith were somewhat puzzled; as far as they were concerned, their mission was to promote the sale of papermaking machines.

In the next three days, Johnson and Smith were totally involved in a very busy schedule. They visited the paper mill, looked around the workshops, and had a full-day meeting with Wang and several engineers; they spent half a day with officials from various government departments, including those in charge of the paper mill. The Americans had expected the meetings to focus on specifications, data, price, and contract terms, but most of the time was spent on introductions and descriptions of the Chinese mill and the American company. The Chinese spent a significant amount of time explaining the importance of the purchase and the expansion of paper productions in China.

In the remaining day and a half, the Americans were escorted for sightseeing tours and treated to two full meals a day, with ten or more courses each. Mr. Wang was with them at each dinner (he said he wanted to be sure his visitors were treated well). The night before they returned to the U. S., Johnson and Smith were given a farewell dinner, with one toast after another, and one course after another. The atmosphere was full of hospitality.

The Americans were touched by the kindness and generosity of their hosts, but they were disappointed because neither of them could figure out whether the Chinese had any intention of buying their papermaking equipment. The talk of "friendship" and "long-term working relationship" had perplexed them; they didn't want to waste time on a relationship until they had a contract. In addition, the tight schedule had exhausted them. On the one hand, they had been well looked after, but on the other hand, they had felt constrained.

After their return to the U. S., Johnson and Smith sent a "thank you" note and an invitation to Mr. Wang and his colleagues to visit the American company. Two weeks later, Mr. Wang accepted, and the visit was scheduled for the early fall.

In the meantime, the Chinese had also invited Mr. Pierre, the president of a French papermaking machinery company near Paris. He and his senior engineer arrived for a four-day stay and were treated as the Americans had been. Three weeks after returning to Paris, Pierre sent three company representatives — an engineer, a salesperson, and the public relations director — to visit the Chinese mill again. They stayed for two weeks, spending most of their time in the workshops, chatting with the engineers, workers, and Mr. Wang himself. They also spent time with government authorities at different levels. They were aware of their competitor in the U. S., who had better technology than theirs. Through their casual conversations, the French learned the price range and the specific equipment features the Chinese were looking for. They also learned that the Chinese wanted the manufacturer to provide training and other after-sales services.

Hospitality, American style vs. French style

In the early fall, Mr. Wang, a senior engineer and an interpreter visited the American company. They arrived on a Sunday to find a taxi waiting for them at the airport. They were taken to a nice hotel and were notified that their dinner was arranged at 6:30 p.m. at the hotel. They dined alone on salad, steak, steamed vegetables, and mashed potatoes, all of which tasted strange and pretty awful to them.

The next morning, a taxi picked them up and took them to the American company, where Mr. Johnson and his colleagues greeted them at the gate and escorted them to a conference room. Three piles of materials were ready and waiting for the Chinese visitors, including the American company's brochure and technical information. The Americans had prepared full professional presentations with slides, but the meeting went slowly because of the difficult translations. A lunch of sandwiches was served in the conference room. The Americans felt that they had done their best to impress the visitors with their technology and facilities, but they got no clue to how their presentation was received. When Johnson sounded out the interpreter, the response was, "Not bad." That evening, the Americans held a dinner for their guests at a French restaurant, but the beautiful tableware and elaborately prepared French food did not seem to stimulate the visitors' appetites. After dinner, the Chinese were presented with pens and leather briefcases as gifts.

A month later, Mr. Wang, his senior engineer, and a French interpreter left China for Paris. Although they arrived on Sunday, they were met by Mr. Pierre and his assistant. The French drove their guests to the hotel, helped them settle in, and then took them to a Chinese restaurant for dinner. During the next three days, the visitors met with Pierre, his senior engineer, and salespeople. They were shown around the workshops and watched demonstrations of the operational process. The Chinese realized that some of the specific features of the facility were not as advanced as those of the American's. Moreover, the French firm's price was higher, but it offered to provide free training besides after-sales services. During their four days in Paris, the Chinese ate mostly Chinese cuisine; Pierre took them to a French restaurant just once. On their last day, the Chinese were escorted to a sightseeing tour by their host.

At the farewell dinner, Wang told Pierre that he would send a letter of intent as soon as he got back to China, and both sides could then prepare for formal negotiations. He stated that the Chinese felt comfortable working with their French host. There was one toast after another to friendship and a long-term working relationship.

Discussion:

1. Why did the Chinese company choose the French company to cooperate?
2. Any ideas could we learn from this case?

Part V *Typical Cases in Intercultural Business Communication*   213

 Case analysis:

The above case illustrates that the cultural differences between China and the United States can generate misunderstandings during business interactions, and can even cause the loss of deals. The Americans lost the attractive potential deal while the Chinese lost the opportunity of obtaining the comparatively more advanced equipment. The Chinese finally decided to work with the French because they felt comfortable working with the French. Mr. Pierre turned his company's disadvantage into an advantage and won the contract because he correctly interpreted the Chinese side's needs and behavior, and observed the Chinese etiquette. The Americans lost the potential deal because they were less sensitive to the Chinese culture, and some of their behaviors were just misunderstood by the Chinese. The cultural differences causing misunderstandings between the Chinese and the Americans are analyzed here by applying some of the international negotiation variables.

Concept of negotiation

During the banquet set for the Americans, the Chinese mentioned several times "friendship and long-term working relationship." The expectation of the Chinese was to establish a business relationship first, then to start future business. Therefore, during the meeting of the second day, the Chinese spent most of the time on the introduction of their company and on emphasizing the importance of the Chinese market. However, Americans were pragmatists, and they preferred to get the job done in a minute. To them, their mission in China was to promote the sales of their machines. They expected the meetings to focus on specifications and contract terms rather than general information. In their minds, the hard facts of their technology and facility could help them win the order from the Chinese. But unfortunately, it turned out that hard facts were not Mr. Wang's first concern. In addition, the Chinese spent a lot of time on banquets, and escorted the Americans at every dinner and sight-seeing tour. All these were the non-task sounding activities of the Chinese aiming to establish harmonious relationship between the negotiating parties. The French were clever enough to utilize these opportunities to gain the information of what the Chinese expected to get from the future deal, and thus won an advantage over their American competitor. Being not sensitive enough to the cultural differences, the Americans felt disappointed at leaving China being empty-handed, though they were impressed by the hospitality of the Chinese host.

Concern with protocol

Johnson was warmly welcomed by both the leaders of the Chinese company and the local government officials immediately after they had arrived China. They were treated with banquets and sight-seeing tours. To the Chinese, the busy and tight schedule for the Americans showed their care and respect for their guests. However, the Americans felt like losing independence and freedom by this tight schedule, and they were not used to these relationship-building activities. On the contrast, there was only a taxi waiting for Mr. Wang and his colleagues after their arrival in the United States. Most of the time, the Chinese were left alone. Mr. Johnson's failure to meet Mr. Wang and his colleagues at the airport and spend time showing them around the city made Mr. Wang feel disrespected by the Americans. Mr. Johnson might well respect Mr. Wang, but he showed his respect in his American style, which was misunderstood. What's more, the gifts from the Americans were petty and small, which showed no generosity and sincerity of the Americans in the eyes of the Chinese.

Complexity of language

When Mr. Johnson asked Mr. Wang what would be the next step, Mr. Wang responded that he had to report to his authorities to make a decision. But his response to the French was that he would send a letter of intent as soon as he got back China. Mr. Wang might have the decision-making power, but he was unwilling to pick the American company as the supplier, for he felt that the better equipment and the better price could not make up his perceived slight from the Americans. This indirect and vague answer was to avoid embarrassment and save face for both parties, and still to leave room for future negotiation.

In China, letter of intent with general principles stated is often the form of negotiation outcome to show the friendship and mutual trust between the negotiation parties.

Case 2　It's hard to understand!

Tom Forrest, an up-and-coming executive for a U. S. electronics company, was sent to Japan to work out the details of a joint venture with a Japanese electronics firm. During the first several weeks Tom felt that the negotiations were proceeding better than he had expected. He found that he had very cordial working relationships with the team of Japanese executives, and in fact, they had agreed on the major policies and strategies governing the new joint venture. During the third week of negotiations Tom was present at a meeting held to review their progress. The meeting was chaired by the president of the Japanese firm, Mr. Hayakawa, a man in his mid-thirties, who had recently taken over the presidency from his 82-year-old grandfather. The new president, who had been involved in most of the negotiations during the preceding weeks, seemed to Tom to be one of the strongest advocates of the plan that had been  developed to date. Also attending the meeting was Hayakawa's grandfather, the recently retired president. After the plans had been discussed in some detail, the octogenarian past president proceeded to give a long soliloquy about how some of the features of this plan violated the traditional practices on which the company had been founded. Much to Tom's amazement, Mr. Hayakawa did nothing to explain or defend the policies and strategies that they had taken weeks to develop. Feeling extremely frustrated, Tom then gave a fairly strongly argued defense of the plan. To Tom's further amazement, no one else in the meeting spoke up in defense of the plan. The tension in the air was quite heavy and the meeting adjourned shortly thereafter. Within days the Japanese firm completely terminated the negotiations on the joint venture.

 Discussion:

1. How do you understand the Japanese company's decision?
2. What would Tom do next time when he negotiated with Japanese?

 Case analysis:

The essence of Tom's problems reflects the cultural differences in the business negotiations between the U. S. and Japan. The failure of the negotiations was caused by the different negotiation style of the two cultures and the concrete operation in the process of the negotiation. As far as Tom was concerned on behalf of the United States, during the early weeks of negotiations, it is a process to refine the problem, prepare carefully for the ultimate success and cooperate with each other. However, as

Japanese partners showed him thoughtful courtesy during the negotiation, Tom thought that Japanese representatives were as great sincere and confident as themselves. In addition, after Tom came terms with the new person in charge, Tom misunderstood that just like Americans, one person could decide everything in Japan during negotiation, which made Tom fully confident. But the concept of negotiations is greatly different between Americans and Japanese: first, the performance of Japanese during early weeks of the negotiation is to establish a good relationship between the two sides which can pave a good way for the following negotiation stage; second, Japan's culture determines the way by which they face the problem is a circuitous manner, even if the problem is acute, they will take evasive attitude in order to maintain the face of both sides for harmony. Therefore, the courtesy Japanese representatives showed in the last few weeks of the negotiation in the case might be only a kind of politeness, which was not as optimistic as Tom thought; third, Japanese culture pays close attention to the views of the mass, so individuals can not make decisions on major issues, and they have to consult the collective views. The older generation often enjoys a high authority in the collectives. Therefore, when the current head proposed any dispute, the negotiations reached deadlock.

As one can imagine, the negotiations ended in failure. From the failure in the negotiations, certainly Tom is extremely dissatisfied with Japanese performance, and would think that the other party does not cooperate sincerely, and Japanese strongly dislike Tom's hard-line rude manners and are certainly very unpleasant. So understanding the different cultures is the key to the success of the collaborative negotiations.

Case 3 Why left me alone?

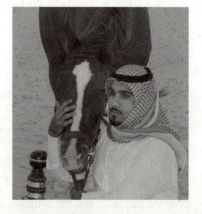

Some German business people would complain about the inefficiency of their Arabic partners. Schneider's experience might be a typical one. Schneider paid a visit to Abdullah, one of his potential clients in the Mid-East, and was hospitably received. But Abdullah dwelt very long on small chatting and Schneider got a bit impatient. But as he had been advised before that Arabic people value friendship very much and a long chatting before setting to business is a norm, he exercised his patience. Schneider tried to keep his step to that of Arabic and instead of presenting the program as how benefiting it would be to Abdullah, he said that he himself would benefit a great deal, which always sounded persuasive and pleasant in Mid-East business field. Abdullah was pleased that he could help Schneider and agreed to set an arrangement for the further talk on the program.

On the appointed day, Schneider arrived on time and was again received with a long chatting before the talk started. However, in the midst of the talk, someone entered the room and said something to Abdullah, and then Abdullah stood up and apologized for an excuse. Schneider was left in the meeting room for another two hours. Schneider, well-organized and scheduled as his native people, was very upset with the unexpected pause during the talk. He couldn't help worrying about his dating on the very evening as the talk might be ended later than he had supposed.

Finally, Abdullah returned and said in a casual way that one of his friends had just dropped in and so he had to excuse himself to have a cup of coffee with the visitor. That's really the last straw for Schneider. He regretted very much that he had not followed his Arabic background friend's advice, who suggested he get a local agent to settle business there.

Discussion:

1. Why would Arabic business people rather be helpful than helped?
2. Why should Schneider get a local agent to settle business in the Mid-East?

Case analysis:

Mutual benefiting is a trading principle in most parts of the world. But Arabic business people prefer to be helpful. They value friendship very much and if their partners pay their visit first they will be very pleased. As they have a cultural trait of relation-driven (unlike the Americans and Germans task-driven features), they place friendship above business benefits. If they think one is really friendly and sincere, they would like to do business with him or her.

Arabic people also value in-group relation very much though they may be a bit wary to the people outside their culture. They will not leave their own native folk waiting though there is an important business meeting with some foreign partners.

It is advisable to find some local people as your agents in Mid-East as they can win more trust and contracts there than you — an outsider there.

Case 4   Who is cleverer?

Wang Ming, a trading staff member in a Chinese company, is attending a fair where his company has got a booth to display their products. A Russian businessman is interested in their items and starts trying to make a deal with Wang. As Wang has a lot of experience in making deal with  Russian people, he gets the quote made in different versions — one is bearing higher prices and the other lower. His assistant, an intern, is very curious about this and Wang explains to her:

"Russian business people are very smart. They take price into great account and always try to get the suppliers' price lower and even lower. As a matter of fact, no matter how rational your first quote is, Russian buyers will reject it. They will use some cheating strategy as to say to the supplier: Your price is not competitive at all. Your competitor has quoted a favorable price."

"So, we show them a price list first with higher prices," said the assistant. "After their exhausting haggling, we show the true price list as to make them believe they win the haggling."

"Yes, that is the strategy and it always works well," said Wang Ming.

 Discussion:

1. Why would Russian trading makers like to keep cutting down?
2. Do you know how to cut the price down on the negotiation table?

 Case analysis:

Russia is a country with complicated cultures — one mixed with collectivist as most of its land is in Asia and individualist as its earliest founded cities are in Europe and most of its elite people are nurtured by European cultures. The USSR was, in fact, a regime on the foundation of collectivism, which lasted more than 70 years and affected people's behavior. Therefore, their performance is a combination of different cultures. For instance, the way of haggling shows they would often use high-contextual device. Russian business people usually make big deals so only large orders could draw their attention. But they are very strict or picky with trading terms and also try hard to haggle over the price. In order to reach their goal, they may be even threatening and cheating to their partners (usually knocking the table in a rage), but an experienced worker should not be threatened. Stick to your point and they will be back again and if you give in then you have to give in all the time in future. Anyhow Wang's strategy is worth trying.

Russian people are one of the best educated in the world, so they are always decent at the negotiation table — well dressed, neat hair, and they also expect their business partners well dressed and mannered. If you were not careful with your appearance and manners at the table, they would not be pleased with you and even quit you no matter how promising the deal will be.

Case 5 No bargaining!

Zhang is a buyer of a motor company. He has to travel a lot to find adequate suppliers so he can often be seen at some big motor and vehicle fairs. He is very famous in his circle and a smart buyer. But recalling early career, Zhang would tell you one of his failure at his purchasing job.

Scan was a very famous vehicle and motor parts manufacturer based in Sweden. Zhang knew the products of Scan were reliable so he tried to talk with Scan's salesman at an international fair, with the intention to get a deal done. Everything seemed going on well as the both sides started, but when Zhang tried to bargain over the air was getting tense.

"Our quote is based on careful calculation, there is no room for any cutting down," the Scan's salesman said politely but firmly.

Zhang insisted, as that was a common practice. And what surprised him was the Scan's salesman picked his case and left.

Discussion:

1. Why is haggling not practical with Swedish business people?
2. What will you do to make the price strategies?

 Case analysis:

There is a great similarity between Scandinavian people and German-speaking people, which is that they all are very concerned about details. In terms of anthology this is a cultural trait titled "Low-Context." People bearing such trait are very precise and they count what is said or written very much. So Swedish business people, as well as people from Germany, Finland and Norway, usually believe that they carefully calculate every figure and there is little room for revising or improvement.

On the other hand, Chinese people, as most people from collectivist culture background, value more than what is said, so they are not so careful about what is really meant. You may often catch the sight of some written signs as to remind people of doing something from no smoking and spitting. In business circle, like most business people, Chinese people also like to haggle, as they are likely to estimate their counterparts' quote has large room for shrinking; they do so also partly because they think what in black and white may not mean so much.

So when people just haggle over the price without pointing out what fault is in the calculation or what exact improvement should be made about the contract, Swedish business people may get very annoyed and they won't give up their principle easily. For outside, they seem a bit rigid, but they are very honest in the price and they will not compromise with price and then replace the good material with less-quality one.

 Cases for students' practice:

Case 1

Xiao Li once participated in a negotiation on the third day when a U. S. manager in a U. S. -Chinese business negotiation did not receive the information he was expecting in a report, he asked the Chinese negotiator who was responsible for the

Part V Typical Cases in Intercultural Business Communication

report for a meeting to discuss his needs. The Chinese politely put him off. The next day, he was informed by the Chinese manager that there was no problem with the report, the report had the information it always had, and the report could not be changed.

Case 2

An American team of two men representing Canwall, a wallpaper printing equipment manufacturer, went to a town in the north of Shanghai in the province of Jiangsu, China, to negotiate a sale to a new wallpaper production company. Charlie Burton, president of Canwall, traveled with his marketing director, Phil Raines. The company had never before sold its equipment outside the United States, and the two Americans were delighted with the warm reception they enjoyed in China. This was not the first meeting between the American company and the Chinese wallpaper factory. The manager of the Chinese company, Mr. Li, had been a member of a delegation to the United States. He had met with one of Canwall's senior salespersons and the director of manufacturing. Subsequently a trade representative from America had been in China representing Canwall's interests to the Chinese manager. After these meetings and numerous letters and faxes, Canwall's top people were now ready to negotiate the sale.

The day they arrived they were met at the airport in Shanghai by Manager Li himself and transported in a chauffeur-driven car to the town. Their accommodation was in a newly built hotel, and although it was not luxurious, it was certainly comfortable. A few hours after their arrival they were treated to a 12-course banquet given by their host, with several high-level municipal officials present. This red carpet treatment made them feel optimistic about the sale.

The next day they were taken to see the sights nearby: a large, new port for container ships and several factories that indicated the prosperity of the region. They were eager to begin discussing the sale, but after lunch they were given time to rest. In the late afternoon one of the manager's English speaking employees came by with the news they would be taken to see a local dance company's performance that night.

The third day they finally sat down to meetings. Progress seemed very slow — each side giving generalizations about itself that seemed unrelated to the sale. After listening to various apparently unrelated points, the American thought, "So what?"

The Chinese also spent a lot of time talking about the American trade agent who had been in their town earlier. Burton wasn't able to tell them much about that *person, since he had never met him personally.*

Case 3

Pacific Dunlop is a diversified American-managed manufacturer and marketer of footwear, optical fiber cables and batteries. The company has gone from strength to strength in China, partly thanks to the influence of its managing director Paul Winestock who has been the chief negotiator in developing businesses for the company.

Winestock negotiates in the Chinese way. He says, "I negotiate as it goes. I did not know this when I started doing business with Chinese in the 1970s. Before leaving for China we would telex an outline of all the things we wanted to discuss and send a rough timetable. But when we arrived, everything would be changed. We would perform days and days. We would sit at the table and go over the issues point by point then go back to them all over again. Sometimes we could not reach a conclusion, but we would not give up. I would come back two months later. Sometimes we could reach a conclusion, but two months later, we had to discuss it again. Some contracts took me a week, some took me a year."

In the following business negotiations with his Chinese party, Winestock did not go directly towards discussion topics and instead, he gave enough patience to Chinese typical reception and tried to establish long-term good relationship with Chinese partners. He talked about the history and development of his company and the intention of establishing friendship with Chinese negotiators on the negotiating table.

The result was the agreement he wanted.

Part VI

Tips for Successful Intercultural Communication

    The world we live in consists of a diversity of cultures. In our daily life, people will encounter individuals from completely different cultural backgrounds. When this occurs, we will experience a certain degree of anxiety. What ways of communication are appropriate? What are the taboos of the other or others? If we know nothing about their cultural background, the result can be, without exaggeration, a true disaster. Cross-cultural communication tips are the most important remedies to help people overcome the barriers that arise as a result of this ignorance. These tips can help us communicate successfully.

    A good command of communication skills is therefore of critical importance for us to achieve success in intercultural communication. Without communication skills, we will be deaf, dumb, and blind. We will not be able to allow others to know our thoughts, feelings, or ambitions. It will be impossible for us to build a good relationship with our partner, resolve conflicts smoothly and achieve success. In this part we will set out some tips that will enable you to improve your communication skills.

Chapter

1

Tips for ordinary intercultural communication

Intercultural communication can be a dynamic and creative affair but occasionally, due to the inability to interpret people correctly, it can be a real problem. Building an understanding of other people's cultures, their communicative styles and behaviors can go a long way toward improving relationships and being more successful in an intercultural environment. Here are some tips for the building of success in ordinary intercultural communication.

Tip 1 The desire to communicate

The first step toward effective communication is that you should have a strong desire to communicate. No matter how skillful you are, if you don't want to communicate, all your efforts are fruitless. So the desire to communicate with others is the strongest motivation to success. If you have the desire, you will try to express yourself clearly. If you have the desire, you will ask questions and try to get some information. If you have the desire, you will listen to others attentively. The effort you make to express yourself and to understand others will lead you along the path to successful communication.

Tip 2   Know about other cultures

On account of the differences of living environment, thinking patterns, and languages, people from different cultures have different ways of organizing their lives, perceiving the world, expressing ideas, dealing with daily matters, and so on. If we are familiar with these aspects of our partner's culture, it will greatly help us to communicate effectively. So try to find out something about their culture before you decide to communicate with a foreigner.

"The best way to learn a foreign language is to live in the country which speaks the language." This saying has been regarded as commonsense by linguists. However, it can equally well be applied to communication. We can also say, "The best way of understanding a foreign culture is to live in that culture." Though living in a foreign culture can help understand that culture, it is usually costly and hard to arrange, thus putting it beyond the reach of ordinary people.

There are many other less expensive ways to experience foreign cultures. For example, you can search on the Internet. You can now find almost any information you want there. So you can use it to learn many things about the foreign cultures without ever leaving your house.

Regularly visiting the library is also a good way to learn about the foreign culture. In a library, you can find many newspapers, magazines, journals, travel books and similar materials, that can be of enormous help to you in this respect.

Foreign films can also provide you with information about their cultures if you know where to find good ones. By choosing movies that match your interests, you can know about things around the world. From watching movies, you learn the foreign culture, entertain yourself and prepare for your future interaction with a foreigner, all at the one time.

Lastly, please remember that having a friend of another culture is of great help for you to know that culture.

Tip 3   Seek similarities

When dealing with people from other cultures, we should look for similarities. People from different cultures have many differences, but what unites people is much greater than what separates people. For example, ways of parenting may differ, but the common bond of a mother and a child crosses many barriers. According to

Maslow's hierarchy of needs, people's basic needs are common. All people have to eat, wear clothes, and want to be free from external restraints.

As human beings, we not only have similar physical needs and feelings, we also have common values. It is these similarities that unite us, and in a very real sense make us one community. There are many differences between cultures but there are just as many similarities.

Tip 4 Rid yourself of assumptions

Assumptions are ideas that are taken for granted. They are beliefs that are thought to be true, which are often not true. Assumptions are usually influenced by subjective factors and everyone makes or has assumptions about those with whom they are communicating.

Since assumptions are usually not true, we should pay special attention to them. Whenever we rely on our assumptions, we first need to reflect on why we think in this way and openly discuss them with others to ensure that they are true. By doing so, we take a large step to overcome the intercultural communication barriers.

We should bear in mind that people from other countries, probably speak, act, dress, or even eat differently. Don't take it for granted that they share your values and attitudes, however strongly you believe in them. Take it as a fact that their cultures are different and respect those differences.

If our assumptions about other people's culture are based on incorrect information, mistakes will occur in cross-cultural conversations. Our incorrect information usually comes from sources such as rumors, friends, jokes, even unprejudiced news reports. If you want to know whether something you heard is true or not, please check with people from that culture. However, you should adopt certain strategies when asking questions. For example, if you want to confirm whether the statement "Native Africans don't celebrate Christmas" is true or not, you'd better ask an African in this way, "What festivals do you celebrate?" rather than "You really don't celebrate Christmas?" Asking questions directly, especially about one's beliefs, may sometimes offend the other person.

Tip 5 Avoid stereotypes

A stereotype is a commonly held belief about specific social groups or types of individuals. Differences in socioeconomic status, religion, or dialect are often reflected in stereotypes. However, these differences can be found within any culture; we cannot use them to distinguish one culture from another. It is better therefore to suspend judgment, avoid misconceptions, narrow perspectives, and immature reactions. Although stereotypes often subsume elements of truth, those elements cannot be generalized to characterize an entire culture. To have a complete understanding of one culture, we should be critical about the sayings that prevail about its people and their behaviors.

We should not make judgments about others on the basis of what we see or hear. When we judge others from stereotypes, we should think carefully about what is true and what is not true because we can be wrong and may offend other people. Each culture is different, and this is the way the world is made. When not offending others, making stereotypes about other cultures is not bad. As researchers in this field have discovered, we cannot avoid thinking in stereotypes so we should ensure that they are positive ones.

When communicating with a people from a different culture, we should bear in mind that we are meeting and interacting with an individual whose background and beliefs may be different from those shared by those of the society from which they come.

Tip 6 Slow down

This tip is to overcome language barriers. Speaking slowly is particularly important in a cross-cultural context. Generally speaking, most people's command of a foreign language cannot be as good as that of native speakers. So while talking to them, you should not speak as fast as when talking to your own countrymen. If it is hard for you to understand your partner because of his accent and unclear pronunciation, it is probably hard for him to understand you, too. The faster you speak, the more difficult it will be to communicate.

For example, while delivering lectures to Chinese, some Americans speak very fast. The result is that they lose their audience. No matter how excellent your ideas are, if you can't make yourself understood, they mean nothing. Chinese usually don't ask their speakers to repeat what they have said because it is considered impolite to do so. If they don't understand you, they'll just sit there letting your thoughts and ideas pass over their heads. So please do speak slowly in intercultural communication. The importance of speaking slowly is more evident for interpreters. If you speak too fast, they will simply ignore what they don't understand. Asking for clarification may suggest a lack of competence, so Chinese translators will not ask you to repeat something because they fear they'll lose face.

Tip 7　Accept and respect others' culture

When communicating with people from other cultures, we are often confronted with different world views. These differences often challenge our own beliefs, and they may give us reason to examine the world from a different point of view. For most of the time, people are tolerant of these differences, but they seldom really accept them. To create a world based on equality and respect, differences between cultures should be accepted. When you encounter a difference, ask yourself if you are tolerating it or truly accepting it. If you are tolerating it, ask yourself why you don't accept this difference. Only by accepting the differences can we enjoy the richness that the world has to offer.

Respect is the foundation of all intercultural communications. By respecting others, you can get respect and mutual respect helps build up more open and fruitful relationships.

The reciprocity of respect mentioned above is, however, often overlooked. There is a duty to respect values and practices in other cultures and there is a reciprocal right to have one's own cultural values and practices respected. When cultural values and practices are only tolerated but not respected, those belonging to the tolerated culture tend to be looked down upon from a distance. They strongly resent this and will show their resentment in different ways, perhaps even flaunting their differences. In such a case, no side benefits.

Tip 8　Be patient

Intercultural communication often involves conflicts, which will lead to frustration on one or both sides. When this happens, things may not get done as expected. Communication will become tiresome and responses may be inappropriate. Being patient with others and yourself will help you overcome such issues and avoid similar incidents in the future.

Patience is an art, a kind of willingness to stop and wait without being annoyed and angry. In a multicultural group, when we negotiate among different cultures, social norms, expectations and assumptions, patience is of paramount importance. When we are working across cultures, the following tips for cultivating patience should be considered:

• Ask yourself what your real intention is;

• Don't enforce your expectations, leave the other person free to act as they wish;

• Realize that social norms and customs may vary between cultures and try to avoid making personal judgments.

It is essential to exercise patience with regard to others; it is also important that we be patient with ourselves. We often see the world in the light of our own beliefs, social values and norms. Through patience, we can help ourselves and others to interact in a way that takes into account everyone's social background and individuality.

Tip 9   Watch your body language

Some body language, such as gestures (e. g. pointing directly at others) or our unconscious habits (e. g. maintaining direct eye contact) may be offensive in some cultures. Watch, investigate and then get to know the appropriate and inappropriate behaviors in the culture where you are speaking.

Body language is an important form of nonverbal communication. We continuously give and receive many wordless signals consciously or unconsciously from the person with whom we are communicating. All of our nonverbal behaviors — the speed with which we speak, the tone of our voice, the frequency of eye contact, our gestures, the way we sit, the distance we keep from our interlocutor — send strong and countless messages to others.

How you listen, look, move, and react tells others whether you are listening to them, and whether you care about what they are saying.

Tip 10   Observe the rules of etiquette

Every culture has its own rules of etiquette for communicating. It is therefore necessary to learn at least the most important of those of the target language for intercultural communication.

Tip 11   Avoid sensitive topics

Topics such as income or marriage may be suitable for general conversations in one culture, while they are considered of a very personal nature in another culture. For example, such topics are good ones for conversations in China, but in America they would be considered an encroachment on one's privacy. Making your answer broad and general is an often-used technique to deflect personal questions. It is better to say "People in my field usually make anywhere from $30,000 to $60,000 a year" than "I make $40,000 a year." If you're pressed to give a concrete number, then you can gently give an answer like, "That's a topic that I don't feel comfortable discussing," and move on to a new area.

Tip 12   Be wise

In intercultural communication, we should know how to interact with people with respect and knowledge. The success of the communication to a large extent depends on the wisdom of the communicators. If we have a good understanding of the cultural background and we think twice before opening our mouth or taking action, many of the problems that arise when we are communicating could be avoided.

Tip 13   Ask questions

When you feel confused about the other person's words or behaviors, the best way to resolve the problem is to ask them to explain more clearly. Asking questions can prevent you from making assumptions, and make your interlocutor aware that you have not understood them. But, above all, ask in a pleasant and friendly way.

Tip 14   Be cautious of cultural jargon

Generally it is hard to translate local terminology, popular cultural references, and humor. Even though others may understand the words, the meaning you want to express is lost on them. Where they are concerned, what you are very familiar with may not have any meaning or may have a very different meaning. For example, what you consider humorous in your culture may even be offensive in other cultures.

If cultural references are used in your presentation, please find ones that will resonate with the audience. In the case of humor, if they are specific to your own culture, then explain why they are considered funny. If you use acronyms, explain them, saying what each letter stands for. Generally speaking, it is better not to use jargon and slang.

Tip 15   Avoid Chinglish

Chinglish is often quaint and attractive, expressing the hospitality and unique perspective of the Chinese world-view. Sometimes it is quite amusing, raising a smile for foreign visitors, on other occasions it can be confusing. Sadly, Chinglish is sometimes just plain bad English and shows a careless and unprofessional approach to translation, even by large companies and organizations.

Tip 16   Self-reflect

Take time to reflect on the way you yourself communicate and see in what way you can improve, in the way you speak, the way you present things, your general manner, and so on.

Chapter 2

Recommendations for effective intercultural business negotiations

Effective business negotiations can determine the success of international business relationships. This requires that the negotiators be well prepared. If they know the secrets of achieving international business negotiation outcomes and grasp the elements which are relevant to the process, they can be much more successful in these business  activities. An experienced negotiator knows about not only what to gain but also how to gain. Actually, in negotiations, proper behaviors are necessary for both sides for a measured-up negotiation benefits them both.

2.1 Identification of the partner's culture in advance

In international business negotiations, it is common to have cultural differences between negotiators from different cultures. People from different countries have different cultural values, which can influence international business negotiations in significant and unexpected ways at every stage of a negotiation. The diverse values of partners will lead to different methods of negotiation and variable outcomes. In a negotiation with executives from different cultures, an understanding and adaptability to these differences are strongly required.

2.2 Cultivating cultural awareness and sensitivity

In order to achieve business success, first of all, our Chinese negotiators should reflect upon our own cultural system, which is quite different from that of Western countries. This reflection includes not only being aware of our own values, beliefs and social norms, but also how these cultural phenomena influence our way of thinking and behavior. In this way, we can try to avoid the effects of stereotypes and ethnocentrism in intercultural communication. Secondly, we Chinese negotiators should be culturally sensitive and try to learn more about other cultures. In this process, we may suffer discomfort or emotional stress, but we should try to understand and think in a different way. Negotiators should remember that their foreign counterparts are different from them in many ways. These differences are not only represented in physical features, but also in social beliefs and values. As soon as the differences are identified and understood, negotiators should try to find suitable ways to adjust to them. However, it is not necessary to fully adapt oneself to the other side's culture and we should avoid losing our own judgment by allowing ourselves to be drawn too deeply into another cultural system. For a wise negotiator, one way to overcome cultural differences is to be interested in, know, respect and appreciate the other's culture. Cultural superiority and arrogance must be avoided because they would cause disagreement and could lead to the failure of the negotiation.

Cultural differences should be tolerated and respected by negotiators. Once differences are understood, they should seek ways of accepting them. Besides, respecting your opponent's customs and taboos may help you to control the negotiation process and to sign a favorable deal. Ignorance of the customs and taboos of other cultures will lead to business failures.

2.3 Good preparation before negotiation

Preparation can make one proactive rather than reactive. Planning involves two aspects: technical preparation and cultural preparation. When coming to the negotiating table, many negotiators are well prepared in both respects and expect you to be likewise.

Poor preparation will not only make you fail technically in the negotiation, but it also will give your opponent the impression that you don't take the negotiation seriously.

So how should one prepare well for a business negotiation?

Firstly, you should collect information about your opponent before going to the negotiating table. Information such as the other party's expectations, their team members, their background and negotiating strategies is of great importance, and must be collected before the negotiation. Failures of negotiation are often caused by the lack of such information. After having collected such information, you can make a plan for the negotiation and determine negotiating strategies.

Secondly, in the process of negotiation, you can take advantage of the other side's negotiating styles and win bargaining power. Your knowledge of your opponent's culture can, to a certain extent, as we saw earlier, help prevent cross-cultural conflicts.

Thirdly, pay attention to details. For example, be dressed properly. If you are dressed neatly and formally, that means you respect the other person. If you put on a brand new suit to go to a talk, that means you are an inexperienced businessman because it may make you look and feel quite anxious, even clumsy. Be wise to have proper excuses in hand. Excuses such as "an unexpected visitor" or "a call of nature" are most commonly used at the negotiation table. By such excuses, one can leave the table and get some time to think about a problem you have difficulty resolving. Also, of course, you can pretend to be thirsty so that you can leave to get some water. On the other hand, it is very unwise to ask questions such as "Who are you going to see?" or "Can't you wait until we have finished discussing this point?" when your opponent makes such excuses.

2.4 Improving business communication skills

The cross-cultural negotiation is an essential part of intercultural business communication. Communication skills play an important role in business negotiations. Business communication mainly involves two forms: verbal communication and nonverbal communication. If a negotiator is good at skills of both forms, then he will have a good chance to control the whole negotiation process to his advantage.

Needless to say, it is advantageous to know the language of the other party. English is regarded as the business language internationally, so most business negotiations are carried out in English. One of the prerequisites of an excellent negotiator is that he must have a good command of English. If you are not a native English speaker, you can ask your opponent to speak slowly and repeat the points you want to know clearly. In order to have yourself well understood, you should try to avoid using colloquial expressions, slangs and idioms. Besides, the same word may have different meanings in different cultures, thus make sure that the other party understands what you said in the way you meant it. It is of course important to know something of the other person's language, if only as a sign of respect. The failure of many native English-speaking businessmen to do so has often proved a handicap in negotiating business deals.

On the other hand, nonverbal communication is equally important in the process of negotiation, so we should pay attention to nonverbal cues such as body language and facial expressions. From those nonverbal cues, we can interpret the other person's underlying attitudes and intentions so as to respond correspondingly. In doing so, we should pay special attention to the fact that the same nonverbal cue may have different meanings in different cultures. Therefore, it is necessary for the negotiators to be aware of the cultural differences and use the nonverbal communication correctly to facilitate the negotiation process.

Cross-cultural communication is about dealing with people from other cultures, during which we should minimize misunderstandings and maximize our potential to build up a good intercultural relationship. The above tips are the starting point for us to improve our cross-cultural awareness. Though there are many barriers that exist between cultures, our desire for information and willingness to communicate with others will break them down. It takes time and effort for an individual to become open to new ideas and new people in the process of cross-cultural communication. However, smiles and acceptance will help us to eventually break into an exciting new world characterized by clarity and connectedness.

References

[1] Don Snow. 跨文化交际技巧——如何跟西方人打交道[M]. 上海：上海外语教育出版社,2005.

[2] Joyce Merrill Valdes. Culture Bound[M]. New York：Cambridge University Press, 1988.

[3] Larry A. Samovar, Richard E. Porter, Lisa A. Stefani. Communication Between Cultures[M]. Belmont：Wadsworth Publishing Company,1998.

[4] Linell Davis. 中西文化之鉴[M]. 北京：外语教学与研究出版社,2004.

[5] Paula Saukko. Doing Research in Cultural Studies[M]. London：Sage Publications, 2003.

[6] William B. Gudykunst, Young Yun Kim. Communicating Strangers[M]. New York：The McGraw-Hill Companies, Inc. ,1984.

[7] Yong Yun Kim. Becoming Intercultural[M]. Thousand Oaks：Sage Publications, Inc. , 2001.

[8] 毕继万. 跨文化非语言交际[M]. 北京：外语教学与研究出版社,2001.

[9] 戴凡，Stephen L. J. Smith. 文化碰撞[M]. 上海：上海外语教育出版社, 2006.

[10] 邓炎昌,刘润清. 语言与文化[M]. 北京：外语教学与研究出版社,2003.

[11] 窦卫霖. 跨文化商务交流案例分析[M]. 上海：对外经济贸易大学出版社, 2007.

[12] 顾力行,Michael H. Prosser. 跨文化视角下的中国人：交际与传播[M]. 上海：上海外语教育出版社,2006.

[13] 关世杰. 跨文化交流学[M]. 北京：北京大学出版社,2005.

[14] 胡文仲. 超越文化的屏障[M]. 北京：外语教学与研究出版社,2004.

[15] 胡文仲. 跨文化交际面面观[M]. 北京：外语教学与研究出版社,2004.

[16] 胡文仲. 跨文化交际学概论[M]. 北京：外语教学与研究出版社,2004.

[17] 贾玉新. 跨文化交际学[M]. 上海：上海外语教育出版社,1998.

[18] 李学爱. 跨文化交流：中西方交往的习俗和语言[M]. 天津：天津大学出版社,2009.

[19] 戎林海. 跨越文化障碍——与英美人交往面面观[M]. 南京：东南大学出版社, 2006.

[20] 徐克枢,Jeanette Lochner,邱立中. 白领英语畅谈东西方文化 43 情景主题[M]. 北京:中国水利水电出版社,2009.
[21] 翟华. 东方文化西方语[M]. 北京:中国书店,2009.
[22] 张爱琳. 跨文化交际[M]. 重庆:重庆大学出版社,2003.